Sector
Investing

Sector
Investing

1996 Edition

Sam Stovall

McGraw-Hill

New York   San Francisco   Washington, D.C.   Auckland   Bogota
Caracas   Lisbon   London   Madrid   Mexico City   Milan
Montreal   New Delhi   San Juan   Singapore
Sydney   Tokyo   Toronto

International Standard Serial Number:
Standard & Poor's Guide to Sector Investing
ISSN 1081-051X

McGraw-Hill

A Division of The McGraw-Hill Companies

2 3 4 5 6 7 8 9 0   AGM/AGM   9 0 1 0 9 8 7 6

ISBN 0-07-052239-1

*The sponsoring editor for this book was David Conti, the editing supervisor was Penny
Linskey, and the production supervisor was Suzanne W. B. Rapcavage. It was set in New
Times Roman by Sam Stovall of Standard & Poor's, a division of The McGraw-Hill
Companies, Inc.*

Printed and bound by Quebecor/Martinsburg.

McGraw-Hill books are available at special quantity discounts to use as premiums
and sales promotions, or for use in corporate training programs. For more information, please write to the Director of Special Sales, McGraw-Hill, Inc., 11 West 19th
Street, New York, NY 10011. Or contact your local bookstore.

This publication is designed to provide accurate and authoritative information in
regard to the subject matter covered. It is sold with the understanding that the publisher is not engaged in rendering legal, accounting, or other professional service. If
legal advice or other expert assistance is required, the services of a competent professional person should be sought.

*—From a declaration of principles jointly adopted by a committee
of the American Bar Association and a committee of publishers.*

 This book is printed on recycled, acid-free paper containing a minimum
of 50% recycled, de-inked fiber.

Contents

ABOUT THE AUTHOR

Sam Stovall is editor of S&P's *Industry Reports* and a member of S&P's Investment Policy Committee. He is a frequent guest on CNBC's "Buy, Hold or Sell" program, as well as CNN's "Moneyline." Mr. Stovall is a board member of the New York Chapter of the American Association of Individual Investors and is an adjunct professor of finance at Marymount Manhattan College in NYC.

Introduction

The $63,000 Question

If you were to ask a group of average investors to name the optimal way to make a killing in the stock market, they would probably shout -- market timing! (Market timing is the technique of successfully "buying low and selling high," by pinpointing the peak and trough in stock prices.) And although they might be enthusiastic, they would be wrong. For not only is market timing that classic technique that few have mastered, but it is also less successful than an alternative technique by more than 4 to 1. That technique? Sector investing.

A study performed by CDA/Weisenberger, an investment research firm out of Rockville, Maryland, compared the performances of three investment strategies -- market timing, sector investing, and "buy and hold" -- over a 10-year period. The market timing technique was defined by correctly predicting price changes in the overall stock market of 10% or more in either direction, buying when prices were about to rise and selling when prices were about to decline. The sector selector strategy invested the entire portfolio in one of six sectors -- energy, financial services, gold, health care, technology, or utilities -- at the beginning of each year. The "buy-and-hold" strategy bought and held the stocks in the S&P 500 for the entire 10-year period.

Each investment technique started with $1,000. At the end of the 10-year period, the "buy-and-hold" investor walked away with a little more than $6,000, while the market timer netted almost $15,000. Yet the sector selector amassed nearly $63,000! Not bad for an overlooked investment technique.

An Alternative Investment Approach

A conservative investor will typically take the oft-advised "diversified" approach to investing by putting his money to work in either an index or a broadly based equity mutual fund, which owns hundreds of stocks in dozens of industries. This investor is willing to bypass the big killings (thus lowering the return) in order to reduce the volatility, or risk, of their portfolio.

A more aggressive investor, on the other hand, may place bets on only a few stocks in a limited number of industries, accepting the increased risk in the hope of enhancing the return on their investment.

But for some investors, the above strategies may be too hot or cold. For them, some other discipline may be just right.

Enter sector investing, a technique that is more aggressive than investing in broadly based mutual funds, yet less risky than investing in only a handful of stocks. And, it can be accomplished with either stocks or mutual funds.

Advice on market timing and individual stock picking abound; investors have a plethora of guides to timing the market, allocating assets and selecting stocks. Yet the evaluation and selection of the right sector has been ignored. Almost nowhere can one find a comprehensive guide to understanding sector investing.

Enter *Sector Investing*, a book, updated on an annual basis, that will introduce the reader to an old saying on Wall Street: "A rising tide lifts all boats." That is, if a particular industry is "hot," all stocks within that particular industry will likely benefit. And this adage is based on fact. Studies have indicated that as much as 60% of a stock's price move can be attributed to the direction of the overall market and whether the company's industry group is in or out of favor with investors. The remaining influence pertains to the underlying company-specific factors.

The book will walk you through the "top-down" approach to investing. It will:

■ Analyze the typical economic cycle of recovery and recession, dividing it into five phases and identifying the sectors and industries that perform best during each phase.

■ Describe the tools of measurement used to evaluate growth trends in the overall economy and each of the industries that comprise the S&P 500 Composite Index.

■ Evaluate performances (investment returns, standard deviation, and beta) and valuations (price-to-earnings ratios, relative P/Es, and yields) for all industries.

■ Discuss how to spot over-sold or over-bought industries using 12-month relative strength.

■ Review the definitions, characteristics, and investment outlooks for these industries, as well as display peer comparisons on more than 1,000 component stocks.

■ Provide S&P's economic and investment outlook for 1996.

■ Identify mutual funds by their sector/industry focus.

This book is geared toward the individual investor, to whom Standard & Poor's has been providing information and advice for more than 100 years. And while the book will assume the reader is aware of such terms as P/E, yield, and total return, not much more will be expected. This book will be used to expand upon the reader's basic understanding of investment concepts and techniques.

Sector Investing Is Not for Everyone

It may sound as if everyone could benefit from participating in sector investing. This is not entirely true.

Investors with little time to devote to the successful management of a portfolio, who take the "diversified" approach to investing and typically have a lower risk tolerance, should not engage in sector investing.

More active investors, however, may be willing to expose a portion of their portfolio to a limited number of industries that they think will outperform the general market in the months ahead. These investors have evaluated their tolerance for handling investment risk and are able to accept the increased risk in the hope of enhancing the overall return on their investment. They may engage their entire portfolio in this investment technique, but typically they should use only that portion that has been allocated to aggressive investments.

A Dose of Reality

The reason why sector funds may be inappropriate for passive/conservative investors yet appropriate for active/aggressive investors can be summed up in one word: volatility -- the variability of investment returns. The quantitative measurement of this risk is known as standard deviation, or the amount by which an annual return may differ (or deviate) from the average (or standard) return over a specific period of time. The larger the standard deviation, the greater the risk. And it is this standard deviation that allows investors to compare the risks and rewards associated with the price performance of specific industries, sectors, or the overall market. For example, the S&P 500 Composite Index (a broadly diversified assortment of 500 companies in 90 industries) sported a standard deviation of 14.7 over the 1981 - 1995 period, whereas the Gold, Machine Tools, and Entertainment industries posted standard deviations of 42.3, 33.8 and 35.9, respectively, for the same period. (A complete listing of the S&P industries and their standard deviations can be found in Chapter 3.)

Therefore, it is important to realize that even though a one-year advance of 50% by the S&P Health Care Index in 1991 would have been welcomed by both the passive and active investor alike, it's the active investor who more likely would have had the investment temperament or mindset to weather the near-20% drop recorded for this index in 1992. Indeed, it is prudent for all investors to understand that a buy-and-hold approach is typically not recommended when dealing in sector funds. These funds should be looked upon as short-to-intermediate-term trading vehicles and not long-term total-return instruments. Remember, a 50% loss in one year requires a 100% gain in the next year just to break even!

Acknowledgments

This successful completion of this book would not have been possible without the help of Jim Dunn; David Blitzer, Ph.D., S&P's chief economist; Arnie Kaufman, Editor of *The Outlook*; and the S&P equity analysts, who did the work so that I could take the credit: Alan Aaron, Stephen Biggar, Jane Collin, John Coyle, CFA, Raymond Deacon, William Donald, Robert Gold, Kevin Gooley, Tom Graves, CFA, Ronald Gross, Michael Jaffe, Steven Jaworski, Joshua Harari, CFA, Paul Huberman, CFA, Stephen Klein, Leo Larkin, Richard O'Reilly, CFA, Michael Pizzi, Karen Sack, CFA, Herman Saftlas, Robert Schpoont, Catherine Seifert, Joe-Victor Shammas, Kenneth Shea, Elizabeth Vandeventer, and Peter Wood, CFA. I would also like to thank David Conti, my editor, without whom the idea would not have become a reality.

Sam Stovall

1

The Basics Behind
Sector Investing

What's a Sector?

Before we can begin to discuss how you can improve your investment
awareness and results using sector investing, it's necessary to understand
two key components: *sectors* and *industries*. Many use these terms
interchangeably. But they are not the same. A sector is a group of industries
that have similar fundamental characteristics, whereas an industry is a collection
of companies with similar primary lines of business.

Although the definition is easy, the grouping of sectors and industries isn't,
for there is no uniformly agreed-upon arrangement of sectors and industries
that comprise the universe of companies in which you can invest. The U.S.
Government's Standard Industry Classification (SIC) system offers hundreds
of different SIC codes that provide for a defined breakdown of a company's
primary and secondary lines of business. But many regard this system as too
large and unwieldy, as well as out of date. Other industry breakdowns also
have been established by investment publications and brokerage firms.

But one industry grouping has been embraced by individual and institutional
investors alike as a realistic proxy for the universe of stocks found in the New
York, American, and National exchanges. That universe? The S&P 500
Composite Price Index.

Why the S&P 500?

No other benchmark of stock market performance is more widely followed or more closely analyzed than the S&P 500. It is a market-value-weighted index (shares outstanding times stock price) in which each company's influence on the index's performance is directly proportional to its market value. It is this characteristic that makes the S&P 500 such a valuable tool for measuring the performance of actual portfolios. Although the 500 companies chosen for the S&P 500 are not the largest companies in terms of market value, they are chosen for inclusion because they tend to be leaders in important industries within the U.S. economy. The market value of companies in the S&P 500 represents about 75% of the aggregate market value of common stocks traded on the NYSE, and a little less than 70% of all U.S. equities.

The origins of the S&P 500 go back to 1923 when S&P introduced a series of indices that included 233 companies in 26 industries. Since then, the S&P 500 has grown to encompass 500 companies representing 90 industries, 10 sectors (11 if you count "Other"), and four overall segments. These segments are familiar to many: the Industrials, Financials, Utilities, and Transportation issues. The diagram below illustrates this hierarchy.

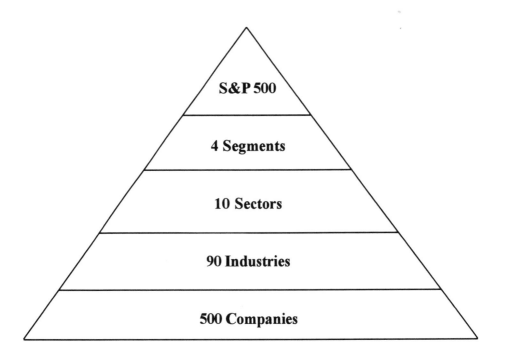

Table 1-1.   The S&P 500 Index: Its Sectors and Industries

Basic Materials
Aluminum
Chemicals
Chemicals (Diversified)
Chemicals (Specialty)
Containers (Metal & Glass)
Containers (Paper)
Gold Mining
Metals (Miscellaneous)
Paper & Forest Products
Steel

Capital Goods
Aerospace/Defense
Electrical Equipment
Engineering & Construction
Heavy Duty Trucks & Parts
Machine Tools
Machinery (Diversified)
Manufacturing (Diversified)
Pollution Control

Consumer Cyclical
Auto Parts
Automobiles
Broadcast Media
Building Materials
Entertainment
Hardware & Tools
Homebuilding
Hotel-Motel
Household Furn. & Appl.
Leisure Time
Manufactured Housing
Publishing
Publishing (Newspapers)
Restaurants
Retail (Department Stores)
Retail (General Merchandise)
Retail (Specialty)
Retail (Specialty-Apparel)
Shoes
Textiles
Toys

Consumer Staples
Beverages (Alcoholic)
Beverages (Soft Drinks)
Cosmetics
Distributors (Cons. Prods.)
Foods
Health Care (Diversified)
Health Care (Drugs)
Health Care (HMOs)
Health Care (Miscellaneous)
Hospital Management
Household Products
Housewares
Medical Products & Supplies
Retail (Drug Stores)
Retail (Food Chains)
Tobacco

Energy
Oil & Gas Drilling
Oil (Domestic Integrated)
Oil (Exploration & Production)
Oil (International Integrated)
Oil Well Equip. & Services

Financials
Insurance Brokers
Investment Bank/Brokerage
Life Insurance
Major Regional Banks
Money Center Banks
Multi-Line Insurance
Personal Loans
Property-Casualty Insurance
Savings & Loans
Financial (Miscellaneous)

Services
Specialized Services
Specialty Printing

Technology
Communication Equip. Mfrs.
Computer Software & Svcs.
Computer Systems
Electronics (Defense)
Electronics (Instrumentation)
Electronics (Semiconductors)
Office Equipment & Supplies
Photography/Imaging
Telecommunications (LD)

Transportation
Airlines
Railroads
Truckers
Transportation (Misc.)

Utilities
Electric Companies
Natural Gas
Telephone

Other
Conglomerates
Miscellaneous

Throughout this book, it will be the industries and sectors found in the S&P 500 Index that will be referred to in the text, tables, and graphs. As of December 29, 1995, this index consisted of this sector/industry breakdown shown in Table 1-1.

See Appendix A for a comprehensive listing of sectors, industries, and companies in the S&P 500 Index.

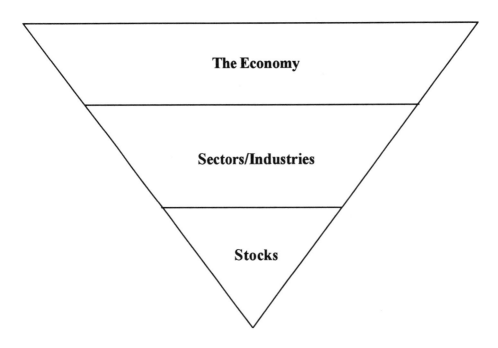

What Then Is Sector Investing?

Now that we know what a sector is, we are ready to understand sector investing, which is as simple a concept as it sounds. Like an inverted pyramid, sector investing starts with an analysis of the big picture (the outlook for the overall U.S. economy) and ends with the identification of stocks worth buying. At the "big picture" level, projections are established to answer such questions as, "Where are we in the economic cycle?"; "Have interest rates peaked?"; and "Is inflation accelerating?" Once these assumptions have been established, the next questions to be answered are "Which industries will benefit from the coming economic developments through an acceleration in earnings growth?" (these are the industries in which to invest, since the outlook for a company's earnings is the key determinant to the movement of its stock price); and "Which industries will experience growth, but at a decelerating rate of speed?" (these should be avoided). Finally, the investor decides "Which companies within those favored industries are projected to perform best?"

And while individual stock selection may be the goal for some, one benefit to sector investing is that significant gains can be obtained without having to select the winners from the losers. Indeed, as mentioned in the introduction, studies have shown that as much as 60% of the price fluctuation of an individual stock can be identified by economic, market, and industry influences, with the remaining 40% dependent on company-specific factors. So whether you prefer to trade in mutual funds or individual stocks, a keen awareness of sector dynamics can help improve your investment results.

Because sector investing is associated with this macro-to-micro, or economy/sector/stock, approach, it also has become known as "top-down" investing. This is in contrast to "bottom-up" investing, where stock selection is based primarily on the interpretation of company-specific, fundamental (supply and demand), and technical (charting and quantitative) factors. Both types of investors can benefit from the guidelines presented in this book.

So where do we start? At the top, with the economy and its influence on the price performances of the underlying industries.

2

How the Economy Affects Industries, Companies, and Their Stock Prices

The first step that you must take to perform sector investing successfully is to be keenly aware of the present and make an educated guess about the future. In order to identify which sectors and industries are expected to outperform the overall market in the coming months, you must ascertain where we are now in the economic cycle and try to get a feel for where we are headed.

Tying Sectors to Cycles

Investment advisors frequently describe stocks as being early-, mid-, and late-cycle performers, or being defensive or interest-sensitive in nature. While this "invest-o-speak" might sound confusing at first, it's really quite straightforward. The economy is cyclical in nature: It continuously meanders through periods of expansion and contraction. What's more, stock prices usually follow a similar, though anticipating, pattern by rising about five months prior to when the economy expands and falling about seven months before the economy begins to contract. Indeed, some industries have demonstrated a pattern of outperforming the overall stock market during certain phases of the economic cycle while underperforming during others. To help pinpoint when industries may perform best or worst, many analysts have broken the complete economic expansion/contraction cycle into five phases: three representing the expansion (early, middle, and late) and two representing the contraction (early and late). And based on this association of industry outperformance and a particular phase within the economic cycle, analysts attempt to get an edge on other investors by anticipating these changes in the economy: They time the purchase of shares that are projected to perform well and avoid those that typically get hammered during a particular phase in the economic cycle. This rolling in-favor/out-of-favor phenomena is also called "sector rotation" since investors rotate the holdings in their portfolios by buying only those stocks or sector funds that are projected to outperform the overall market during the short-to-intermediate term and selling those that have already run their course. For instance, during the early phase of an economic expansion, those stocks that are called "early-cycle" stocks frequently will soar while the overall market posts a healthy gain. And during the beginning of an economic contraction, while the overall market might suffer a double-digit decline, some industries will retreat by a significantly narrower margin. (It is because these industries suffer less, or defend a portfolio from devastating losses, that they are called "defensive" issues.)

Until now, however, empirical evidence linking this sector rotation to the five phases of the economic cycle has been elusive. The National Bureau of Economic Research (NBER), the official keeper of information on economic cycles, indicates that there are two official phases to a complete economic cycle: *expansion* (also known as an economic recovery), and *contraction* (also called recession). An economic expansion is when most major sectors of the economy are advancing; a recession is when most are declining. The NBER's Business Cycle Dating Committee identifies turning points; usually the committee reports within a few months of these turning points. For most people, this definition is a bit nebulous and open to speculation. To satisfy impatient politicians, the economist Arthur Okun (an advisor to Presidents Kennedy and Johnson) suggested that two consecutive quarters of shrinking gross domestic product (GDP) be used to signal a recession. In 1980, however, the United States entered into a recession with only one quarter of declining GDP. In addition, should one use two quarters of advancing or declining GDP as a sole guide, six months could go by before an investor becomes aware of (and the NBER confirms) the existence of an expansion or contraction. Thus, analysts rely on additional characteristics to identify the coming peaks and troughs in the economic cycle. In general, these additional characteristics include monthly figures on employment levels, interest rates, and the rate of inflation. Analysts have also come to learn the fairly regular pattern the economy takes when traversing the expansion and contraction phases of an economic cycle.

Characteristics of the
Economic Cycle

At the beginning of an economic expansion, the picture is one of general despair: Unemployment is high; consumer and industrial demands are low; and consumer confidence is posting successive monthly declines. In an effort to pull the economy out of recession, raise consumer confidence, and increase consumption (since consumers account for two-thirds of all GDP expenditures), the Federal Reserve Board ("the Fed") has been lowering interest rates since the middle of the previous economic contraction by cutting the federal funds and discount rates. (There are 12 Federal Reserve Banks, but none set policy; the Board of Governors of the Federal Reserve System does this.) The only positive aspect of this period in the economic cycle is that since there is a lack of significant demand for goods and services, the inflation rate is either flat or declining.

Soon, these lower interest rates begin to have an effect on the economy by making it easier and cheaper to purchase the goods and services that consumers have deprived themselves of for so long. The confidence that consumers hold for the future improves and they start to spend again. This pickup in spending requires an increase in industrial output and the need for more employees, who in turn join in the demand for goods and services, which requires a further increase in industrial output and the need for more employees, and so on.

You can imagine, then, that as this pent-up demand is released there are a greater number of consumers (demand) chasing a more limited number of goods (supply), thereby putting ever increasing upward pressure on prices. And while two of the Fed's three general economic goals are now beginning to be satisfied (full employment and economic growth), which should make them happy, their third goal of stable prices is being undermined and becomes cause for concern.

Therefore, in an effort to combat this upward spiral of inflation, the Fed typically "leans against the wind" to temper the growth of the economy and the pickup in inflation by raising interest rates. And while the Fed's goal is a slowdown in economic growth to a more manageable level of expansion, what typically happens is that its rate-hiking moves, together with the effects of other business and economic factors, throw the economy into recession. And in a situation that is a reverse image of the early phase of the economic expansion, we find interest rates on the rise, consumer demand beginning to fall, industrial output starting to slacken, and employment levels declining. Only when the Fed realizes that it has gone too far with its interest rate policy does it again begin to ease interest rates to reignite the economic process.

"When to Hold and When to Fold" or Identifying an Industry's Track Record

As can be seen in Table 2-1, there have been nine complete economic expansions in the past 50 years, the shortest of which lasted 12 months, and the longest 106 months; we are currently in the tenth. On average, the duration was nearly 50 months. There also have been nine economic contractions, lasting anywhere from 6 to 16 months and averaging nearly 11 months. The table also shows that while the stock market attempts to anticipate a downturn in the economy, it is not always successful. In fact in 1980, the stock market peaked one month after the start of an economic contraction. In another case, it peaked 13 months in advance. In all, however, the market anticipates an economic contraction by an average of seven months. Yet the market is a bit more successful, and consistent, when it comes to anticipating the start of an economic expansion. The market bottomed as little as three months and as much as eight months prior to an economic revival, or about five months on average.

This difference in consistency and success of anticipating economic expansions and contractions is interesting: Why would investors anticipate an economic downturn through a peak in stock prices by seven months (and quite inconsistently), yet lead a recovery (with more success) by only five months? Is it because of the two emotions that drive the stock market (fear and greed), that most investors are more motivated by fear than greed? (This implies that the risk tolerance of most investors is conservative and they are more willing to bypass an opportunity than give back a gain.) Or is it merely that more analysis on spotting tops in the market than bottoms needs to be done?

In an attempt to establish empirical evidence uncovering a pattern of market outperformance and underperformance by industries in the S&P

**Table 2-1.   Peaks and Troughs in the Economy and Stock Market
November 1945 - December 1995**

Expansion/Contraction		Event	Duration (Months)	Date S&P 500 Peaked (P) or Troughed (T)		S&P 500 Anticipated Economy
Start	Finish					
Nov-45	Oct-48	Expansion	36	T	Jul-45	4
Nov-48	Sep-49	Contraction	11	P	Jul-48	4
Oct-49	Jun-53	Expansion	45	T	Jun-49	4
Jul-53	Apr-54	Contraction	10	P	Jan-53	6
May-54	Jul-57	Expansion	39	T	Sep-53	8
Aug-57	Mar-58	Contraction	8	P	Aug-56	12
Apr-58	Mar-60	Expansion	24	T	Oct-57	6
Apr-60	Jan-61	Contraction	10	P	Jul-59	9
Feb-61	Nov-69	Expansion	106	T	Oct-60	4
Dec-69	Oct-70	Contraction	11	P	Nov-68	13
Nov-70	Oct-73	Expansion	36	T	May-70	6
Nov-73	Feb-75	Contraction	16	P	Jan-73	10
Mar-75	Dec-79	Expansion	58	T	Oct-74	5
Jan-80	Jun-80	Contraction	6	P	Feb-80	-1
Jul-80	Jun-81	Expansion	12	T	Mar-80	4
Jul-81	Oct-82	Contraction	16	P	Nov-80	8
Nov-82	Jun-90	Expansion	92	T	Aug-82	3
Jul-90	Feb-91	Contraction	8	P	Jul-90	0
Mar-91	???	Expansion	57	T	Oct-90	5
Averages:	9 Contractions		10.7			6.8
	9 Expansions (w/o current)		49.8			4.9

Sources: National Bureau of Economic Research; Standard & Poor's

500, each economic expansion was separated into three equal time periods. For instance, the expansion of November 1970 to November 1973 lasted 36 months. The early, middle, and late phases were then defined as lasting 12 months each. The economic contractions, on the other hand, were divided in half. The percentage of gain or loss for each of the industries during these phases for the nine expansions and contractions were calculated and compared with the results for the S&P 500. Table 2-2 shows the number of times that an industry outperformed the S&P 500 in each of these phases. (Appendix B shows the results on a percentage basis.) Take a look at the automobile industry, which is in the consumer cyclical sector on Table 2-2. Since data for this index started to be kept before 1945 (the beginning of this study) it participated in all nine of the economic expansions and contractions. Hence the 9 in both "# of Cycles" columns. (Auto parts, you'll notice, participated in only four each.) Yet during the early phase of the economic expansion, automobile stocks outperformed the S&P 500 eight times, and then experienced a declining consistency of market outperformance in the middle and late expansion phases and in each of the two contraction phases. The stocks in the automobile industry, therefore, appear to be classic (no pun intended) early-cycle performers. The industry also had a batting average of one for five -- more on this later.

Although it was not surprising that automobile stocks were early-cycle performers, an interesting revelation occurred with the manufactured housing industry. In the past, these issues have been characterized by some analysts as non-interest-sensitive (interest-sensitive means they do well when interest rates fall and poorly when rates rise) because earnings were driven by substitution and demographics. In a period of rising interest rates, which typically increases the cost of financing a newly purchased home, consumers were supposed to shy away from the more expensive site-built homes and opt for the more cost-effective manufactured homes. This action is called substitution. In addition, demographics played a longer-term role in the earnings of manufactured housing companies as indicated by the old industry adage that these homes are meant for the "newly wed and the nearly dead." But this analysis shows that the share prices of manufactured home stocks outperformed the market during the period of falling interest rates five out of the five times it participated in this study, leading one to conclude that while this industry's earnings may rise as a result of substitution and demographic trends, its share prices are indeed interest-rate driven.

But just as there are some industries that are classic cyclical plays that

Table 2-2.

	The Number of Times This Industry Beat the S&P 500 in the Past Economic:							
	Expansions				Contractions			Batting
	# of Cycles	Early	Middle	Late	# of Cycles	Early	Late	Average
Basic Materials								
Aluminum	9	6	5	3	9	3	3	2
Chemicals	9	6	4	3	9	5	3	2
Chemicals (Diversified)	2	2	2	1	3	1	1	--
Chemicals (Specialty)	0	--	--	--	1	0	1	--
Containers (Metal & Glass)	9	1	4	5	9	5	3	2
Containers (Paper)	9	6	6	4	9	3	6	3
Gold Mining	9	1	6	4	9	5	7	3
Metals (Miscellaneous)	9	4	4	6	9	5	3	2
Paper & Forest Products	9	7	4	4	9	3	5	2
Steel	9	6	3	4	9	3	2	1
Capital Goods								
Aerospace/Defense	9	6	5	4	9	6	3	3
Electrical Equipment	9	6	7	4	9	2	7	3
Engineering & Construction	0	0	0	0	1	0	1	--
Heavy Duty Trucks & Parts	9	6	4	3	9	1	2	1
Machine Tools	9	5	4	4	9	2	5	2
Machinery (Diversified)	9	5	5	4	9	3	5	3
Manufacturing (Diversified)	0	--	--	--	1	0	1	--
Pollution Control	4	4	3	2	5	2	4	--
Consumer Cyclical								
Auto Parts	4	2	3	1	4	0	2	--
Automobiles	9	8	4	2	9	1	3	1
Broadcast Media	8	8	6	5	9	4	6	--
Building Materials	9	5	2	4	9	1	8	2
Entertainment	9	5	5	4	9	6	5	4
Hardware & Tools	2	1	0	1	2	0	2	--
Homebuilding	4	3	2	1	5	1	4	--
Hotel-Motel	4	4	2	2	5	0	4	--
Household Furn. & Appl.	9	6	4	5	9	2	5	3
Leisure Time	4	4	2	1	5	2	3	--
Manufactured Housing	4	2	1	1	5	1	5	--
Publishing	9	5	5	5	9	2	9	4
Publishing (Newspapers)	4	4	3	2	4	1	2	--
Restaurants	4	3	3	3	5	1	3	--
Retail (Department Stores)	9	5	3	4	9	6	6	3
Retail (General Merchandise)	4	2	2	2	4	1	3	--
Retail (Specialty)	1	1	0	1	1	0	1	--
Retail (Specialty-Apparel)	0	--	--	--	1	0	1	--
Shoes	9	4	4	5	9	3	7	2
Textiles	9	5	5	5	9	3	4	3
Toys	4	3	1	3	5	1	3	--
Consumer Staples								
Beverages (Alcoholic)	9	3	5	5	9	7	6	4
Beverages (Soft Drinks)	9	3	7	6	9	6	8	4
Cosmetics	6	2	5	3	7	3	4	--
Distributors (Cons. Prods.)	1	0	0	1	1	1	0	--
Foods	9	4	3	5	9	8	6	3
Health Care (Diversified)	0	--	--	--	1	1	1	--
Health Care (Drugs)	9	3	6	6	9	8	5	4
Health Care (HMOs)	0	--	--	--	0	--	--	--
Health Care (Miscellaneous)	0	--	--	--	1	1	1	--
Hospital Management	2	1	1	2	3	2	2	--

Table 2-2.   **The Number of Times This Industry Beat the S&P 500 in the Past Economic: (cont'd)**

	Expansions			Contractions			Batting
	# of Cycles	Early	Middle	Late	# of Cycles	Early	Late	Average

	# of Cycles	Early	Middle	Late	# of Cycles	Early	Late	Average
Household Products	9	4	3	5	9	8	8	3
Housewares	0	--	--	--	1	0	1	--
Medical Products & Supplies	4	1	3	2	5	3	4	--
Retail (Drug Stores)	4	4	3	1	4	1	4	--
Retail (Food Chains)	9	3	2	6	9	6	8	3
Tobacco	9	2	5	6	9	7	8	4
Energy								
Oil & Gas Drilling	4	2	2	3	5	3	2	--
Oil (Domestic Integrated)	9	5	4	4	9	3	4	1
Oil (Exploration & Production)	0	--	--	--	1	0	0	--
Oil (International Integrated)	9	5	6	3	9	3	5	3
Oil Well Equip. & Services	9	4	7	6	9	4	5	3
Financials								
Insurance Brokers	0	--	--	--	1	0	1	--
Investment Bank/Brokerage	0	--	--	--	0	--	--	--
Life Insurance	9	6	4	6	9	4	8	3
Major Regional Banks	9	2	3	4	9	4	6	1
Money Center Banks	9	1	3	5	9	5	6	3
Multi-Line Insurance	4	3	1	3	5	1	2	--
Personal Loans	9	4	3	4	9	4	8	1
Property-Casualty Insurance	9	5	1	6	9	4	7	3
Savings & Loans	5	2	2	3	6	1	6	--
Financial (Miscellaneous)	0	--	--	--	1	0	1	--
Services								
Specialized Services	1	1	1	0	1	0	1	--
Specialty Printing	0	--	--	--	0	--	--	--
Technology								
Communication Equip. Mfrs.	2	2	0	2	3	1	1	--
Computer Software & Svcs.	2	2	2	1	3	0	3	--
Computer Systems	9	5	4	5	9	4	6	3
Electronics (Defense)	0				1	1	1	--
Electronics (Instrumentation)	4	2	4	3	4	3	2	--
Electronics (Semiconductors)	4	3	2	3	4	1	2	--
Office Equipment & Supplies	1	0	1	0	1	0	1	--
Photography/Imaging	0	--	--	--	0	--	--	--
Telecommunications (LD)	0	--	--	--	1	0	0	--
Transportation								
Airlines	9	8	4	2	9	3	4	1
Railroads	9	6	2	4	9	2	2	1
Truckers	6	5	4	3	7	1	5	--
Transportation (Misc.)	0	--	--	--	1	0	1	--
Utilities								
Electric Companies	9	2	1	3	9	7	6	2
Natural Gas	9	4	5	3	9	7	3	2
Telephone	0	--	--	--	1	1	0	--
Other								
Conglomerates	4	4	2	1	5	1	4	--
Miscellaneous	0	--	--	--	1	1	0	--

are associated with the early expansion (like automobiles), middle expansion (electrical equipment), late expansion (metals misc.), early contraction (food), and late contraction (life insurance) phases, there are some that performed well in several phases (and are indicated by a batting average of 4 out of 5), or nearly always struck out (1 for 5). The batting average is merely a count of the number of times an industry outperformed the market five or more times out of nine during each of the three economic expansion phases and during each of the two contractionary phases. Batting averages were computed for only those industries that participated in all nine economic cycles (or where 9 appears in the # of Cycles column). Batting averages fell between 1 and 4. Those industries with consistently high batting averages include beverages, entertainment, health care (drugs), publishing, and tobacco. Those with a batting average of only one in five include airlines, automobiles, heavy duty trucks and parts, major regional banks, oil (domestic integrated), personal loans, railroads, and steel.

The knowledge that investors should gain from Table 2-2 and Appendix B is that the performance of the overall market is highly cyclical and that more than 80% of the gains that are likely to be recorded take place during the more investor-friendly stock market environment of the late contraction to mid-expansion phases of an economic cycle versus the late expansion and early contraction phases, when the investing environment appears more hostile. In particular, the market experienced an average loss of around 10% during the first, or defensive, phase of an economic contraction but gained an average 8% during the second, or interest-sensitive, phase of the contraction, and 22%, 12%, and 9% for the early, mid, and late phases of an economic expansion, respectively.

Table 2-2 also suggests that less-aggressive investors who still wish to participate in sector investing should gravitate toward those industries with batting averages of 3 or 4 out of 5 (none was 5 out of 5), and that those investors who are more aggressive and willing to monitor the market's sector rotation may hope to reap greater rewards by investing in industries with batting averages of 1 or 2 out of 5.

Above all, this table shows that one way to be successful with sector investing is to realize that gains and losses come from how skillfully an investor anticipates these sector/industry rotations. The trick is to be able to identify the current economic phase and anticipate the timing of the succeeding phase.

Timing Guidelines

General timing guideposts include:

1. Decide whether the economy is in recovery (expanding) or in recession (contracting).

2. Measure the duration of the current expansion or contraction and compare to the average as indicated in Table 2-1 -- this assumes that the NBER has identified such a date. In reality, however, the NBER will fix the date of an economic contraction after the subsequent expansion has already started. It is advised, therefore, to monitor the reports of well-respected Wall Street economists and use their prognostications, as well as your own input, to estimate the starting and ending dates of economic peaks and troughs.

3. Identify which industries are outperforming or underperforming the overall market and compare them to Table 2-2.

4. Monitor the general trend in those economic indicators that measure the growth or rise in consumer expectations, industrial output, inflation, interest rates, and the slope of the yield curve. This last concept merits further explanation. The yield curve is a pictorial representation of the yields offered on debt instruments from the 3-month Treasury bill through the 30-year Treasury bond; this curve typically demonstrates an upwardly sloping bias with the spread (or difference) between short-term bills and long-term bonds being around 2 percentage points (also referred to as 200 basis points). In the early stages of an economic recovery, however, the yield curve is sharp as the spread expands to 300 basis points or beyond because investors anticipate economic growth to accelerate in the months ahead (as well as a resulting pickup in inflation). Prior to an economic contraction, on the other hand, the yield curve has narrowed to the point where the spread is 100 basis points or less. There have even been times when the yield curve has become inverted, meaning that shorter-term bonds yielded more than longer-term bonds. This happens when investors anticipate a recession in the coming months, which will reduce the longer-term growth in the economy and inflationary expectations.

In general, the five phases of an economic cycle are characterized by:

Early Expansion
Duration: First third of economic expansion, or
                                                 about 17 months on average.

Consumer expectations:	Rising sharply.
Industrial production:	Flat to rising modestly.
Inflation:	Continuing to fall.
Interest rates:	Bottoming out (it leads inflation).
Yield curve:	Steep.

Middle Expansion

Duration:	Second third of economic expansion, or about 17 months on average.
Consumer expectations:	Leveling off.
Industrial production:	Rising sharply.
Inflation:	Bottoming out.
Interest rates:	Rising modestly.
Yield curve:	Moderate.

Late Expansion

Duration:	Last third of economic expansion, or about 17 months on average.
Consumer expectations:	Declining.
Industrial production:	Flattening out.
Inflation:	Rising modestly and beginning to be of concern to investors and the Fed.
Interest rates:	Rising rapidly due to supply and demand of capital and Fed policy to combat projected increase in inflation.
Yield curve:	Flattening out (short rates rising as the Fed combats inflation, whereas long rates may be falling as they reflect future inflationary expectations).

Early Contraction

Duration:	First half of economic contraction, or about 6 months on average.
Consumer expectations:	Falling sharply.
Industrial production:	Declining.
Inflation:	Rising less strongly.
Interest rates:	Peaking.
Yield curve:	Flat (and sometimes inverted -- short rates are higher than long rates).

Figure 2-1: Typical Sector Rotation within a Complete Economic Cycle

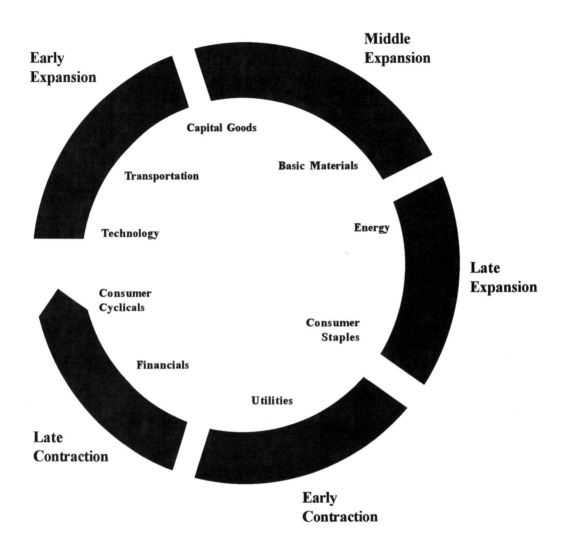

Late Contraction

Duration:	Final half of economic contraction, or about 6 months on average.
Consumer expectations:	Reviving.
Industrial production:	Decline diminishing.
Inflation:	Flat to declining.
Interest rates:	Falling.
Yield curve:	Rising again.

Figure 2-1 is a graphic representation of the rotation of sectors favored by investors as the economy passes through a complete economic cycle of expansion and contraction. As the economy begins to expand, investors rotate through the technology, transportation, and capital goods issues as demand increases, output expands, and inflation heats up. But as the expansion matures, too much of a good thing causes interest rates to rise; investors then begin favoring the more defensive issues as the market averages start to decline. Next, as the Fed looks to pull the economy out of recession by easing its grip on interest rates, the financial issues come to life. And as lower interest rates induce increased consumption and production, the consumer cyclicals begin to take off and the sector rotation process begins again.

Caveats to Consider

There are some definitional factors that you should be aware of. First, since the S&P 500 is a market-capitalization-weighted index, extreme swings in the stock price performance of industry leaders may have skewed the industry index's return during the periods analyzed. For instance, IBM's price slump of 1993-94 will make itself evident when the results for the current expansion are included. Second, the returns calculated do not include reinvested dividends, which doesn't fully portray the investment performances of such total-return industries as electric companies, baby bells, and natural gas pipelines and distributors. And finally, the method of separation of expansion and contraction phases (into thirds and halves, respectively) was chosen for simplicity. A more in-depth analysis could indeed establish a different duration for each of the five phases.

Also, although the findings of this analysis are certainly enlightening and, hopefully, profitable, investors should be aware of one additional fact: The study is a measure of how these industries performed in time under economic, political, and market conditions that were particular to that point in time. And as everyone is aware, conditions constantly change. For instance, aerospace/defense issues appear to be early-expansion stocks in this study. But now that the Cold War has ended, will this continue to hold true? Only time will tell. But this particular question does serve as a perfect way to introduce the next chapter. Although this study has identified general patterns, future industry-specific factors may affect future price performances for these industries. It therefore pays to be informed of the general and specific economic factors that drive certain industry groups as well as other less certain aspects, such as the acceptance of new product introductions. It is with this in mind -- the need to look beneath the general trends -- that we move to Chapter 3, where you will become familiar with the fundamental and investment characteristics of each of the industries in the S&P 500.

3

Industry Profiles
and Projections

Standard & Poor's analysts review hundreds of reports issued by the U.S. government, industry trade organizations, and individual companies, as well as a host of investment reports from other Wall Street research firms. Although the individual investor is not expected to read this massive amount of information — let alone have access to it — there are three things the sector investor must be familiar with in order to make winning investment decisions.

■ The first is a carry through of the top-down framework of sector investing. In order to anticipate which industries will experience an increase or decrease in orders and profits, an investor must become familiar with those economic indicators that will have an influence on an industry's earnings and share price movements.

■ Next, an investor must have a framework from which to judge if an industry is overvalued or undervalued on a historical basis. For instance, even if the projected phase of the economic cycle might indicate that a certain industry should outperform the overall market, if that industry already is trading at a substantial premium, an investor might just be buying these shares at the top rather than at the bottom.

■ Finally, the investor must be familiar with the fundamental characteristics of a particular industry in order to judge whether stocks within that industry might act similarly to past performances or dynamics within the industry will alter future price movements.

This chapter is broken into two sections to help the investor accomplish the above tasks: section one consists of comparative measurements and relative performances, while section two contains investment outlooks.

Comparative Measurements

This first section of this chapter shows the diversity of influences, performances and normal valuations for the industries in the S&P 500 Index. It also discusses how to evaluate these different industry valuations. It starts with three tables that show influencing economic indicators, price performance results, and valuation measurements for the industries within the S&P 500. The tables are arranged by sector, with each member industry then listed alphabetically. Companies that make up these industries are found in appendix A.

Table 3-1 is a quick summary of three indicators, displayed in macro-to-micro (sector specific to industry specific) order, that influence earnings and share prices for those industries in the S&P 500. These indicators are usually economic reports that can be retrieved by an investor on a weekly, monthly, or quarterly basis from most financial publications. For some sectors, like financials, the macro indicators are the same for all industries since the driving force for all of the industries within this sector is the direction (or anticipated direction) of interest rates. When interest rates fall, the prices for stocks in the financial sector rise. This is because investors expect profit margins for financial companies to widen, as the cost to obtain the money that they lend out (through interest on savings accounts, etc.) drops more quickly that the price they charge (through interest on credit cards, auto loans and the like). And the reverse is also true. When interest rates rise, share prices fall because of the anticipated narrowing of profit margins.

Some of the more-micro, or industry specific, indicators may differ within a sector, however, depending on the effects they have on the particular industries. In general, an investor can keep abreast of improving or deteriorating trends by closely monitoring these economic indicators, and thereby increase or decrease investment exposure in industries that will be helped or hurt by these developments.

Table 3-1. Influencing Indicators

Sector/Industry	Indicators (Macro to Micro)		
Basic Materials			
Aluminum	Industrial Production	End Market Expectations	Product Prices
Chemicals	Industrial Production	End Market Expectations	Chem. Production Indexes
Chemicals (Diversified)	Industrial Production	End Market Expectations	Non-Chemical Factors
Chemicals (Specialty)	Industrial Production	End Market Expectations	Raw Material Costs
Containers (Metal & Glass)	Personal Income	Raw Material Costs	Agricultural Output
Containers (Paper)	GDP Growth	Industrial Production	End Market Expectations
Gold Mining	Capacity Utilization	Employment	U.S. Dollar
Metals (Miscellaneous)	World GDP Growth	Housing Starts	Auto Production
Paper & Forest Products	Interest Rates	Housing Starts	Capacity Utilization
Steel	GDP Growth	Auto Production	Construction Spending
Capital Goods			
Aerospace/Defense	GDP Growth	Defense Spending	Contract Awards
Conglomerates	Industrial Production	Consumer Confidence	Interest Rates
Electrical Equipment	GDP Growth	Capital Spending	U.S. Dollar
Engineering & Construction	Capital Spending	Order Levels	Order Backlog
Heavy Duty Trucks & Parts	GDP Growth	Industrial Production	Retail Sales
Machine Tools	GDP Growth	Capital Spending	Machine Tool Orders
Machinery (Diversified)	Interest Rates	Housing Starts	Auto Sales
Manufacturing (Diversified)	Industrial Production	NAPM	Interest Rates
Pollution Control	Industrial Production	Capital Spending	Construction Spending
Consumer Cyclical			
Auto Parts	Consumer Confidence	Personal Income	Interest Rates
Automobiles	Consumer Confidence	Personal Income	Interest Rates
Broadcast Media	Advertising Spending	Interest Rates	Regulatory
Building Materials	Interest Rates	Consumer Spending	Housing Starts
Entertainment	Consumer Spending	New Products	Product Quality
Hardware & Tools	Interest Rates	Housing Starts	New Products
Homebuilding	Interest Rates	Employment	Housing Starts
Hotel-Motel	Consumer Confidence	Travel Costs	Construction Levels
Household Furn. & Appliances	Interest Rates	Consumer Spending	Housing Starts
Leisure Time	Consumer Confidence	Demographics	New Products
Manufactured Housing	Interest Rates	Employment	Consumer Confidence
Publishing	GDP Growth	Consumer Confidence	Paper Costs
Publishing (Newspapers)	GDP Growth	Advertising Spending	Paper Costs
Restaurants	Consumer Confidence	Disposable Income	Cost Pressures
Retail (Department Stores)	Consumer Confidence	Disposable Income	Employment
Retail (General Merchandise)	Consumer Confidence	Disposable Income	Employment
Retail (Specialty)	Consumer Confidence	Disposable Income	Employment
Retail (Specialty-Apparel)	Consumer Confidence	Disposable Income	Employment
Shoes	Consumer Confidence	Disposable Income	Interest Rates
Textiles	Consumer Confidence	Interest Rates	Housing Starts
Toys	Consumer Confidence	Disposable Income	New Products
Consumer Staples			
Beverages (Alcoholic)	Interest Rates	Consumer Confidence	Personal Income
Beverages (Soft Drinks)	Interest Rates	Consumer Confidence	Personal Income
Cosmetics	Consumer Spending	New Products	U.S. Dollar
Distributors (Consumer Prods.)	Inflation	Interest Rates	Consumer Confidence
Foods	Interest Rates	Consumer Confidence	Personal Income
Health Care (Diversified)	Demographics	Gov't Policies	U.S. Dollar

Sector/Industry	*Indicators (Macro to Micro)*		
Health Care (Drugs)	Demographics	Gov't Policies	U.S. Dollar
Health Care (HMOs)	Demographics	Medicare Reimbursement	Regulatory
Health Care (Miscellaneous)	Demographics	Medicare Reimbursement	Employment
Hospital Management	Demographics	Medicare Reimbursement	Regulatory
Household Products	Interest Rates	Housing Starts	New Products
Housewares	Interest Rates	Housing Starts	New Products
Medical Products & Supplies	Demographics	Medicare Reimbursement	U.S. Dollar
Retail (Drug Stores)	Inflation	Disposable Income	Demographics
Retail (Food Chains)	Inflation	Disposable Income	Consumer Confidence
Tobacco	Interest Rates	Consumer Confidence	Taxes
Energy			
Oil & Gas Drilling	Commodity Prices	U.S. Dollar	Refined Product Margins
Oil (Domestic Integrated)	Commodity Prices	U.S. Dollar	Refined Product Margins
Oil (Exploration & Production)	Commodity Prices	U.S. Dollar	Refined Product Margins
Oil (International Integrated)	Commodity Prices	U.S. Dollar	Refined Product Margins
Oil Well Equip. & Services	Commodity Prices	U.S. Dollar	Refined Product Margins
Financials			
Insurance Brokers	Interest Rates	Policy Sales	Policy Pricing
Investment Banking/Brokerage	Interest Rates	Employment	Stock Market Outlook
Life Insurance	Interest Rates	Employment	Personal Savings
Major Regional Banks	Interest Rates	Inflation	Employment
Money Center Banks	Interest Rates	Inflation	Employment
Multi-Line Insurance	Interest Rates	GDP Growth	Pricing
Personal Loans	Interest Rates	Employment	Consumer Confidence
Property-Casualty Insurance	Interest Rates	GDP Growth	Policy Pricing
Savings & Loans	Interest Rates	Employment	Housing Prices
Financial (Miscellaneous)	Interest Rates	Employment	Stock Market Outlook
Services			
Specialized Services	GDP Growth	Consumer Confidence	Capacity Utilization
Specialty Printing	Interest Rates	Advertising Spending	Paper Costs
Technology			
Communication Equip. Mfrs.	GDP Growth	Inflation	Regulatory
Computer Software & Svcs.	Employment	Computer Sales	New Products
Computer Systems	Capital Spending	U.S. Dollar	New Products
Electronics (Defense)	GDP Growth	Defense Spending	Contract Awards
Electronics (Instrumentation)	Capital Spending	U.S. Dollar	R&D Spending
Electronics (Semiconductors)	Capital Spending	U.S. Dollar	Book-to-Bill Ratio
Office Equipment & Supplies	Capital Spending	Interest Rates	Employment
Photography/Imaging	Demographics	Consumer Confidence	Personal Spending
Telecom. (Long Dist.)	GDP Growth	Inflation	Regulatory
Transportation			
Airlines	GDP Growth	Consumer Confidence	Fuel Costs
Railroads	Industrial Production	Construction Spending	Weather
Truckers	Industrial Production	Interest rates	Fuel Costs
Transportation (Miscellaneous)	Industrial Production	Retail Sales	Fuel Costs
Utilities			
Electric Companies	Interest Rates	Industrial Production	Regulatory
Natural Gas	Interest Rates	Industrial Production	Product Prices
Telephone	GDP Growth	Inflation	Regulatory

Table 3-2 on the next page summarizes industry performances, displaying each industry's 1-, 5-, 10-, and 15-year price performances (dividends are not included), along with its standard deviation and an "Averages Since" column to tell the reader if an industry index has a shorter than 15-year average. In general, this table informs investors of the magnitude of average returns and volatility that may be experienced when investing in separate industries.

What is interesting about table 3-2 is the return/risk tradeoff that each industry has provided to investors in the past. Take a look at gold mining stocks. It shows that if you held gold mining stocks in your portfolio as a hedge against inflation, as many asset allocators suggest, you would have realized only a 2% average annual price gain during the past 15 years. Yet the volatility, as indicated by a standard deviation of 42, would have been unbearable. Standard deviation is simply the percent by which returns fluctuate, or deviate, from the average, or norm, 66% of the time. So combining these return/risk factors, you would see that during two out of every three years, gold mining stocks provided an average annual return of 2%, give or take 42%! That means that your gold stocks could have risen by as much as 44% (2 + 42) or fallen as much as 40% (2 - 42). To win with this industry, your timing had to be impeccable!

For less aggressive sector investors, however, the key is to look for those industries that have high long-term returns, but low standard deviations. Take the food industry, for instance. In the past 15 years, its average annual return was 19.9 and its standard deviation was 20. Therefore, on average, you could expect a fluctuation range from a plus 40% to a minus 0.1%. Not bad!

One final note, as this has to do with the benefits of diversification on volatility (but at the expense of potential returns). The standard deviation on the S&P 500 over the past 15 years was only 11. Yet there are less than a handful of industries that have an equal or lower standard deviation. This interesting phenomena proves that holding a large basket of stocks from a wide variety of industries significantly decreases your portfolio's overall fluctuation of returns.

Table 3-2. Industry Performances and Volatility (Data through 12/29/95)

Sector / Industry	Average Annual % Change				Std. Dev.	Avgs. Since
	1995	5 Yrs.	10 Yrs.	15 Yrs.		
Basic Materials						
Aluminum	21.1	9.1	9.8	6.3	24	1981
Chemicals	26.8	15.2	12.8	11.3	19	1981
Chemicals (Diversified)	29.1	16.5	13.7	12.5	15	1981
Chemicals (Specialty)	29.4	12.2	8.9	NA	15	1984
Containers (Metal & Glass)	5.5	13.7	15.3	17.8	20	1981
Containers (Paper)	-4.6	7.7	9.6	12.8	25	1981
Gold Mining	11.6	6.1	6.9	2.0	42	1981
Metals (Miscellaneous)	8.0	8.8	13.0	7.0	25	1981
Paper & Forest Products	7.4	10.2	9.0	9.6	19	1981
Steel	-8.4	13.5	7.7	2.9	24	1981
Capital Goods						
Aerospace/Defense	62.1	20.9	12.0	11.0	26	1981
Electrical Equipment	36.7	17.0	11.3	11.3	18	1981
Engineering & Construction	40.2	8.8	11.7	NA	17	1983
Heavy Duty Trucks & Parts	3.8	12.2	3.1	5.7	27	1981
Machine Tools	11.3	9.4	-4.0	-4.2	34	1981
Machinery (Diversified)	20.7	14.5	10.6	5.1	21	1981
Manufacturing (Diversified)	38.6	16.8	14.1	NA	11	1983
Pollution Control	11.8	-1.5	10.6	12.5	40	1981
Consumer Cyclical						
Auto Parts	20.8	21.4	9.1	10.1	26	1981
Automobiles	14.4	14.9	7.9	11.0	31	1981
Broadcast Media	30.6	17.7	17.7	21.7	30	1981
Building Materials	33.4	15.5	10.0	10.5	24	1981
Entertainment	19.4	14.6	17.2	16.1	36	1981
Hardware & Tools	43.3	14.3	7.7	8.2	13	1981
Homebuilding	41.3	19.5	8.6	4.5	38	1981
Hotel-Motel	17.2	26.7	9.3	11.3	46	1981
Household Furn. & Appl.	18.8	15.1	6.9	10.8	31	1981
Leisure Time	24.0	16.0	3.7	8.7	42	1981
Manufactured Housing	31.8	16.6	6.9	11.3	36	1981
Publishing	23.8	14.1	8.5	13.1	27	1981
Publishing (Newspapers)	23.1	10.0	5.4	10.8	24	1981
Restaurants	48.9	23.4	14.9	19.9	36	1981
Retail (Department Stores)	12.1	9.2	11.4	16.9	29	1981
Retail (General Merchandise)	10.5	10.0	11.3	15.3	29	1981
Retail (Specialty)	-3.4	12.3	10.7	NA	24	1982
Retail (Specialty-Apparel)	9.7	6.8	7.5	NA	42	1985
Shoes	33.8	22.3	19.9	19.7	38	1981
Textiles	10.0	5.3	6.0	10.5	38	1981
Toys	35.8	32.1	13.7	11.9	39	1981
Consumer Staples						
Beverages (Alcoholic)	24.8	9.5	13.2	17.9	28	1981
Beverages (Soft Drinks)	47.2	22.2	24.3	23.9	26	1981
Cosmetics	30.1	22.6	21.2	15.4	24	1981
Distributors (Cons. Prods.)	22.3	13.3	11.0	NA	15	1982
Foods	24.7	11.1	15.5	19.9	20	1981
Health Care (Diversified)	44.5	12.5	15.5	NA	17	1983
Health Care (Drugs)	67.1	16.0	18.9	17.4	18	1981
Health Care (HMOs)	28.8	NA	NA	NA	9	1992
Health Care (Miscellaneous)	57.9	11.5	6.2	NA	34	1983

Sector / Industry	Average Annual % Change				Std. Dev.	Avgs. Since
	1995	5 Yrs.	10 Yrs.	15 Yrs.		
Hospital Management	39.4	6.9	8.3	8.6	34	1981
Household Products	36.6	14.5	17.6	17.7	18	1981
Housewares	5.7	14.0	17.1	NA	23	1984
Medical Products & Supplies	66.9	14.6	14.8	14.0	23	1981
Retail (Drug Stores)	40.2	15.7	13.3	15.7	34	1981
Retail (Food Chains)	25.9	11.5	17.6	19.0	21	1981
Tobacco	49.5	11.2	23.2	19.8	19	1981
Energy						
Oil & Gas Drilling	36.4	0.2	0.3	-7.4	43	1981
Oil (Domestic Integrated)	9.5	-0.6	3.9	2.1	23	1981
Oil (Exploration & Production)	16.2	-11.2	NA	NA	12	1989
Oil (International Integrated)	28.9	10.5	13.0	9.0	18	1981
Oil Well Equip. & Services	35.4	3.2	7.2	-1.8	32	1981
Financials						
Insurance Brokers	10.8	2.5	5.2	NA	25	1984
Investment Bank/Brokerage	50.1	NA	NA	NA	21	1992
Life Insurance	39.5	15.2	8.8	14.3	23	1981
Major Regional Banks	51.7	24.3	8.8	5.4	21	1981
Money Center Banks	57.7	25.8	9.0	11.3	20	1981
Multi-Line Insurance	45.0	19.4	9.4	12.0	21	1981
Personal Loans	44.8	24.7	10.6	13.5	25	1981
Property-Casualty Insurance	32.9	13.0	8.3	11.3	18	1981
Savings & Loans	60.0	16.6	7.7	8.5	30	1981
Financial (Miscellaneous)	56.6	24.6	NA	NA	21	1990
Services						
Specialized Services	32.4	2.5	3.1	NA	16	1982
Specialty Printing	23.9	NA	NA	NA	17	1990
Technology						
Communication Equip. Mfrs.	49.2	21.9	15.3	12.5	22	1981
Computer Software & Svcs.	40.3	30.2	14.9	18.0	20	1981
Computer Systems	31.9	0.8	-1.5	3.0	20	1981
Electronics (Defense)	95.8	26.4	16.7	NA	13	1983
Electronics (Instrumentation)	53.1	34.4	13.4	11.4	29	1981
Electronics (Semiconductors)	35.2	37.7	19.4	14.8	30	1981
Office Equipment & Supplies	38.2	22.1	9.4	NA	21	1982
Photography/Imaging	40.7	NA	NA	NA	20	1990
Telecommunications (LD)	32.0	16.7	11.3	NA	24	1984
Transportation						
Airlines	45.9	3.3	4.2	8.4	30	1981
Railroads	42.9	20.7	13.5	10.8	25	1981
Truckers	-12.5	4.2	1.6	8.2	28	1981
Transportation (Misc.)	19.0	17.7	NA	NA	27	1988
Utilities						
Electric Companies	23.1	5.1	5.4	7.8	16	1981
Natural Gas	37.0	4.9	5.0	4.6	23	1981
Telephone	43.9	8.7	11.2	NA	16	1984
Other						
Conglomerates	27.3	14.0	9.3	8.3	27	1981
Miscellaneous	17.3	12.1	10.3	NA	11	1985
S&P 500 Composite	**34.1**	**13.4**	**11.5**	**10.7**	**11**	**1981**

And, finally, Table 3-3 provides the investor with an industry-by-industry comparison of fundamental valuation measurements: It shows the industry's 1996e price-to-earnings ratio (P/E) and average P/E from 1981-1995; 1996e and average relative P/E (P/Es for the individual industries relative to the P/E of the S&P 500); and dividend yield for year-end 1995 and average yield. A 15-year average (1981-1995) was chosen since it is long enough to encompass several economic and stock market cycles, as well as short enough not to include results that reflect yesteryear influences. The small "e" referenced above means estimated by S&P analysts. And what usually is the case, not only for S&P but also for most all Wall Street analysts, is that estimates made early in the year are generally optimistic, and the year-end actual results are typically less. So bear that in mind when comparing projected P/Es and relative P/Es against long-term averages.

Investors can still benefit from this table, however, by becoming aware of characteristics of a particular industry. If you were asked whether a P/E of 15 was high or low, the first question you should ask is "for which industry?". A P/E of 15 is very high for an automobile stock, as the group's long-term average is 7.4. It would be wise, then, to avoid this investment. Yet if it were a semiconductor stock, it would be trading at a 25% discount to its long-term average and could look like a bargain.

In the past, investors compared current dividend yields to long-term average yields to see if an industry was overvalued or undervalued. With chemicals, for instance, their 15-year average was 4.76%, but their year-end rate was sharply lower. One might presume, therefore, that chemical shares were overpriced and would soon fall to bring the dividend yield back in line. Yet during the 1990s, the way investors look at dividend yields has changed, since capital gains are taxed at a lower rate than dividends and investors would prefer to be rewarded with an increased return on equity than an increase in dividends. As a result, income-seeking investors should use the current dividend yield table merely as a guide to find those industries that offer the highest dividend yields, not to spot overvalued and undervalued situatons.

Table 3-3. Industry Valuations (Data as of 12/29/95)

Sector / Industry	P/E Ratios		Relative P/E		Dividend Yield		Avgs. Since
	1996e	Avg.	1996e	Avg.	1995	Avg.	
Basic Materials							
Aluminum	8.2	12.2	0.58	0.77	1.92	3.63	1981
Chemicals	11.2	17.4	0.79	1.10	2.77	4.76	1981
Chemicals (Diversified)	13.7	17.2	0.97	1.08	1.90	3.74	1981
Chemicals (Specialty)	16.1	16.1	1.14	1.01	1.22	3.20	1984
Containers (Metal & Glass)	16.4	16.6	1.15	1.05	0.40	2.83	1981
Containers (Paper)	7.4	15.2	0.52	0.96	3.07	2.61	1981
Gold Mining	32.5	33.5	2.29	2.29	0.85	1.63	1981
Metals (Miscellaneous)	8.9	15.1	0.63	0.95	2.60	2.65	1981
Paper & Forest Products	7.2	19.3	0.51	1.22	2.74	3.71	1981
Steel	9.6	13.8	0.67	0.87	1.22	2.66	1981
Capital Goods							
Aerospace/Defense	16.3	11.1	1.15	0.70	1.68	3.22	1981
Electrical Equipment	16.9	15.2	1.19	0.96	2.40	3.35	1981
Engineering & Construction	20.1	26.8	1.42	1.69	1.19	2.30	1983
Heavy Duty Trucks & Parts	11.0	23.3	0.78	1.47	3.23	3.23	1981
Machine Tools	12.3	27.5	0.87	1.73	1.13	3.13	1981
Machinery (Diversified)	10.9	19.8	0.77	1.25	2.32	3.27	1981
Manufacturing (Diversified)	14.4	18.4	1.02	1.16	1.49	2.59	1983
Pollution Control	14.4	20.7	1.02	1.31	2.04	1.69	1981
Consumer Cyclical							
Auto Parts	12.0	15.6	0.85	0.98	2.36	3.27	1981
Automobiles	7.0	7.4	0.50	0.47	3.71	5.31	1981
Broadcast Media	35.8	31.8	2.53	2.00	0.13	1.12	1981
Building Materials	13.0	17.4	0.92	1.09	1.65	3.12	1981
Entertainment	34.5	24.1	2.43	1.52	0.51	1.29	1981
Hardware & Tools	15.4	19.1	1.08	1.20	2.00	3.10	1981
Homebuilding	15.1	18.9	1.07	1.19	0.92	1.99	1981
Hotel-Motel	17.3	19.1	1.22	1.20	0.89	3.30	1981
Household Furn. & Appl.	12.9	17.6	0.91	1.11	2.34	3.85	1981
Leisure Time	13.0	15.0	0.92	0.95	1.76	3.08	1981
Manufactured Housing	14.7	15.0	1.04	0.95	2.33	2.77	1981
Publishing	16.8	20.5	1.18	1.29	3.51	2.78	1981
Publishing (Newspapers)	17.5	18.7	1.23	1.18	1.94	2.66	1981
Restaurants	19.3	15.3	1.36	0.96	0.66	1.34	1981
Retail (Department Stores)	10.1	12.2	0.72	0.77	2.71	2.94	1981
Retail (General Merchandise)	14.0	14.0	0.99	0.88	1.25	3.31	1981
Retail (Specialty)	16.4	21.0	1.16	1.32	0.74	1.01	1982
Retail (Specialty-Apparel)	15.2	18.4	1.07	1.16	1.67	1.21	1985
Shoes	15.9	12.4	1.12	0.78	1.05	3.03	1981
Textiles	12.9	13.5	0.91	0.85	1.86	2.83	1981
Toys	14.8	13.7	1.04	0.86	0.85	1.04	1981
Consumer Staples							
Beverages (Alcoholic)	17.7	14.2	1.24	0.89	2.28	2.30	1981
Beverages (Soft Drinks)	23.9	17.4	1.68	1.09	1.26	3.10	1981
Cosmetics	21.4	17.1	1.51	1.08	1.66	4.05	1981
Distributors (Cons. Prods.)	17.0	17.2	1.20	1.09	2.32	1.85	1982
Foods	17.3	15.5	1.22	0.97	2.32	3.28	1981
Health Care (Diversified)	17.6	17.2	1.24	1.08	2.46	3.15	1983
Health Care (Drugs)	19.7	16.7	1.39	1.05	2.22	3.16	1981
Health Care (HMOs)	15.2	23.1	1.07	1.45	0.94	1.59	1992
Health Care (Miscellaneous)	23.3	34.7	1.64	2.18	0.03	0.24	1983
Hospital Management	14.6	17.5	1.03	1.10	0.20	2.17	1981

Sector / Industry	P/E Ratios		Relative P/E		Dividend Yield		Avgs.
	1996e	Avg.	1996e	Avg.	1995	Avg.	Since
Household Products	18.0	15.0	1.27	0.94	2.10	3.75	1981
Housewares	14.7	17.7	1.04	1.11	2.04	1.70	1984
Medical Products & Supplies	20.9	23.8	1.48	1.50	1.13	2.06	1981
Retail (Drug Stores)	19.2	16.1	1.36	1.02	1.67	2.29	1981
Retail (Food Chains)	14.9	14.3	1.05	0.90	1.61	3.30	1981
Tobacco	12.3	11.0	0.87	0.69	4.39	4.37	1981
Energy							
Oil & Gas Drilling	36.4	26.9	2.57	1.70	0.78	1.40	1981
Oil (Domestic Integrated)	15.4	23.6	1.09	1.49	3.62	5.03	1981
Oil (Exploration & Production)	34.4	34.0	2.42	2.14	0.96	3.12	1989
Oil (International Integrated)	15.5	11.8	1.09	0.74	3.56	6.38	1981
Oil Well Equip. & Services	20.5	26.2	1.45	1.65	2.10	3.02	1981
Financials							
Insurance Brokers	14.1	18.7	0.99	1.18	3.26	3.81	1984
Investment Bank/Brokerage	8.2	9.9	0.58	0.62	1.81	2.39	1992
Life Insurance	11.0	9.5	0.77	0.60	2.75	3.95	1981
Major Regional Banks	9.9	18.3	0.69	1.15	3.44	4.91	1981
Money Center Banks	8.5	9.4	0.60	0.59	3.27	5.65	1981
Multi-Line Insurance	12.1	13.8	0.85	0.87	1.51	3.21	1981
Personal Loans	11.1	10.4	0.78	0.65	2.85	5.54	1981
Property-Casualty Insurance	11.8	12.6	0.83	0.79	1.83	4.91	1981
Savings & Loans	11.2	16.2	0.79	1.02	2.56	4.00	1981
Financial (Miscellaneous)	12.1	10.9	0.85	0.69	2.19	3.11	1990
Services							
Specialized Services	19.9	19.7	1.40	1.24	1.75	3.17	1982
Specialty Printing	17.2	18.1	1.22	1.14	2.93	2.77	1990
Technology							
Communication Equip. Mfrs.	22.5	20.8	1.59	1.31	0.25	1.01	1981
Computer Software & Svcs.	22.1	22.9	1.56	1.44	0.18	0.93	1981
Computer Systems	10.5	16.8	0.74	1.06	0.74	3.24	1981
Electronics (Defense)	17.0	13.8	1.20	0.87	1.13	2.13	1983
Electronics (Instrumentation)	16.2	18.7	1.14	1.18	1.54	1.08	1981
Electronics (Semiconductors)	10.3	20.0	0.72	1.26	0.49	1.06	1981
Office Equipment & Supplies	14.9	18.8	1.05	1.18	2.31	4.67	1982
Photography/Imaging	16.2	24.2	1.15	1.52	2.30	4.34	1990
Telecommunications (LD)	16.1	19.2	1.13	1.21	1.85	3.93	1984
Transportation							
Airlines	11.7	18.8	0.82	1.19	0.12	0.88	1981
Railroads	13.3	12.8	0.94	0.81	2.25	3.56	1981
Truckers	15.0	21.7	1.06	1.37	2.12	2.93	1981
Transportation (Misc.)	12.0	22.7	0.85	1.43	0.74	1.30	1988
Utilities							
Electric Companies	12.0	10.3	0.85	0.65	5.83	8.31	1981
Natural Gas	15.8	16.1	1.11	1.02	2.82	5.50	1981
Telephone	16.7	14.5	1.18	0.91	3.89	6.01	1984
Other							
Conglomerates	10.8	13.2	0.76	0.83	2.36	4.03	1981
Miscellaneous	18.9	NA	1.33	NA	2.00	NA	1985
S&P 500 Composite	**14.2**	**15.0**	**1.00**	**1.00**	**2.29**	**3.88**	**1981**

Relative Performance

Another way to measure whether an industry is overvalued or undervalued is to look at its price performance in comparison with the overall market over a 12-month period, and then see how this compares to its historical trend.

The reason investors actively buy and sell stocks and/or mutual funds, other than for recreational purposes, is to achieve a return that is better than that for the overall market (or the return one would receive by investing in an S&P 500 index mutual fund). Therefore, investors continually evaluate the performance of their portfolio on a "relative" basis. And if their portfolio underperformed the market, these investors take steps to improve their results, by selling the laggards and replacing them with leaders.

It is because of this portfolio adjustment that lagging industries tend to get beaten down even further than the fundamentals justify, and that leading industries get bid up significantly beyond their historical fundamental averages. Just look at what happened to steel (laggard) and semiconductors (leader) stocks in 1995 and you will understand.

And since humans are involved, you can be sure that whether its investing or dieting, things tend to get overdone both to the upside and to the downside. What is important and profitable to remember, however, is that after a period of extreme price movements, these prices generally will tend to gravitate back toward the mean or average. That is the reason for the old investment saying "buy straw hats in winter and overcoats in summer." Consumers may not want them then (when prices are low), but they will want them later (when prices are high).

One way to spot buying or selling opportunities due to price extremes is by comparing an industry's 12-month price performance against that for the S&P 500. If, over a 12-month period, the price performance for a particular industry equaled that of the overall market, then that industry's relative performance would be 100. If the industry underperformed the market, its relative performance would be below 100. And if the industry outperformed the market, you guessed it, its relative performance would be above 100. (A 12-month period allows for the development of a trend and causes the graph not to look like an investor's EKG diagram.) The profit potential lies in spotting those industries that currently have extreme relative performances and taking appropriate buy/sell action.

Take a look at the graph on page 33 for the first industry reviewed in this chapter -- Aerospace/Defense. At the end of 1995, its 12-month relative performance was 121. Yet in the past 15 years, two-thirds of all relative performance results (one standard deviation) fell within the band from 114 to 88. Or, in other words, once the relative performance went above 114, the share prices for the component companies in the S&P Aerospace index started to look expensive. Therefore, as we entered 1996, investors eyeing this industry because of the prior year's results might want to be careful as this industry may soon enter a period where its performance merely equals or even underperforms that of the S&P 500. Conversely, investors who looked at this chart in late 1992 would have seen that the relative price performance had dipped below 88, signaling a buying opportunity.

Industry Outlooks

The next section of this chapter is a snapshot of each industry in the S&P 500, providing a five-part review of the industry:

■ An investment outlook *box* displaying the projected price performance of an industry based on its relative performance and a market-capitalized weighting of STARS (see Chapter 4) for the companies in the index. Outlooks can be positive, neutral, or negative.

■ An investment *outlook* for each industry, highlighting what the S&P analyst believes lies ahead for the companies within each industry over the coming year and beyond. (These outlooks were updated as of December 29, 1995, so all referenced statistics and reports were the most current available.) Investors will come to rely on this section to learn to judge whether stocks within each industry may act similarly to past performances or if dynamics within the industry might alter future price movements.

■ A *description* of the index components and their products and/or services provided.

■ A discussion of the *characteristics* of the industry, including the influencing indicators listed in Table 3-1, and other industry-specific factors that could affect share prices for companies within this industry, such as seasonal price variations and the effect of government regulations.

■ Finally, a *graph* showing up to a 15-year trend in 12-month relative price performance is included to help the investor spot industries that may be overvalued or undervalued based on past relative price performance.

Completing the picture is Chapter 4, which offers a financial digest for more than 1,000 companies that are followed on an analytical basis by S&P analysts. Projected earnings, P/Es, and dividend yields, as well as buy, sell, or hold rankings, are listed for each company. These peer company listings are arranged alphabetically within each of the following 90 industries.

Aerospace/Defense

Outlooks	
Relative performance:	*Negative*
Fundamental (STARS):	*Positive*

Outlook

In 1996, defense industry stocks will continue to be affected by the fortunes of the commercial sector and the continued squeeze on military spending. In 1995, the S&P Aerospace/Defense Index soared 62%, as companies benefited from restructuring activities and, in the later half of the year, indications that the commercial aircraft market was beginning to recover. The performance surpassed the 34% returned by the S&P 500 for the year.

Although the parts of the defense budget that go to U.S. companies (known as procurements and RDT&E) may have bottomed in fiscal 1995 (ending September), defense contractors should continue feeling the pinch as increases in the fiscal 1996 budget are not expected to reach the level of inflation. Accordingly, we recommend the accumulation of selected military contractors that are adapting to cope with the relatively lower level of government orders. Activities range from growing foreign sales to reducing operating costs. Some companies are divesting or expanding (primarily through acquisition) business units to achieve the critical mass required under current defense spending

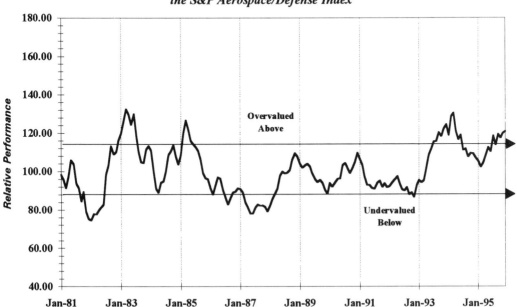

Trend in 12-Month Relative Performance for the S&P Aerospace/Defense Index

levels. The 1995 merger of Martin Marietta and Lockheed is the most far-reaching example. Also, there's Northrop Grumman which, in January 1996, agreed to pay a sweet $3.6 billion for the defense business of Westinghouse Electric. We expect the group to react positively to further consolidation activities in the industry.

Another opportunity for growth is in the commercial sector. Accordingly, we favor companies with defense operations that are supplemented by strong commercial activities. Although there are many opportunities in the space sector, the market for new aircraft is by far the largest commercial segment. Production rates of the major jet airplane manufacturers have fallen in recent years, but should rebound in 1996. The airline industry, which produced disastrous financial performance in the first half of the decade, is benefiting from higher air fares and continuing increases in traffic. Orders for new aircraft improved dramatically in late 1995, and this trend should only gain momentum in coming months. The overall comeback should lead to improved earnings in 1996. It should be noted that share prices are normally driven more by order recovery than by the ensuing earnings pickup.

Description

The aerospace segment, quite simply, produces flying vehicles: aircraft, for both commercial and military marketplaces, as well as manned and unmanned spacecraft, helicopters, and missiles. It also produces the component parts. The defense segment produces such military items as ships, submarines, tanks, and armored personnel carriers.

Characteristics

The primary, and highly cyclical, factors affecting the performance of aerospace stocks are defense spending and the ordering of aircraft by the commercial transport companies. Each cycle can extend over several years and may not necessarily coincide with one another or with conditions in the general economy. Defense spending trends are primarily a product of the state of international relations, while commercial transport ordering reflects the equipment needs of the airline industry. Profits of military contractors can be affected by policy changes of the Defense Department, such as new contracting regulations that result in cuts in profitability for many companies. Share prices of individual companies also are influenced greatly by contract awards.

Airlines

Outlook

Airline stocks soared in 1995 as the industry made progress in its attempt to establish profitability. During 1995, the group jumped 45.9%, versus a 34.1% rise for the S&P 500; indications of higher revenues, lower costs and greater load factors (average aircraft occupancy) could support a further intermediate-term advance. The performance is vastly improved from 1994, when the S&P airline Index plunged 30%, while the S&P 500 fell only 1.5%.

The emergence of low-fare operations by small airlines and large full-service carriers kept revenues of the major carriers flat in 1994. In reaction, the majors have adjusted their route networks to focus on the full-service traveler. Consequently, the average fare has steadily improved through the first ten months of 1995. In October, fare growth reached 8.1%, year to year. When combined with the continued increase in passenger traffic, industry revenues were up 4.0%, year to date. We see further revenue improvement through the remainder of 1995 from several factors, including continued strong passenger traffic and further improvement in industry-wide fares.

Trend in 12-Month Relative Performance for the S&P Airlines Index

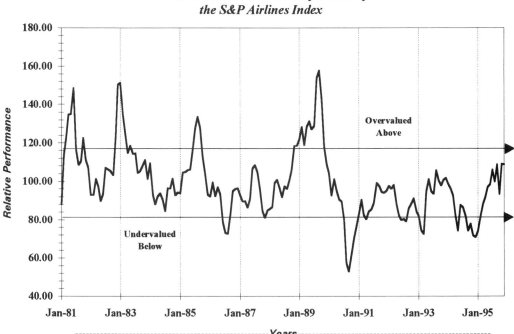

35

Also benefiting air carriers has been their restraint in keeping domestic capacity growth lower than traffic growth. Keeping capacity tight, in general, lifts the airlines ability to limit fare discounting and also raises their capacity utilization. With capacity up only 0.4% through October 1995, the load factor climbed 1.0 percentage points to 66.0%. Moreover, by delaying or reducing new aircraft orders, carriers can reduce their capital expenditures and improve their cash position.

A key element in the emerging profits of the industry is an intensified focus on the control of operating costs. Most of the major carriers have initiated cost-cutting programs that include reductions in the work force, elimination of unprofitable routes, retirement of older planes, limitations on travel agency commissions and general economies. One technique adopted by several carriers has been to offer employees equity positions in exchange for wage and benefit cuts. As a result, unit cost of capacity is generally running below year-earlier numbers. This trend is only expected to intensify given the competitiveness of the industry.

Description

The airline industry provides transportation services to individuals over scheduled routes, and to a lesser extent through chartered flights. Freight is also carried. The individual airlines are classified according to their routes as international, domestic, or regional.

Characteristics

The airline stocks are influenced by factors affecting the trend in passenger travel, the most influential of which is the change in the economy. As corporate profits are reduced, so too is the amount of business travel — business people are the primary users of full-fare tickets. Other important factors include trends in disposable income and their effect on leisure travel as well as the result of across-the-board fare increases and fare wars. The cost factor that influences profit trends the most is that of fuel; as oil prices rise, profits decline. Historically, fuel expenses have made up about 15% of total operating costs. The third quarter (summer season) generally provides the bulk of airline earnings as passenger traffic is highest. Stock prices have shown a tendency to rise late in the year, particularly if there is general optimism toward the overall economy in the coming year. A downtrend sometimes develops in the following spring-to-summer months if the economy does not perform to expectations.

Aluminum

	Outlooks	
Relative performance:	*Neutral*	
Fundamental (STARS):	*Neutral*	

Outlook

After nearly two years of rising stock prices, the group is due for a breather. The S&P Aluminum Index outperformed the market in 1994, rising 20.5%, in contrast to a 1.5% decline for the S&P 500; the group underperformed the market in 1995, rising 21.1%, versus a 34% gain in the S&P 500. Through November 30 of 1995, the group tracked the market, rising 30.3% versus a 31.8% gain for the "500." A 7.1% decline in December 1995 caused the group to underperform for 1995.

Following an accord (known as the memorandum of understanding) in early 1994 among Western producers and Russia that was designed to cut output and reduce the global surplus of aluminum, demand has outstripped supply. But, by late 1995 and early 1996, some signs of a negative change in the supply/demand equation have become evident. On October 17, 1995, Alcan Aluminum said that it planned to lift production in excess of prestrike levels. In mid-November, Alumax announced plans to increase output, and Pechiney SA and Alusuisse-Lonza Holding AG also announced decisions

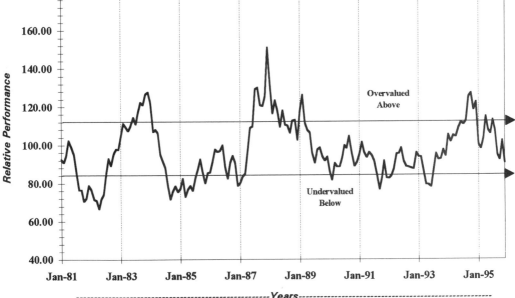

Trend in 12-Month Relative Performance for the S&P Aluminum Index

to raise production. On January 17, 1996 American Metals Market reported that ingot prices fell to a 16-month low and supplies of aluminum on the LME had reached 616,675 tons, the highest level in over six months. On the demand side, the Can Manufactures Institute reported that aluminum beverage can shipments through September totaled 75.367 billion cans, or 2.6 billion cans less than 1994's pace. American Metals Market also reported that U.S. primary production totaled 3,375,241 tons in 1995, up from 3,298,507 tons in 1994.

Assuming 2.7% U.S. GDP growth in 1996, stable business conditions in the rest of the world, and rebuilding of inventories by distributors, shipments should increase and ingot prices about track 1995's level of approximately $0.85 a pound. This will permit higher sales and earnings. We do not anticipate a large earnings gain and if weakness in ingot persists, we would change our outlook for profits. Critical to our forecast for stable prices is that the price weakness in late 1995 and early 1996 deters both Western producers and Russia from increasing production in excess of demand.

Description

Aluminum ingot is a metal that is not found in a natural state. It is derived from alumina through the smelter reduction process. Alumina, in turn, is refined from Bauxite, the raw material that is mined. The ingot can be upgraded to make fabricated aluminum products, such as the lightweight aluminum needed in beverage cans and the aluminum made to fine tolerances for airplanes.

Characteristics

Aluminum ingot prices are sensitive to the balance between supply and demand, and influence the prices of fabricated aluminum products. Fabricated aluminum product prices are more stable than commodity-like ingot quotes, and profit margins of the former are generally higher than margins of the latter. Factors that influence the share prices for these firms include the outlook for industrial activity; the prospects for aluminum's most important markets, such as containers/packaging, transportation, and building/construction; and finally, since most major aluminum companies' product mix is more heavily weighted toward fabricated products, their share prices tend to correlate more closely with fabricated product quotes than ingot prices. Earnings for most aluminum companies are usually strongest in the second quarter as beverage container manufacturers order sheet to meet the high summer demand.

Auto Parts

Outlook

The S&P Auto Parts Index underperformed the market in 1995 and may continue to do so in 1996. Yet we remain positive on select members of the group. Some original equipment manufacturers (OEMs) are benefiting from secular growth in demand for certain components, and several aftermarket (replacement) parts companies (APMs) are benefiting from an ongoing industrywide consolidation. For the OEMs growth opportunities arise from several sources. First, there is the rush to add high-tech features to vehicles in order to distinguish them and to comply with safety and emission regulations. Also, opportunities are improving to gain business from Japanese automakers in the U.S. and in Japan following the 1995 trade accord. Global expansion is also aiding those parts producers that are structuring their businesses to support U.S. automakers' efforts to consolidate designs across their international operations and expand their international businesses. Finally, tightening standards for emission and inspection programs should boost demand for replacement parts over the next few years.

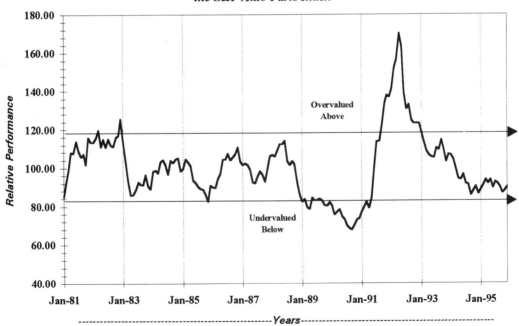

Trend in 12-Month Relative Performance for the S&P Auto Parts Index

39

While the 1995 trade accord was purposely vague, due to Japanese reluctance to compose an agreement which might later be construed as a guarantee, pledges were obtained to open up the Japanese market for replacement parts to independent aftermarket parts suppliers. In addition, Japanese automakers pledged to increase original equipment purchases by $9 billion. OEMs will also benefit from efforts by GM and Ford to rationalize their design and engineering so that common parts are used around the world. Also, most major automakers are developing plans to expand into emerging markets in Asia and South America, and have demanded that their suppliers be prepared to follow or even lead them into these markets. The reason suppliers might be asked to lead into emerging markets is to permit countries such as India and China to develop export markets for auto parts. The economic growth engendered would in turn permit them to buy modern vehicles. Parts makers will also benefit from an expected rise in demand for replacement parts and services, due to new emissions regulations which although delayed should be implemented in 1996 and 1997. The new rules require more rigorous testing using dynamometers at varying speeds, versus the 30-second idling test previously performed.

Description

The auto parts industry manufactures parts and accessories for motor vehicles, including autos, trucks, and off-road vehicles. The industry is divided into two segments: original equipment (parts and accessories for new vehicles) and replacement or aftermarket parts.

Characteristics

Original equipment sales depend on the number, size, and complexity of cars and trucks produced, as well as the portion of vehicles produced captively by their manufacturers. These companies are closely tied to the cyclical auto and truck industries, the sales for which are affected by personal disposable income, consumer confidence, and interest rates. The third quarter is typically the weakest in terms of sales and earnings for these companies, as they are affected by auto plant shutdowns in the summer and model changeover periods. Aftermarket parts sales depend on the number of vehicles in their prime repair years and the number of miles driven annually by the vehicles. Replacement parts sales tend to rise during recessions due to the increased propensity of vehicle owners to repair their vehicles rather than replace them.

Automobiles

Outlooks

Relative performance: *Positive*

Fundamental (STARS): *Neutral*

Outlook

We maintain a neutral ranking on the auto stocks, due to the late stage in the economic cycle, the continuing weak sales trend of recent months, and uninspiring growth expectations overseas. Although we project relatively strong 1995 earnings results, we recently cut our earnings estimates for 1996. As a result, we do not believe the stocks will outperform the S&P 500 in 1996. The stocks will be penalized by the aging of the economic expansion and greater investor focus on non-cyclicals. Although the auto industry posted modest price gains in 1995, we expect a flat year at best in 1996.

We do not think that the Big Three's export opportunities are materially altered by shifts in currency relationships. The domestics already export vehicles to receptive markets. Many of the most promising foreign markets are attempting to develop their own motor vehicle industries and do not allow open access to U.S. products. The automakers are entering newly emerging markets such as China, but these are longer-term plays. GM and Ford produce vehicles in most developed markets overseas and cannot

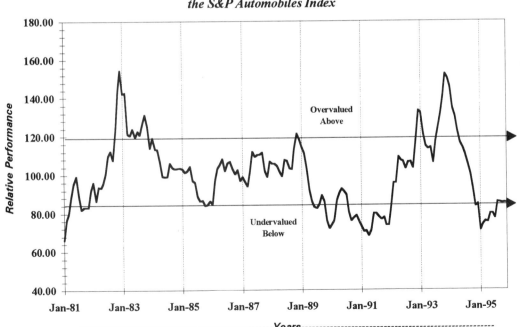

Trend in 12-Month Relative Performance for the S&P Automobiles Index

substantially increase exports from North America to those markets. Meanwhile, potential gains in domestic market share, due to rising prices for imports, may be limited because of a lack of availability of the Big Three's most popular truck models. Any strengthening of the U.S. dollar could undo share gains that have resulted from the currency-impacted price advantage. The outlook for Europe has also deteriorated. Economic growth on the continent has not been strong enough to support a robust expansion in demand. Only a 2% increase in vehicle sales is expected in Europe in 1996. Latin American vehicle demand will also remain slow due to economic problems in Mexico and Brazil. While we still believe that the Big Three are doing many of the right things, including improving productivity, vehicle quality, and balance sheet strength, we think that the weak macroeconomic picture will prevent this group from outperforming the S&P 500 for the balance of this cycle.

Definition

These companies manufacture and sell automobiles and light trucks (under 10,000 pounds). The "Big Three" is composed of General Motors, Ford, and Chrysler.

Characteristics

The U.S. auto industry has evolved into a highly competitive struggle among some 30 manufacturers located worldwide. Although there remain but three domestically owned manufacturers, nine Japanese manufacturers (called transplants) are assembling cars and trucks in North America, either independently or jointly with other Japanese or U.S. auto makers. Worldwide capacity has expanded rapidly in the past 10 years and much of the new production is aimed at the United States, which has few trade barriers. Sales of vehicles in the United States are influenced by general economic conditions, particularly changes in disposable personal income, consumer confidence, and interest rates.

Beverages (Alcoholic)

Outlook

Although up nearly 25%, the S&P Alcoholic Beverages Index modestly underperformed the S&P 500 in 1995, in contrast to the group's outperformance in 1994. The group's recent gains have been buoyed by improved investor sentiment toward these defensive stocks in a slow economy. Nevertheless, our near-term investment outlook on the alcoholic beverages group remains neutral, primarily due to flattish alcoholic product consumption trends in many important markets, such as the U.S. and Europe.

The U.S. alcoholic beverages industry was given a collective reprieve from higher federal excise taxes with the demise of the Clinton Administration's health care reform proposal. But industry members have not toasted yet, as the issue could be debated again in the near future. Meanwhile, U.S. alcoholic beverage consumption continues its steady decline, reflecting growing consumer consumption shift toward lighter, less- and non-alcoholic beverages.

The U.S. brewing industry extended its flattish shipment mode in 1995.

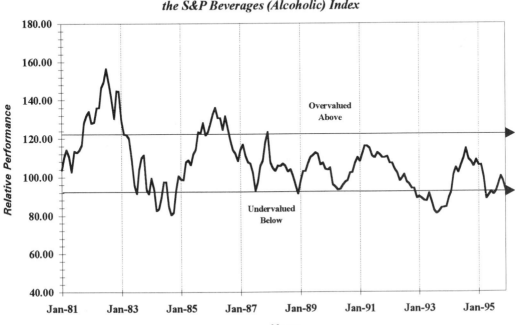

*Trend in 12-Month Relative Performance for
the S&P Beverages (Alcoholic) Index*

43

For 1995 (year-end figures not yet available), S&P projects U.S. shipments to decline by about 1%, reflecting continued moderation drinking trends and a dizzying array of beverage choices, both alcoholic and non-alcoholic. For wine and spirits, U.S. shipments are expected to be in line with 1994 results, both presumably still somewhat restrained by lingering effects from 1991's federal excise tax increases and more moderate consumer drinking habits.

Despite the above negatives, many of the leading U.S. alcoholic beverage companies have significantly diversified their operations over the years, both geographically and by product line, in order to help offset declining consumption patterns in the U.S. Seagram boldly redefined its corporate makeup in April 1995 by selling most of its large du Pont equity stake, and buying an 80% stake in MCA, an entertainment company. In October 1995, Anheuser-Busch (BUD) said it will divest many of its non-brewing businesses (baked goods, snacks, and the St. Louis Cardinals baseball franchise) in order to better focus on its U.S. market-leading beer business. BUD expected to incur a large charge to earnings in 1995's fourth quarter.

Description

This group includes producers of beer, distilled spirits, and wine products.

Characteristics

As defensive issues (those with earnings that are not generally tied to the overall health of the economy), any economic indicator that points to economic weakness will influence these issues favorably as it makes them more attractive to investors than the economically sensitive industries. Such indicators would include interest rates, consumer sentiment, and personal income growth. Investors should realize, however, that many of the leading U.S. alcoholic beverage companies have significantly diversified their operations over the years, both geographically and by product line, in order to help offset declining consumption patterns in the United States.

Beverages (Soft Drinks)

Outlook

The S&P Soft Drink Index (+47%) substantially outperformed the S&P 500 Index in 1995, marking the group's second consecutive year of market outperformance. The gains have been driven by sharp rises in the shares of both Coca-Cola (KO) and PepsiCo (PEP), which were pushed higher by good earnings trends, and by increased investor demand for companies with significant overseas business operations in light of the sluggish U.S. economy. Although the valuations of these equities are either at, or near, historically high levels, we expect most non-alcoholic beverage stocks to further outperform the S&P 500 in the near term, assuming earnings do not materially disappoint.

Sales and earnings are expected to remain in a solid uptrend for U.S. soft drink concentrate producers in 1996, driven principally by increased unit case volume growth (projected by S&P at 4%), higher selling prices, and wider margins. Principal reasons for our optimistic outlook for sales volume growth include: growing U.S. consumer income and spending; and

Trend in 12-Month Relative Performance for the S&P Beverages (Soft Drinks) Index

45

increasing consumer demand for non-alcoholic beverage products (particularly for soft drinks, ready-to-drink teas, juices, bottled water and sports drinks), which should continue to boost non-alcoholic beverage consumption levels. In addition, the U.S. beverage industry should continue to reap growing profits in fast-growing international regions, where demand has risen with recent political changes and market openings. An eventual upturn in the economies of key overseas markets (such as Germany and Japan) would give these companies an added lift.

Our near-term outlook for U.S. bottlers is generally positive. We believe that the major U.S. bottlers have effectively offset 1995's cost pressures (primarily higher aluminum can prices) through higher prices, operating efficiencies, favorable packaging, and product mix trends. We strongly recommend purchase of the shares of Coca-Cola Enterprises (CCE) given the stock's rising earnings and low valuation relative to CCE's growing cash operating profits (operating income before depreciation and amortization charges). Whitman Corp. is also enjoying rejuvenated profit growth for its Pepsi General bottler unit, although overall company profits may be held near term somewhat by costs incurred with bottler expansion in Poland, and weakness at its Hussmann refrigeration product unit.

Description

The non-alcoholic beverage group includes companies that principally manufacture soft drink concentrates (Coca-Cola, Dr. Pepper/Seven-Up); those that primarily bottle the final product (Coca-Cola Enterprises); and those companies that make other non-alcoholic beverage products that may not be their sole product line (Pepsico).

Characteristics

As defensive issues (those with earnings that are not generally tied to the overall health of the economy), any economic indicator that points to economic weakness will influence these issues favorably as it makes them more attractive to investors than the economically sensitive industries. Such indicators would include interest rates, consumer sentiment, and personal income growth.

Broadcast Media

Outlook

The investment outlook for cable television stocks is favorable, now that Congress has passed the long-awaited deregulatory laws, which boost the attractiveness of cablers for outright takeover, merger, or joint ventures. The positive impact on cash flows from loosened rate regulations adds to the industry's attractiveness. The legislation also lifts ownership limits on radio and television broadcasters. With good operating prospects and heavy station trading activities likely to continue at least through 1997, we expect the TV and radio broadcast stocks to outperform the market.

The operating prospects for cablers are positive in the near term. New Congressional legislation will keep price restraints on basic cable services in large markets until 1999, but will remove all restrictions now in markets that cover less than 1% of the nation's subscribers. FCC rules now in effect provide for positive cash-flow growth over the next several years by allowing limited rate increases on selected services. Although Congress also removed competitive barriers between the phone companies and cablers, full-scale

Trend in 12-Month Relative Performance for the S&P Broadcast Media Index

47

compteition is at least several years out, and the largest cablers should be able to compete profitably. The legislation also frees a cable system from rate regulation when a telephone company offers comparable cable service.

Congress also raised the limits on television station ownership to 35% from 25% coverage of the nation's TV audience. Due to very high asking prices for television stations, we do not expect an acceleration in station trading, which had already been robust in anticipation of the loosened legislation, but they should stay healthy, nonetheless. Boosted by political and Olympics spending, we see total broadcast TV advertising climbing more than 10% in 1996, following a gain of nearly 8% estimated for 1995. The rise in total broadcast TV advertising in 1994 was 14.5%.

Congress removed most restraints on radio ownership, which will keep the heat under station trading, as well as prices for the foreseeable future. After a roughly 8.5% rise in advertising in 1995, we see radio advertising gaining another 8% in 1996, with a 6% to 7% gain projected for 1997.

Description

This group consists of television broadcasters, radio broadcasters, and cable TV system operators.

Characteristics

Television and radio broadcasters benefit from trends in advertising spending, the health of the local economy in which they operate, changes in consumer sentiment/spending, and interest rates. Broadcasters also are driven by advertising revenues and costs of programming, with advertising largely a function of general economic activity. While cable operators are also affected by interest rates, FCC regulations that affect pricing and competition and the increase in their subscriber base are more important measures of this segment's growth opportunities. In addition, because of the capital-intensive nature of the industry, cash flow is generally a better measure of the health of a cable system operator than is net earnings, which can include sizable amounts of noncash charges. Thus, these companies are generally valued in the stock market and in private transactions based on a multiple of cash flow. There are no pure-play television broadcasters among the major media stocks, thus the outlook for entertainment, cable, and assorted publishing sectors must also be taken into consideration; it would be wise to evaluate each company on its own merits.

Building Materials

Outlooks	
Relative performance:	*Neutral*
Fundamental (STARS):	*Positive*

Outlook

The S&P Building Materials Index rose 33% in 1995, which was a touch below the 34% gain recorded in the S&P 500 in that period, and a far better performance than the 28% decline posted in 1994. Most of the appreciation in 1995 has been related to much improved interest rate trends, which was in stark contrast to the tightening interest rate environment that dragged down building related stocks in 1994. Given our belief that the current buyer-friendly interest rate picture will remain in effect, we have a favorable investment outlook for the sector over the next 12 months.

The major source of our optimism about the building materials group has been the recent revival of the homebuilding market. After struggling through much of the first half of 1995, as the Fed's credit tightening program of 1994 impacted order rates, the housing market has experienced a considerable pickup since long-term interest rates plummeted in the spring of 1995. The more favorable interest rate environment resulted in a substantial strengthening of existing home sales and new home sales since

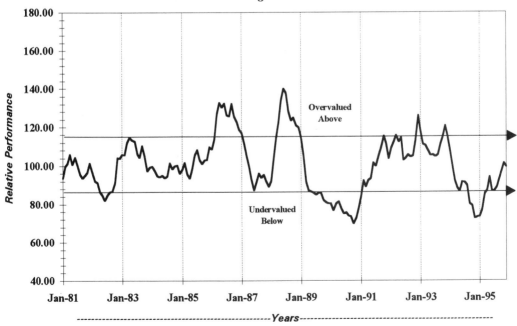

Trend in 12-Month Relative Performance for the S&P Building Materials Index

that time (despite some modest declines in recent months), which in turn have generated a pickup in housing starts; although a slight downtrend has occurred since August. Building materials sales should also benefit from continued strength in repair and remodel markets, along with the recovery of non-residential construction markets, with both driven in part by improved interest rate trends.

Although we have a favorable outlook for the building materials sector as a whole, it should be noted that the performance of the various segments will differ, based on industry specific conditions. For instance, despite a period of difficulties in the building sector, gypsum markets have remained strong, as a larger and aging housing stock has stimulated the repair and remodel markets. The virtual absence of domestic capacity expansion in recent years in the cement industry has kept that industry firm, but the lumber market has suffered from oversupply, on rising imports from Canada and high production to fill the need for wood chips in the paper market. However, despite the varying industry specific performances, the overall performance of building materials stocks tends to move in the opposite direction of interest rates.

Description

Building materials are the items used to build a residential structure: lumber, structural panels, glass, insulation, doors, cement, gypsum wallboard, and plumbing.

Characteristics

Since building materials are the items used to build a home, their sales, earnings, and share-price movements are similar to those that affect homebuilding and household furnishings and appliances: interest rates, personal income/spending, and housing starts. Demand for these items typically increases as the weather warms up.

Chemicals

Outlook

We are less bullish than we have been for commodity chemicals stocks given the industry's less favorable earnings outlook for the next few quarters. Due to concerns regarding the sluggish U.S. economy and declining chemical prices, the S&P Chemicals Index rose only 27% in 1995, well below the 34% gain for the S&P 500. We see the industry's profitability rebounding during the latter half of 1996, however, on expected modest growth in the economy and in demand for chemicals and plastics. Key end markets, such as housing, automotive, and manufacturing, are showing signs of strengthening after bottoming in the second quarter. Little new chemical production capacity will be added over the next couple of years. The industry is also benefiting from the cost reductions implemented over the past few years. In addition, with the European economies advancing, U.S. chemical companies with foreign operations should benefit further. Fertilizer markets, which have improved greatly since 1994, will likely remain strong going into 1996 on good global demand.

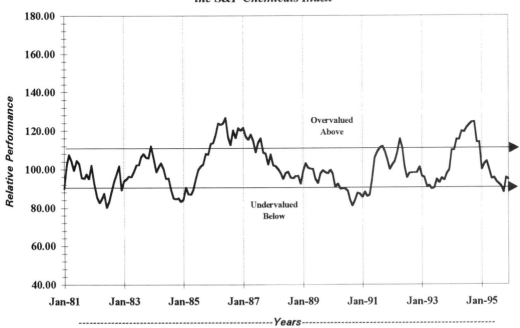

Trend in 12-Month Relative Performance for the S&P Chemicals Index

S&P expects chemical and products production to rise about 3% in 1996, a slightly lower rate than the projected 3.8% gain for 1995 as a result of a slowdown in the growth of the U.S. economy. Chemical output in November 1995, as measured by the Federal Reserve production index for chemicals and products, was at 126.5 (1987=100), up 2.7% from the year-earlier level, but down from the previous month. The industry's operating rates should remain at healthy levels, as we expect only modest capacity expansions over the next year. In November 1995, the utilization rate was 80.8%, versus 80.6% for the year-earlier period. Prices for many petrochemicals and plastics, which have declined since early summer in response to the slowing of the U.S. economy and cutbacks in imports of chemicals by China, may remain soft going into 1996. The producer price index for chemicals and products in November was 141.6 (1982=100), up 3.2% from the year-earlier level, but down versus the prior few months. The industrial chemical price index has also declined since mid-1995.

Virtually all of the major chemical companies reported increases in sales and net income in the third quarter versus 1994, reflecting higher selling prices and profit margins for key products. However, profits for commodity producers generally have declined from the first half due to lower prices, and we expect difficult profit comparisons in the early part of 1996.

Description

The U.S. chemicals industry produces a variety of products, including plastics, fibers, pesticides, paints, and detergents, as well as inorganic chemicals. Most products are used by other industries and, to a lesser extent, directly by consumers. Chemical products can be either high-volume, low-price commodities, or lower-volume, higher-valued specialty products. The S&P Chemicals Index is comprised of traditional commodity producers.

Characteristics

The industry is generally cyclical, driven by changes in economic growth and industrial production. The industrial segment of the economy accounts for about two-thirds of demand for chemical products. The largest end users are the automotive (tires, plastics, and rubber) and housing-related markets (carpeting, furniture, paint, and vinyl siding). Longer-term growth is commonly projected at about 1.5 times real economic growth. Research and development expenditures as a percentage of sales are typically 50% more than for all manufacturing companies.

Chemicals (Diversified)

Outlooks	
Relative performance:	*Neutral*
Fundamental (STARS):	*Neutral*

Outlook

The investment outlook for this industry is similar to that of the commodity chemical industry. Investors are advised also to review the investment outlooks of the nonchemical businesses in which these companies are engaged.

Description

These are companies whose largest individual business is chemicals related, but who also have major interests in other businesses. For example, FMC Corp. produces industrial and agricultural chemicals, while also owning defense, machinery, and gold mining businesses.

Characteristics

The factors that influence the sales, earnings, and share prices of companies in this industry are similar to those in the commodity chemical industry. Depending on the nonchemical businesses, trends in these areas could dampen or magnify the cyclical chemical factors.

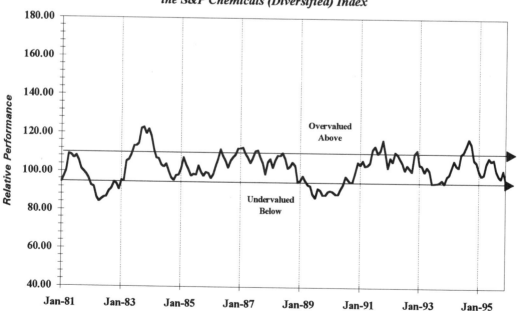

Trend in 12-Month Relative Performance for the S&P Chemicals (Diversified) Index

Chemicals (Specialty)

Outlooks	
Relative performance:	*Neutral*
Fundamental (STARS):	*Neutral*

Outlook

S&P is neutral on the investment outlook for the majority of specialty chemicals stocks, reflecting a broad mix of earnings prospects and valuations for the individual companies. The S&P Specialty Chemicals Index underperformed the S&P 500 in 1995, posting a 29% gain versus 34%, respectively. Specialty chemicals generally lagged the overall market rise in 1995 on economic concerns, following the poor performance in 1994 when many were adversely impacted by investors' fears of higher costs for commodity chemicals.

Based on S&P's forecast for real GDP to show modest growth in late 1995 and 1996, the specialty chemical industry's sales and earnings generally should continue to do well. Positive conditions in the important domestic markets are boosting demand for a wide variety of specialty products. As the European economies continue to advance, U.S. companies with foreign operations should also benefit, though currency exchange rates are now less favorable than previously. Softer prices for commodity chemicals should

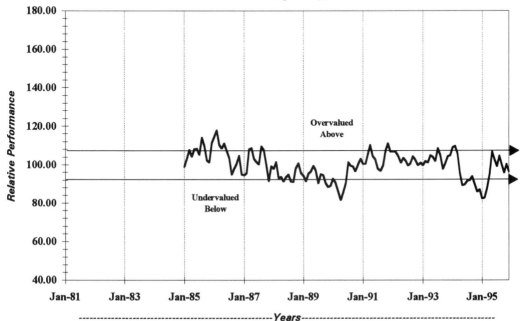

Trend in 12-Month Relative Performance for the S&P Chemicals (Specialty) Index

begin to be a positive factor for specialty chemical producers, although the impact varies by company. Even though long-term prospects vary widely for different types of specialty producers, depending on their individual market conditions, overall industry sales growth is projected at about 6% a year.

Description

Major categories of specialty chemicals include water treatment, manufacturing, processing, additives, coatings, pesticides, catalysts, adhesives, and sealants. Specialty producers are generally smaller in terms of dollar size than traditional commodity producers; some focus on only one product line, while others boast a diverse product mix.

Characteristics

Specialty chemicals products, which are of higher value than commodity chemicals, sell on performance specifications rather than on price. Specialty chemicals also help customers meet increasingly stringent environmental regulations. Although specialties require higher R&D spending and incur a greater amount of marketing and customer service costs, their production is typically less capital intensive than commodities. Specialty chemical producers are generally less affected by changes in the economy and supply/demand balances than are commodity producers, and thus will not see the same earnings softness that commodity producers are beginning to experience. Major categories of specialty chemicals include water treatment, manufacturing processing, additives, coatings, pesticides, catalysts, adhesives, and sealants. Specialty producers are generally smaller in terms of dollar size than traditional commodity producers; some focus on only one product line, while others boast a diverse product mix.

Communications Equip. Mfrs.

Outlooks	
Relative performance:	*Neutral*
Fundamental (STARS):	*Positive*

Outlook

The S&P Communications Equipment Index again outperformed the market in 1995, gaining 49.2% versus a 34.1% rise in the S&P 500; in 1994, this industry rose 14% versus the market's 1.5% decline. Our near-term outlook for the group is positive, especially for companies having a strong presence in wireless and fiber optic equipment, as the telcos target spending to revenue opportunities. Over the longer term, we expect the group as a whole to benefit from spending on infrastructure by developing nations, and as telephone companies and cable operators upgrade their networks for the provision of new service offerings. The group is likely to exhibit extreme volatility in the foreseeable future as shares move with regulatory actions and contract awards.

The group is trading in line with its average premium to the S&P 500, as equipment orders were expected to take their typical seasonal track in 1995's fourth quarter. Stronger growth in access lines and clearer regulatory policy have prompted renewed growth in spending by the major U.S. telephone

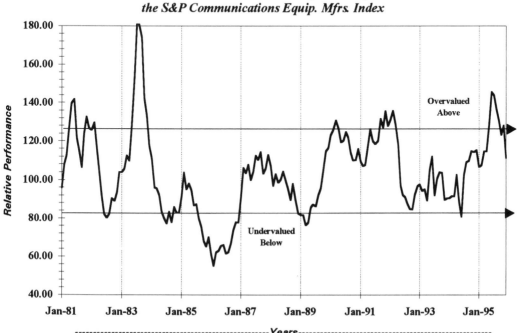

Trend in 12-Month Relative Performance for the S&P Communications Equip. Mfrs. Index

57

companies. As regulators and lawmakers have loosened regulatory restraints on telcos and cable operators, spending over the longer term on infrastructure upgrades for the provision of advanced interactive services should increase. Sharp interest in recent auctions of wireless spectrum licenses portend accelerated spending by wireless service providers as cellular carriers move to upgrade their systems and companies begin building infrastructure for competing wireless technologies.

International growth opportunities are bright long term. Many nations are investing in their telecommunications infrastructure, replacing outdated and inadequate networks to attract foreign investment. The near-term outlook, however, could be affected by recent emerging market currency uncertainties. Spending in regions such as the Far East and Latin America is likely to grow rapidly; spending in the former Soviet Union should also expand, although funding concerns may limit expenditures. Opportunities in more developed regions also exist. Western Europe's unification creates a huge market, while the EC has opened the terminal equipment market to U.S. manufacturers.

Description

These companies manufacture communications equipment ranging from fiber optic cables and wireless antennas used to transmit calls, to end-user equipment such as office phone systems and consumer telephone sets.

Characteristics

Sales, earnings, and share prices are influenced by trends in the overall economy, inflationary expectations, and government regulation. Economic growth influences growth in demand for communications services, and therefore growth in demand for communications equipment. Inflation impacts the manufacturers both through the effect on the prices of their end products and through its impact on interest rates, which will increase customers' cost of capital. And, finally, regulatory policy can either encourage or discourage communications services companies' investment in infrastructure.

Computer Software & Services

Outlook

During 1995, S&P's Computer Software and Services Index rose 40.3%, versus a 34.1% rise for the S&P 500. During 1994, the index rose 17.9% versus a 1.5% fall in the broader S&P 500. In light of conflicting signals over the economy's strength, growth stocks have performed well in the current market environment. Our outlook for the computer services segment remains positive. The software market is one of the fastest growing segments of the computer industry and, as such, is an attractive area for investment. Software stocks continue to outperform the market. We also believe the investment outlook for software stocks remains positive, in general, and believe the best strategy lies with investing in leaders of the various software markets.

Demand for computer services remains strong, fueled by: improvements in the price/performance of increasingly complex hardware; difficulties in integrating hardware from different vendors into a networked environment; advances in software technology; strong demand for customized software;

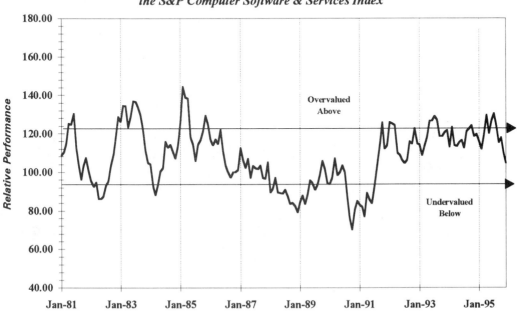

Trend in 12-Month Relative Performance for the S&P Computer Software & Services Index

a shortage of computer science professionals; inefficiencies associated with maintaining an in-house data processing staff; and complex and diverse information needs of the current competitive business environment.

Unit sales of mainframes are showing some strength, and many of the software vendors that have traditionally served this market should do well. In addition, the PC segment is attractive; sales should rise over 20% in 1996. Software vendors have tapped the expanded capabilities of today's newest PCs and are bringing increased usefulness to the desktop, spurring even greater demand for the PC and its software. The number of programs installed on each PC continues to rise. "Windows 95," the newest version of Windows, has delivered a more robust environment in which to develop more graphically intensive and functional PC software programs. Increased access to the Internet will also provide opportunities for the industry. The database and networking markets are also growing fast, driven by users' need to access and manipulate ever-increasing amounts of information, from different computing environments.

Description

Software is a series of coded computer-language instructions that direct a computer's operation. The major categories are systems software, which controls the management of a computer's resources, and applications software, which provides the computer with instructions for the performance of individual tasks. Computer service vendors (processing, professional, and information) help those who can't help themselves when it comes to using computers.

Characteristics

Sales of software are influenced by the sale of computer hardware products. However, the software industry is primarily product driven. A new software product which increases productivity or enhances quality will be in great demand. Computer services are more generally tied to the overall economy. For example, processors of weekly payroll checks will be influenced by employment rates. However, the trend is for organizations to "outsource" their computer-related resources. Service providers often offer organizations cheaper and better computer resource management by offering economies of scale through spreading the costs of hardware, software, development, and maintenance over a large base.

Computer Systems

Outlook

Our 1996 investment outlook for companies in the S&P Computer Systems Index is positive, but we caution that these stocks may continue to be volatile near term. This volatility is stemming from profit taking in the group following above-average share price returns in 1995 and some investor concerns about slowing growth in 1996. In 1995, the index gained 32% versus a 34% rise in the S&P 500. Companies not represented in this index, namely selected networking stocks and firms focusing on client-server technology, also remain attractive because of more positive longer-term structural trends.

The fundamentals in the computer industry remain strong, mainly due to a growing global appetite for technology products that increase productivity. Worldwide competition is forcing companies to become more productive, a task being accomplished largely through the employment of technology. While this trend is favorable for computer system vendors, the industry is still dominated by intense competition that can quickly render today's leaders tomorrow's losers. The new computing paradigm demands that vendor's

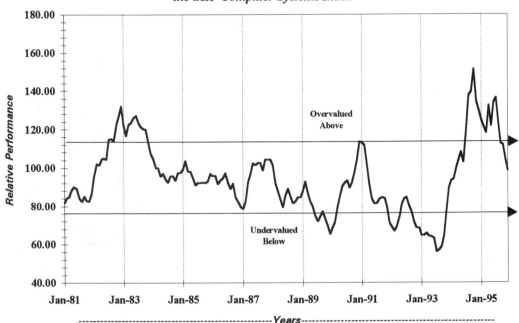

Trend in 12-Month Relative Performance for the S&P Computer Systems Index

61

constantly introduce new, more powerful and cheaper versions of successful products, while keeping a tight rein on operating expenses.

A profitable trend in the computer industry during 1996 is expected to be the continued evolution toward client-server computing. This model promotes the use of networks of cheap, yet powerful, PCs and PC servers, versus larger, more expensive and proprietary mainframe computers. Computer networking stocks should also be strong in 1996, as firms seek to connect standalone desktop systems into local and wide area networks (LANS and WANs). Networking is becoming a strategic imperative for multinational firms that want more flexible access to mission critical information. The PC industry should also benefit from good demand trends in 1996, particularly on the international front. Microsoft's new Windows 95 operating system should fuel a major product upgrade cycle transition, but fierce competition will present challenges to all participants.

Description

Computer systems, which encompass supercomputers, mainframes, minicomputers, workstations, and personal computers, are known for their ability to process huge amounts of information and to run popular software applications for home and business uses.

Characteristics

The key factors used to gauge the overall strength of an economy include capital spending trends by businesses, the general direction of interest rates, and the value of the U.S. dollar. The computer systems industry is known for short product life cycles, which can last as briefly as 6 months. Investors increasingly perceive the computer systems to be a cyclical, not growth, industry. However, not all industry segments worldwide have identical business cycles. Furthermore, most of the large computer companies have not been able to benefit from the relatively strong capital spending in the United States. The computer industry by nature is deflationary. Due to rapid price performance improvements, greater computing power is available at a lower cost each year. As a result, more units have to be shipped to reach the same dollar amount. Rather than focus on macroeconomic indicators to value these stocks, we believe that investors should focus on each company's internal product cycle.

Conglomerates

Outlook

In 1995, the economy weathered the slowdown induced by the Fed's high interest rates in 1994. By the summer of 1995, housing was rebounding, consumer spending was seeing some growth, and exports were outpacing even optimistic forecasts. The economy started 1996 with very low inflation, low unemployment, and enough momentum to keep on advancing for a quarter or two.

As we head into 1996, we have a 2% economy, consisting of 2% inflation and 2% or so of growth. While the Fed may be pleased with 2% inflation, the rest of us are anything but satisfied with 2% growth. The near term answer to getting out of the rut is to lower interest rates. Without lower interest rates, we see the economy gradually deteriorating, setting the stage for a downturn late in 1996 or early in 1997. Unemployment will creep up, consumer spending growth will slowly dissipate, and almost any unexpected setback could tip things over the edge.

Yet lower interest rates won't prevent a recession forever, but it should

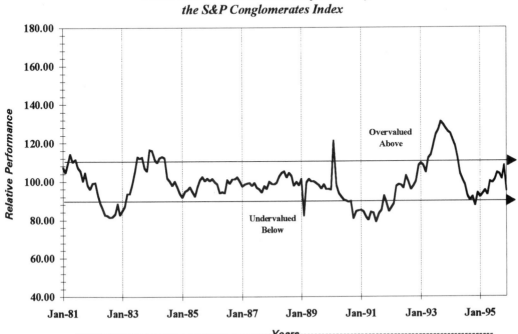

Trend in 12-Month Relative Performance for the S&P Conglomerates Index

keep the current expansion going through 1996. With somewhat lower interest rates, a rise in unemployment will be stemmed, corporate layoffs will be less severe and consumer confidence should remain strong.

Our analysts are looking for an 18% gain in 1996 earnings on the S&P 500, while on a top-down, or macroeconomic basis, we are estimating only a 5% rise. Our analysts were pretty much on target in 1995, but the macro estimate may be closer to the mark this year, assuming the current sharply reduced payout ratio (dividends relative to earnings) of only 38% is at least partly a sign that corporations are concerned about profit prospects. Historically, when the payout ratio falls to a cyclical low, which it did in 1995, earnings in the following years are flat or down.

Specifically, S&P Economics projects annualized GDP growth of 2.8% for 1995 and 2.4% for 1996. Industrial production is forecast to grow 2.8% and 2.5% in 1995 and 1996, with capacity utilization expected to have peaked in the first quarter of 1995. Capital spending should surge 12.7% in 1995 and 4.1% in 1996. Finally, the yield on the 30-year Treasury bond is likely to remain around 6.0% for the remainder of the first half of 1996.

Description

This industry consists of a variety of companies that offer a broad array of products and services to the industrial and consumer marketplaces.

Characteristics

The companies within this industry are less likely to be affected by sector-specific events than they are by the direction of macroeconomic components: GDP growth, industrial production, consumer confidence, interest rates, imports and exports, and the value of the U.S. dollar.

Containers (Metal & Glass)

Outlook

The overall packaging market in the U.S. has been characterized by slow growth, primarily due to a relatively slow-growing population. This has resulted in severe competitive pressures in the U.S. and steady consolidation in the industry via mergers and restructuring. In an effort to enhance operations, packaging companies have focused on faster growing regions of the world that are still developing the use of disposable containers, including Europe, Asia and the Middle East. Particularly attractive markets include Russia, Eastern Europe, and China.

We believe that a new round of consolidation was kicked off by the May 1995 merger agreement between Crown Cork & Seal and CarnaudMetalbox, which will combine the leading North American and European container companies to form the world's largest packaging company. The combination should form a more efficient entity that can benefit from greater economies of scale on a global basis. The combined entity should be aided by significant competitive advantages versus smaller

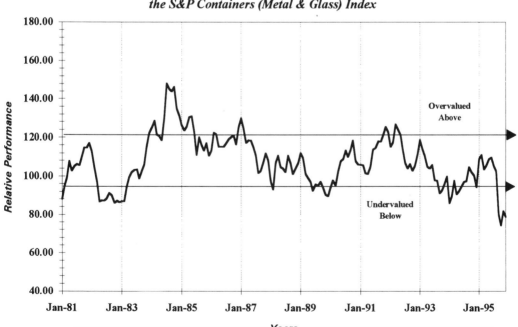

Trend in 12-Month Relative Performance for the S&P Containers (Metal & Glass) Index

competitors, and should also benefit from opportunities to reduce their combined raw materials and overhead costs, as well as a variety of other operating expenses. The creation of a powerful global competitor could prompt other North American and European container companies to consider similar alliances to maintain their competitiveness.

Description

The metal and glass containers industry supplies cans and bottles to beverage and food companies, as well as other users of such containers.

Characteristics

Most of the market segments are highly competitive with products sold primarily on a basis of price, service, quality, and performance. Manufacturers of such products tend to sell a substantial portion of their output to relatively few, but large, customers. The packaging business is capital intensive, requiring significant investments in machinery and equipment, and sensitive to production volumes, the cost of significant raw materials, such as aluminum and steel, and the cost and availability of energy resources. The commodity nature of the industry has resulted in a continuous drive to lower operating costs, maximize use of plant and equipment, and product differentiation. A long-term trend has been to substitute aluminum or plastic containers for steel and glass, making steel and glass containers, in essence, declining market segments.

Containers (Paper)

Outlook

After outperforming the broader market in 1994, stocks of paper container manufacturers performed far to the opposite extreme in 1995, with the 4.6% fall for the S&P Paper Containers Index sharply trailing the 34% gain in the S&P 500 during the year. The weakness in the Containers Index has largely been related to a sluggish demand pattern stimulated by slowing economic conditions and inventory buildups, the ramp up of some of the substantial new industry capacity announced for 1995-1997 and a recent upward revision in the industry's capacity base.

The conditions facing paper container manufacturers are a far cry from the very positive state of affairs in 1994 and the early part of 1995. After suffering through an extended period of difficulties following the last industry up cycle of the late 1980s, the long-awaited profit recovery for the group was finally stimulated by a strengthening of global economies. A surge in domestic and overseas demand led to a very favorable supply/demand situation for producers, prompting sharp containerboard price hikes from

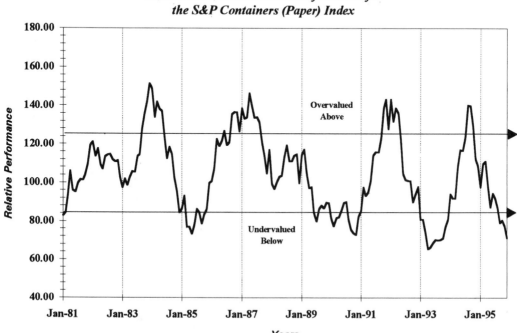

Trend in 12-Month Relative Performance for the S&P Containers (Paper) Index

67

late 1993 through the early part of 1995. However, those exceptional conditions began to be jeopardized by moderating global economic trends during much of 1995, along with 1.1 million tons of containerboard capacity (at peak operating levels) put in place in the first half of 1995. Those factors, along with customers receiving double and triple-orders placed during the period of tight supply and a long string of year-over-year declines in corrugated box shipments, brought about a 54% increase in inventory levels at box plants and mills from a trough of 2.12 million tons in October 1994 to a peak of 3.25 million tons in July 1995.

What has transpired since that time is that converters have been drawing down inventories and holding back on orders in expectation of a continuation of price cuts that have developed in recent months. As such, although inventories at box plants have fallen 547,000 tons from their July 1995 peak, and stood near a level deemed as "normal," those at mills remain high. In addition, the American Forest & Paper Association released its capacity survey in mid-December, and besides showing that substantial capacity expansion would be undertaken over the next few years, also featured an unexpectedly high upward revision in the industry capacity base. Given all of those factors, it could take quite some time for trends to improve in the containerboard industry.

Description

Paper containers are corrugated boxes, as well as the linerboard used to produce them.

Characteristics

Linerboard, the heavy brown paper used to make corrugated boxes, tracks changes in industrial production very closely because corrugated containers are used mainly to ship finished goods; of course, the potential for rapid pricing changes exists on both the upside and downside. Industry earnings also are magnified by the generally high level of balance sheet leverage in the group. A large percentage of sales for both corrugated containers and specialty packaging is made to the food industry. Demand from food producers is relatively stable, compared with other industrial customers. But while stable food industry demand moderates the fluctuations in aggregate demand, changes in overall economic activity have a greater impact on pricing.

Cosmetics

Outlooks	
Relative performance:	*Neutral*
Fundamental (STARS):	*Positive*

Outlook

Our near-term investment outlook for the overall cosmetics industry is positive, based on above-average earnings growth forecasts. Stocks in this industry have underperformed the market in 1995 (although they did outperform the market in October and November), which we attribute to investors focusing on other sectors this year, and since cosmetic issues substantially outperformed the market in 1994. The three major cosmetic companies -- Avon Products, Gillette, and Alberto Culver -- are now all trading toward the low end of their historical price earnings multiple ranges, based on estimated 1996 earnings. Each company reported higher and "as-expected" earnings in the quarter ending September 30, and we feel these stocks are somewhat undervalued and should be accumulated, particularly Avon, which could appreciate over 20% in the next 12 months.

The fundamental outlook for the cosmetic industry for both the near- and long-term differs geographically. Domestically, the cosmetic industry is mature

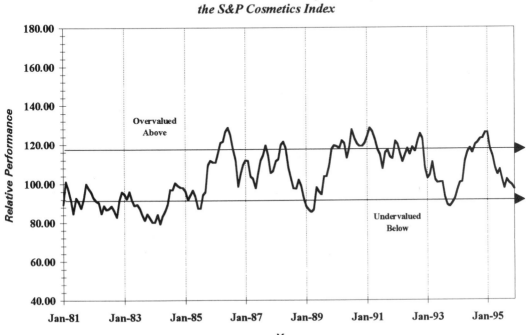

*Trend in 12-Month Relative Performance for
the S&P Cosmetics Index*

and consolidated. According to the Commerce Department, wholesale shipments of beauty care products are projected to rise only 4.0% annually in the years ahead. High usage rates in the U.S., along with the slow growth, are the reasons for heavy competition within the industry. Currently, only 10 manufacturers control 60% of the market. In order to preserve or gain precious shelf space, these manufacturers continue to consolidate, keep rolling out new products, and spend more on marketing and advertising. Significant earnings growth for cosmetic companies in the U.S. is therefore unlikely, and if there is much at all, it is likely to come from the reduction of the company's cost structure and the decrease in debt levels.

During the remainder of this year and onward, growth at cosmetic companies will mainly be driven by expansion into fast-growing markets in Latin America and the Pacific basin. Avon Products and Gillette already have a substantial and growing presence in these markets, which are the main reasons why we like these stocks. Population levels are high in these regions and economic expansion is stimulating rapid growth in per-capita income. Meanwhile, usage levels of cosmetics are low, and this translates into a vast potential market for Avon and Gillette. Longer term, cosmetic companies will be looking to China, India, Russia, and Eastern Europe for substantial volume growth.

Description

The cosmetics industry consists of six major product categories: hair care (29% of total volume), fragrances (22%), skin care (10%), deodorants (9%), dentifrices (7%), and a miscellaneous category that includes mouthwashes, shaving preparations, and sun-care products (7%).

Characteristics

The top 10 producers control more than 60% of the market, while the rest of it is split among 500 smaller producers. Influencing factors include consumer spending patterns, new product introductions, and the value of the U.S. dollar, as most of this industry's future growth is projected to come from international marketplaces.

Distributors (Consumer Products)

Outlook

The near-term investment outlook for the distributors of consumer products continues to be weak. The major factor hurting both food and drug wholesalers is price deflation. The longer-term outlook is more favorable, however, as managements focus on technological enhancements to reduce costs and increase productivity. For all of 1995, the S&P Distributors (Cons. Prods.) Index gained 22.3% versus a 34.1% rise in the S&P 500.

Strategies that worked in the past can no longer come to the rescue of distributors. With moderate-to-high levels of inflation the norm in the past decade, food and drug wholesalers turned price inflation to their advantage. In times of price inflation, increases were passed along to customers more easily as consumers grew accustomed to rising prices. Food wholesalers also would stock up on inventory that could later be sold to chains at higher prices. Price increases thereby aided sales comparisons. Since 1990, however, producer prices have been falling, reflecting ample supplies and weak demand. High drug price inflation -- typically twice the CPI -- has

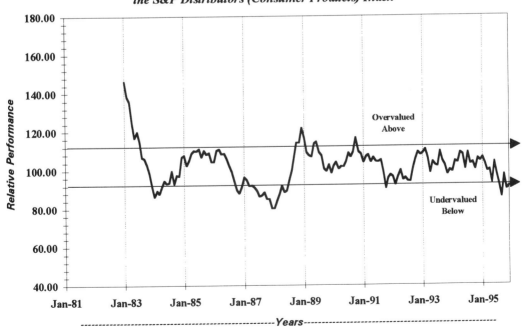

Trend in 12-Month Relative Performance for the S&P Distributors (Consumer Products) Index

kept drug wholesalers' sales advancing at a healthy pace in recent years. But as drug price inflation moderated, sales comparisons declined and profit margins were squeezed. Although we expect inflation to creep back into the system, competitive pressures are anticipated to force wholesalers to forgo significant price increases over the near-to-intermediate term.

To offset the absence of food-price inflation, wholesalers have focused on cost-cutting efficiencies to improve longer-term corporate profitability. Increased productivity has become the industry buzzword, and we expect companies to continue to monitor every aspect of operations and to invest in technology that will boost overall productivity. The resulting economies of scale, coupled with the deep pockets of the major players, should continue to put pressure on the smaller companies; industry consolidation will likely continue. The food wholesaling industry is a $100 billion business that has consolidated dramatically over the past decade, reducing by nearly one-half the number of food distribution companies to some 200. The top two companies, SUPERVALU INC. and Fleming Cos., having merged with competitors, now account for over one-third of the industry's total sales. In drug wholesaling, three companies account for over 50% of the industry's $30 billion in sales.

Description

This industry is mainly made up of food and drug wholesalers. They are the "go-betweens" for the manufacturer and retailer, by distributing or buying and reselling manufacturers' products to the retailers.

Characteristics

The three influencing factors on revenues, earnings, and share prices are inflation, interest rates, and consumer confidence.

Electric Companies

Outlook

Electric utility stocks rallied sharply on lower interest rates in 1995 with a 23% advance in share prices, recovering nearly all the ground lost in the 1993-94 downdraft when interest rates were rising. We expect the group will continue in an uptrend in 1996, reflecting optimism that the Federal Reserve Board will again ease interest rates, but gains will likely lag the S&P 500 performance as will earnings growth in this increasingly competitive, mature industry. Still, combined with an above-average dividend yield, prospects for an above-market average total return are good, and we are recommending a number of low-cost producers for purchase at this time.

Overall prospects for earnings growth in the year ahead are good, despite pricing pressure from industrial customers and regulatory caps on rates that have weakened top line revenue growth. Demand for electric power is growing in many areas of the Southeast and Southwest, areas where expanding population and electricity-intensive industries are boosting kilowatt hour sales, adding to utilities' production efficiencies. Less robust demand

Trend in 12-Month Relative Performance for the S&P Electric Companies Index

73

in sluggish northeast and mid-Atlantic states is cushioned by ongoing headcount reductions and increased computerization of accounting and power generation and delivery functions. The trend to merge, kicked off by neighboring Northern States Power and Wisconsin Energy last spring, is likely to continue.

Regulatory matters still to be settled cloud the longer term outlook for investors, however. Issues include utilities' ability to recover from customers the cost of "stranded assets" (generating plants that are underutilized or have long-term purchased power contracts that cannot be recovered through rate-setting mechanisms) as customers move to a lower-cost energy provider. Whether independent power pools many states are proposing will cripple high cost generators is another. While many states are adopting a go-slow approach to separation of generation from transmission and distribution functions, we expect limited growth in secular demand for electricity will eliminate the very highest cost producers as well as those in economically weak regions such as the Northeast and California. Survivors are likely to be utilities that focus on paying down debt, lowering dividend payouts, pursuit of customers outside their service area, and adding new, unregulated products and services.

Description

Electric utilities are regulated monopolies that have an obligation to provide electricity to customers within their service area. The extensive state and federal regulations that govern these companies include rates charged, safety and adequacy of service, purchase and sale of assets, issuance of securities, accounting systems used, and rates of return allowed on investment.

Characteristics

Since these stocks usually are purchased for dividend yield, they often are viewed as proxies for the 30-year Treasury bond. Electric utilities, therefore, tend to perform poorly in a rising interest-rate environment. The earnings of electric companies also are affected by interest rates. Since these companies are capital intensive, and must borrow substantial amounts of money to fund their fixed investment in plant and equipment, higher interest rates result in increased interest expense, thereby reducing earnings. As a partial offset, regulators periodically examine whether equity investors are being undercompensated relative to fixed investors after adjusting for the relative level of risk. Weather-related earnings variations have little effect on stock-price performance.

Electrical Equipment

Outlooks

Relative performance: *Neutral*
Fundamental (STARS): *Positive*

Outlook

Our near-term investment outlook for the electrical equipment industry is positive. Electrical equipment stocks have, for the most part, trended upward following third-quarter earnings releases. The secular outlook for capital spending, which drives electrical equipment companies' earnings, remains bright. Also important is the strengthening of economic conditions in Europe.

Sector participants have also taken aggressive steps to reduce costs and improve productivity, which primarily has been responsible for their earnings growth in recent years. Well-positioned General Electric is ranked a "buy" in the belief that its earnings expansion can be maintained in an environment of slowing economic growth, while most of the other stocks are ranked "accumulate." We raised General Signal to a "buy" following the appointment of a new chairman who was has signaled a return to core fundamentals. We believe that General Signal's September 21, 1995, announcement that its 1995 earnings would fall below expectations has already been discounted in that stock's price.

Trend in 12-Month Relative Performance for the S&P Electrical Equipment Index

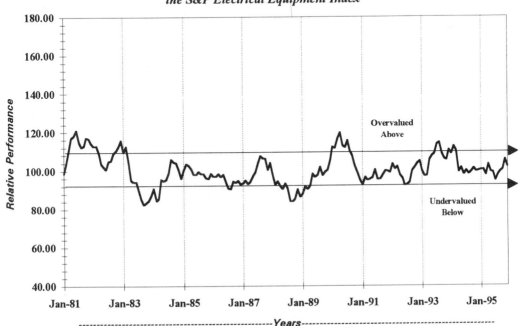

More encouraging news came from the November 28, 1995, analyst meeting hosted by Emerson Electric. The company painted a positive outlook for long-term growth, reflecting an aggressive new product introduction program and international expansion. Adding to the positive sentiment on the group was Thomas & Betts, which reported sharply higher year-over-year, third-quarter sales and earnings. Investors in the company were greeted by additional good news on December 4, 1995, that Moody's Investors Services placed Thomas & Betts debt under review for a possible upgrade. Continuing to attract attention in the group has been Westinghouse Electric's recent acquisition of CBS for $5.4 billion in cash. As part of the proposed acquisition, Westinghouse will, over the next 18 months, sell certain existing businesses to raise approximately $1.5 billion to $2.0 billion to reduce debt incurred in the acquisition of CBS. Helping the new combination's future cash flow will be Westinghouse's tax-loss carryfoward, which would be used to shield expected CBS' profits.

Description

Electrical equipment companies produce a wide range of electrical components used in both the industrial and consumer marketplaces.

Characteristics

These companies typically perform strongly in the later stages of an economic expansion because the capital spending that fuels their sales usually lags the economy. The major determinant of performance in the electrical equipment industry, therefore, is the projected trend for capital spending (the official name for which is nonresidential fixed investment). Since this industry is highly export-driven, fluctuations in the value of the U.S. dollar also have a significant impact on the performance of these stocks.

Electronics (Defense)

Outlook

Despite the clouded outlook for defense spending in the intermediate term, certain defense electronic stocks should continue to outperform the general market in the coming months. For all of 1995, the group rose 95.8%, versus 34.1% for the S&P 500, largely in response to the pace of merger and acquisition activity by defense companies. Further gains could develop for companies expected to benefit from the industry's consolidation or for companies that have successful commercial activities to supplement defense operations.

As defense markets have declined in the past few years, most industry members have focused on cost-cutting efforts in order to improve operating margins and cash flow. An extensive consolidation movement is also underway to remove excess capacity and properly size the industry to smaller demand. Some firms have bought operations in order to gain or retain a dominant position in a particular area of the industry. The most aggressive in this regard was Martin Marietta, which merged with Lockheed in March

Trend in 12-Month Relative Performance for the S&P Electronics (Defense) Index

77

1995. Also extremely active in the acquisition movement has been Loral Corp., which in May, acquired the defense business of Unisys. Feeling pressure to act, Raytheon purchased E-Systems for a sweet $2.3 billion. These and other combinations provide opportunities for increased profitability.

Although the defense budget continues to shrink, we forecast many opportunities within this constricted market. To save money, the Pentagon appears to be emphasizing the upgrade of existing platforms (ships, planes, missiles) with technologically advanced electronics systems rather than the building of new models. In addition, when new platforms are to be built, the government has generally been favoring programs that apply off-the-shelf technology to the project, rather than those that require enormous R&D investments. Consequently, companies with a broad library of technologies and the ability to adapt their technologies will be more likely to prosper. In addition, we favor companies that are able to develop commercial uses for their technologies. Opportunities exist in the aviation, telecommunications and commercial satellite manufacturing markets. And finally, with the weaker dollar, those companies pursuing sales in international markets should benefit.

Description

The defense electronics industry produces a wide variety of equipment involved in weaponry and other devices used by the military. Examples include navigational devices for aircraft and missiles, targeting equipment, surveillance and reconnaissance devices, radar, command, control and communications equipment, and electronic-based training systems.

Characteristics

The major influence on earnings and stock prices is the level and future trend of spending for electronic warfare equipment in the federal defense budgets. The overall defense budget is influenced by world affairs and threats to national security. Individual stocks are influenced by programs winning the largest appropriations.

Electronics (Instruments)

Outlook

Electronics-instrument stocks have performed strongly this year with a stunning 57% rise through November. The gains have reflected a broad-based strengthening of demand, especially in Europe, and better-than-expected earnings by Tektronix. In addition, the rise in Perkin-Elmer's shares has reflected takeover speculation, new management and benefits from a fourth- quarter restructuring of its analytical instruments business, and plans for further restructurings. Perkin-Elmer and Tektronix are ranked "accumulate."

The continued growth of the U.S. economy has begun to benefit instrument sales, which typically lag an economic recovery. In addition, demand from the long-depressed European market is now quite strong. The pharmaceutical industry is once again ordering in volume following weakness while health care reform legislation was debated. The biotechnology industry should also continue to fuel demand. In addition, regulatory changes should boost demand for instruments as environmental regulations are more

Trend in 12-Month Relative Performance for the S&P Electronics (Instruments) Index

79

aggressively enforced and recent changes in laws requiring more precise food labeling and analysis boost demand. Somewhat offsetting has been weakness in the Japanese market, which was largely due to lower purchases by the Japanese government.

Longer term, a rapidly growing biotechnology industry is especially promising, since this is a prime market for instrument manufacturers. For instance, Beckman Instruments is placing greater emphasis on the biotechnology-based portion of its life sciences business.

Recent earnings reports have generally been encouraging. Tektronix jumped in mid-September when it reported that its fiscal first-quarter earnings increased to $0.68 a share from $0.54 on a 31% sales gain. Among other companies, Beckman Instruments' earnings have benefited from cost reductions, while gains at Varian Associates have been led by surging sales of its semiconductor production equipment. The exception to this favorable news was Perkin-Elmer. Its earnings from continuing operations for its fourth quarter ended June 30, 1995, declined to $0.40 a share from $0.41 before a $23 million restructuring charge. However, the company has indicated that it plans to take additional restructuring steps in an effort to enhance profitability. The company also recently elected a new chairman, president, and CEO.

Description

Electronic instruments are used to analyze substances in a wide range of activities from biotechnology research to criminal investigations.

Characteristics

The major determinant in the instrument sector is technology-related capital spending, which typically lags the economy. Other factors that have an influence on instrument demand include private- and government-funded research and environmental regulation requiring analysis of air and water. The electronic instrument stocks benefit from continued emphasis on quality control, the rapidly growing biotechnology industry, efforts to clean the environment, as well as the expanding life sciences and advanced materials markets.

Electronics (Semiconductors)

Outlooks	
Relative performance:	*Neutral*
Fundamental (STARS):	*Positive*

Outlook

Despite retreating from their summer highs, semiconductor stocks outperformed the overall market during 1995. The rally initially was sparked by strong fiscal 1994 fourth-quarter earnings reports and better-than-expected orders. It subsequently gained momentum on more optimistic forecasts for industry growth over the next several years and extremely strong earnings reports in 1995's first nine months. While the group is expected to remain volatile in the near term, due to ongoing profit taking, we still believe the fundamentals are excellent for continued above-average share price appreciation over the next 12 months.

The semiconductor industry has historically been subject to intense boom and bust cycles that all but the most risk tolerant investors were willing to endure. However, the semiconductor industry in 1995 is dramatically different in size and diversity from as little as five years ago. In 1990, worldwide semiconductor consumption totaled some $50 billion, versus estimated 1995 totals of between $140 to $150 billion. In addition, the 15%-20%

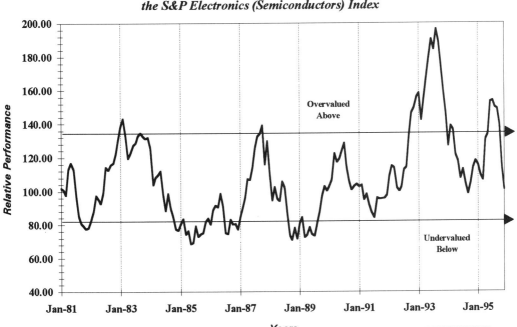

Trend in 12-Month Relative Performance for the S&P Electronics (Semiconductors) Index

industrywide growth that is projected through the end of the decade would bring worldwide consumption to $300 to $350 billion in the year 2000.

This growth is being fueled by a number of converging factors including the mass market adoption of personal computers, the increasing content of semiconductors in electronic equipment, appliances, cellular phones, and automobiles, and the insatiable demand for these products in emerging countries. For example, PC unit volume is expected to reach 60 to 65 million units in 1995, up from some 48 million in 1994 and should remain on a 15% to 20% growth curve as the demand in emerging countries accelerates. The leading beneficiaries of this growth will be microprocessor suppliers like Intel and memory makers Texas Instruments and Micron Technology.

These strong secular growth trends and demand drivers suggest that the cyclicality experienced in the semiconductor industry in the past is likely to be reduced in favor of a period of more sustainable and predictable growth. This should ultimately result in continued above-average share price appreciation potential for investors.

Description

A semiconductor is a single chip of silicon that can store a million bits of information. The industry has two main product categories: discrete devices and integrated circuits. A discrete semiconductor is an individual circuit that performs a single function affecting the flow of electrical current. Integrated circuits, as the name suggests, combine two or more transistors on a base material, usually silicon. There are three types of integrated circuits: memory, logic, and those with logic and memory.

Characteristics

Companies in this industry are influenced by trends in the overall economy, nonresidential fixed investment (capital spending), and the research and development spending by such industries as biotechnology and pollution control. In addition, since much of the industry's business is international, the value of the U.S. dollar can dramatically impact a company's bottom line. The primary indicator of industry health is the book-to-bill ratio, which measures the number of orders being placed compared with the number of orders being filled. A number above 1.00 (or parity: booked orders equals fulfilled orders) indicates that there are more orders being placed today than in the past and that the industry is growing.

Engineering & Construction

Outlook

Our near-term investment outlook for the engineering & construction industry remains positive, based on strong fundamentals that include rising sales and earnings, in addition to balance sheets that contain little or no debt. E&C stocks outperformed the market in 1995, rising 40.2%, versus a 34.1% rise in the "500." Despite the strong showing relative to the market in 1995, E&C stocks should outperform in 1996 as well, due to a continued acceleration in sales and profits.

The fundamental outlook for engineering & construction sales and profits for 1996 is positive. Acquisitions, oil projects worldwide, together with continued strength in chemical, pulp and paper, and power industries, should boost backlogs and aid future sales. Longer term, the reconstruction of Eastern Europe and the former Soviet republics, expansion of process industries in Asia/Pacific, along with requirements of the Clean Air Act of 1990 and worldwide growth in electrical power, are projected to enhance E&C growth during the balance of the 1990s.

Trend in 12-Month Relative Performance for the S&P Engineering & Construction Index

83

We currently rate two E&C companies that we cover "accumulate" and one "hold." Shares of FWC have underperformed the market during most of 1994 but rebounded sharply in 1995. We believe the shares will outperform again in 1996 as acquisitions lead to an acceleration in revenues and earnings. At the end of 1995's third quarter, FWC's backlog reached a record $5.8 billion, the highest level in the company's history, partly the result of the Enserch Environmental acquisition in November 1994. More recently, FWC acquired Ahslstrom Corp.'s Pyropower unit, a manufacturer of fluidized bed combustion systems. This latter acquisition will enhance FWC's energy equipment business while the former will aid FWC's already solid environmental business. We think JEC is attractive as an earnings turnaround. Over the last three years JEC's earnings have been flat and the share price has suffered. However, we think JEC is about to regain its revenue and earnings momentum, and stock price should follow as perceptions change. JEC earned $1.27 in fiscal 1995 and we estimate earnings of $1.45 in fiscal 1996. Based on its fiscal 1995's second-half earnings, it appears that JEC has turned the corner. In late November 1995 we downgraded Fluor to "hold" from "accumulate" based on price. Currently selling at 21 times our 1996 estimate of $2.30, FLR is fairly valued for the near term.

Description

The S&P Engineering & Construction Index is composed of companies that provide design, engineering, and building services to the chemical, petroleum, environmental, and electric power industries (also known as process industries). The only company in the index involved in civil construction, such as building dams, bridges, and major infrastructure projects, is Morrison Knudsen.

Characteristics

The principal factors affecting stock prices in the E&C industry are industry order levels, backlog growth, and capital spending by the process industries. Backlog in this industry can be erratic, which makes it difficult to identify a developing trend. Backlog and orders do not always rise in direct response to greater economic activity.

Entertainment

Outlook

Our near-term investment outlook for entertainment stocks is moderately positive, with Disney being our favorite among the stocks we cover. In recent months, prices of various entertainment-related stocks have been boosted by the latest round of takeover activity, which includes Disney's offer to acquire Capital Cities/ABC and Westinghouse's agreement to purchase CBS. During 1995, the S&P Entertainment Index gained 19%, versus a 34% rise in the S&P 500.

Meanwhile, our longer-term outlook for entertainment stocks is generally positive, particularly for those companies that own and create sizable amounts of filmed entertainment programming. Currently, the ownership and supply of U.S. movies and TV shows largely revolves around seven diversified entertainment companies -- Disney, News Corp., Seagram (80% owner of MCA and its Universal filmed entertainment businesses), Sony Corp. (owner of Columbia Pictures), Time Warner, Turner Broadcasting System, and Viacom (owner of Paramount). We expect demand for programming to get

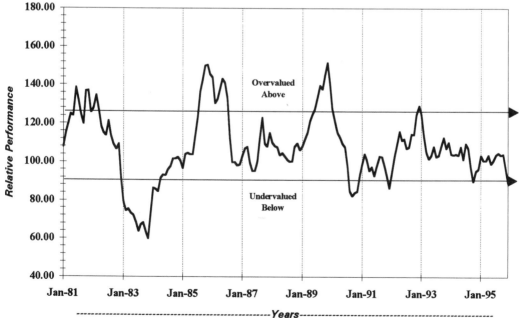

Trend in 12-Month Relative Performance for the S&P Entertainment Index

85

a boost from cable, telephone, and satellite companies seeking to deliver more content directly to consumers' homes. However, some of the large content suppliers, such as News Corp., Time Warner, and Turner, are also owners of distribution outlets, such as TV networks, channels, or cable systems.

For movies, theatrical performance accounts for a much smaller portion of a film's overall revenues than it did in the past. However, TV and home video demand will be influenced by how well a film does in theaters. In home video, we expect further movement toward consumers purchasing tapes, including stimulus from lower prices. But, VCRs are now in more than 70% of U.S. households, and we do not expect domestic video demand to provide the kind of revenue growth to suppliers of movies that it has in years past. With increasingly sophisticated cable television systems, the addition of more channels and improved pay-per-view capabilities are expected to boost future revenues for program suppliers. However, current revenue from pay-per-view is still relatively small. In overseas markets, the development of home satellite and cable TV businesses should provide additional growth opportunities for U.S. suppliers of filmed entertainment.

Description

Companies in this industry emphasize providing enjoyment to consumers through the production of video or audio media, such as movies, TV programs, recorded music. The emphasis here is on their production; broadcast media firms provide the on-air distribution of an entertainment company's product.

Characteristics

This industry's influencing indicators include consumer confidence and consumer spending, the development of new technology, and the quality of the product, or, in other words, Is the movie industry making films that people want to see? This industry is increasingly dominated by large, worldwide conglomerates. At least 80% of domestic box office dollars typically go to movies released by Time Warner, Sony (Columbia/Tri Star), Matsushita (Universal), Viacom (Paramount), and News Corp. (Fox). The worldwide recorded music industry is also dominated by Time Warner, Sony, Bertelsmann A.G., Thorn EMI, and Matsushita. These companies also have a variety of other entertainment-related interests, such as manufacturing VCRs, operating theme parks, and owning TV stations and cable networks.

Financial (Misc.)

Outlook

The investment outlook for the diversified financial industry is mixed, since the group is composed of a broad array of consumer-oriented financial service companies, offering, among other things, credit cards, personal loans, second mortgages, and automobile loans. The outlook for the interest-sensitive sector as a whole is positive because of the favorable impact on profit margins from projected lower interest rates.

Interest rates are up sharply since late 1993, but have declined in recent periods. As of January 3, 1996, yields on short-term government bills were 5.20%, up from 3.63% in September 1993, but down from 7.75% in January 1995. The yield on long-term government bonds was 6.04%, down from 8.18% in November 1994 but up from 5.87% in October 1993. We anticipate that short-term rates and long-term rates will decline through mid-1996.

The slope of the yield curve (gap between the typically higher yield on 30-year bonds and lower-yielding 3-month Treasury bills) is an important

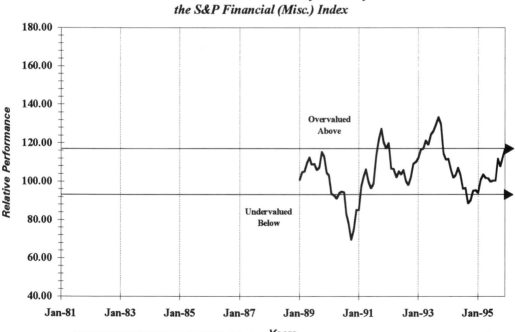

Trend in 12-Month Relative Performance for the S&P Financial (Misc.) Index

determinant of financing spreads (the return on assets less the related cost of funds) for many financial firms. S&P projects the yield curve to widen slightly by mid-1996.

A healthy economy is generally favorable for financial firms, in that it stimulates borrowing and leads to reduced credit losses. In a recession, borrowing slackens and credit losses rise. The U.S. Gross Domestic Product (GDP) grew at a 4.2% rate in the third quarter of 1995, and we project growth at 2.1% for the fourth quarter, 2.9% for the first quarter of 1996, and 2.7% for the second quarter of 1996.

Most financial businesses are characterized by low returns on assets and shareholders equity resulting from intensely competitive and highly cyclical industry conditions and few barriers to entry. There are, however, a handful of well-capitalized high-return, growth companies in the universe. The market consistently values certain financial firms at modest P/E ratios because they are by their very nature highly leveraged and perceived to carry a high level of credit risk, although actual losses in many instances are modest.

Description

This group is composed of a broad array of consumer-oriented financial service companies, offering, among other things, securities brokerage services, credit cards, and mortgages.

Characteristics

The level and direction of interest rates is a key determinant of this industry's profitability. In addition, the slope of the yield curve (gap between the typically higher yield on 30-year bonds and lower-yielding 3-month Treasury bills) is an important determinant of financing spreads (the return on assets less the related cost of funds) for many financial firms. Other influencing factors include the level of unemployment, which correlates to the number of loan defaults, and the outlook for the stock and bond markets, as two components of this index are investment firms.

Foods

Outlooks

Relative performance: *Positive*

Fundamental (STARS): *Neutral*

Outlook

The S&P Food Index rose nearly 25% in 1995, but still below the torrid growth of the broader S&P 500 Index. Our near-term investment outlook remains mildly bullish, as the relatively defensive group is likely to stay in favor given our expectations of further U.S. economic sluggishness ahead. Earnings for most major food companies in 1995 were generally favorable, helped by benefits accruing from late 1994's wide-scale cost-cutting efforts, and a modest improvement in net pricing (price increases minus promotional spending). Companies with substantial international presence also benefited from favorable foreign currency exchange translations (except for Mexico). We believe that these trends are likely to continue well into 1996, thus allowing profits to resume their low-teen growth rate for the foreseeable future.

Record harvests of important grains in late 1994 helped keep commodity costs down for U.S. food processors in 1995's first half. However, heavy spring 1995 rains in the Midwest hampered plantings of these crops, causing

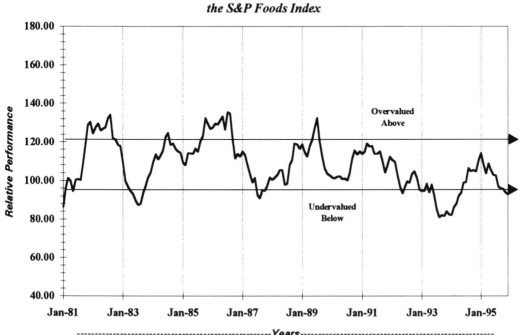

Trend in 12-Month Relative Performance for the S&P Foods Index

89

smaller than expected crops of major grains, and rebounding prices. Although the lasting impact of the recent surge in grain prices will likely be short-lived, we recommend that investors take a cautious stance toward those companies that would be negatively impacted by a sustainable level of high grain prices, such as Archer-Daniels-Midland and Tyson Foods. However, we remain very positive on the shares of IBP, Inc., the world's largest meatpacker.

The shares of branded packagers, such as Campbell Soup, Sara Lee, Hershey Foods, CPC International and H.J. Heinz, have risen steadily since mid-1994, helped largely by increased investor demand for these highly defensive issues in the midst of a slow economy. Combined with projected good earnings trends, these issues should get a further lift in coming months.

Longer term, the packaged food industry's ability to meet evolving consumer lifestyles and tastes should enable these companies to sustain their long, successful record of higher sales and profits. In addition, rising U.S. and world standards of living, increasing world trade liberalization, and the significant adoption of progressive economic policies throughout the world should provide U.S. food packagers adequate opportunities for long-term growth.

Description

This group includes food processors at both the early stages of packaged food production (agricultural processors such as Archer-Daniels-Midland and ConAgra) as well as the later stages (cereal and general food processors and packagers such as Kellogg and General Mills).

Characteristics

As defensive issues (those with earnings that are not generally tied to the overall health of the economy), any economic indicator that points to economic weakness will influence these issues favorably as it makes them more attractive to investors than the economically sensitive industries. Such indicators would include interest rates, consumer sentiment, and personal income growth. Investors should note, however, that demand for food is generally price inelastic; these influencing indicators are not as sensitive to stock performance for this group as they are for others.

Gold Mining

Outlooks

Relative performance: *Neutral*

Fundamental (STARS): *Neutral*

Outlook

Gold shares underperformed a very strong stock market in 1995 gaining 11.6%, versus a 34.1% increase for the S&P 500. This meager gain is remarkable given that the average price for gold in 1995 was $385.40/oz., up just 0.3% above 1994's average price of $384.30/oz. As the price of gold moved sideways in late 1995, share prices for mining issues swung wildly. Investors know quiet periods often are followed by outsized movements, but money managers lack conviction as to which direction the next big move in gold may be. We believe the next few months will be critical for gold. The recent deterioration in silver, platinum, and palladium bodes ill for gold.

The fundamental case for higher gold prices is weak. The economy slowed markedly in 1995's second quarter with industrial output slipping 0.6% from the first quarter, the first such quarter-to-quarter decline in production since 1991's first quarter. The rebound in the third quarter was tepid and early reports on Christmas sales show consumers remain in a funk. We would

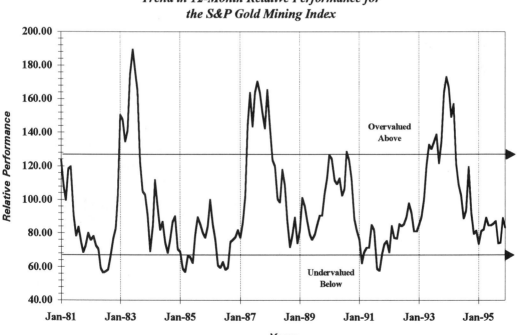

Trend in 12-Month Relative Performance for the S&P Gold Mining Index

conclude that the economy lacks sufficient vitality to threaten higher inflation rates particularly since industrial capacity utilization remains well below the 85% flashpoint. A recent survey conducted by the Federal Reserve Bank of Philadelphia found that 10-year inflation expectations among economists had dropped to 3.0%, from nearly 4.0% in 1992. In the real world — measured by the Journal of Commerce's Index of 18 industrial commodities — deflation rather than inflation appears the worry of the moment. After being flat since January, the JOC Index moved to new lows in October paced by weakness in copper and base metals. The index stabilized in November but renewed its fall in December. Finally, with the dollar in an uptrend since April, higher inflation via import prices appears unlikely.

Apart from jewelry, the largest use of gold is for investment. Though inflation remains benign, we see signs that supply/demand equation may soon favor a short-lived rally. One bit of evidence supporting this view was the brief rally in late November when the gold lease rate, the cost to borrow physical gold, jumped to 3% from below 1%. This phenomenon reflects a habit of gold producers to sell forward, thus increasing amounts of their production. With such high rates, however central banks are expected to lend more of their 30,000-ton gold hoard and alleviate this temporary "shortage."

Description

Gold is a precious metal. Gold mining companies mine for gold, and may also mine silver and other precious metals.

Characteristics

Speculative demand is the main swing factor for gold prices. This demand is derived from gold's role as a hedge against inflation or financial crisis. Inflation does not usually accelerate until well into an economic recovery when sufficient slack has been taken up. This is usually indicated by a factory capacity utilization rate of 84%-85% or higher and an unemployment rate of 5.5%-6.25% or lower. Gold tends to be inversely related to the value of the U.S. dollar. Gold mining shares move in the same direction, but fluctuate more than the price of gold. Among the most volatile of all groups, gold stocks are capable of bucking a stock market trend for sustained periods.

Hardware & Tools

Outlook

The investment outlook for this industry is neutral. During 1995, the S&P Hardware & Tools Index outperformed the market, gaining 43.3% versus a rise of 34.1% for the S&P 500.

The "do-it-yourself" (DIY) market is expected to hit $95.8 billion by 1997, from $73 million in 1992 and $27.5 million in 1977. This parallels the professional home-improvement market, which is expected to reach $46.2 billion in 1997, from $32.5 billion in 1992 and $10.7 billion in 1977.

The DIY market has grown rapidly for a number of reasons. The increased presence of huge home centers, such as Home Depot, has encouraged people to do some home projects on their own. The popularity of the DIY market is also bolstered by the personal satisfaction and the cost savings customers realize. We expect the leading suppliers of DIY products to benefit from increased DIY activity in the 1990s. New products, partnership relationships with customers, quick delivery, and a solid

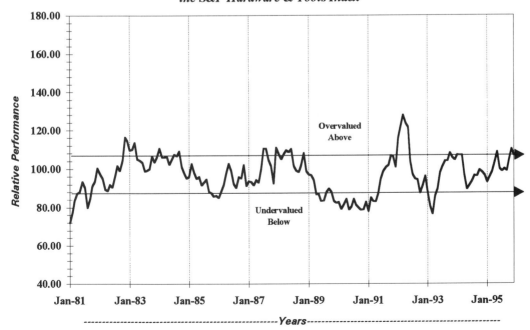

Trend in 12-Month Relative Performance for the S&P Hardware & Tools Index

understanding of the marketplace are the keys to future success for these companies.

We believe one reason why consumers want to remodel and/or effect repairs on their homes is related to the age of the existing housing stock in the United States. Between 45%-50% of the nation's dwellings were built before 1960. And even though precise statistics regarding the upkeep of these dwellings are unavailable, we believe it is likely that many of these houses need a face-lift.

A subdivision of the DIY market is the "buy-it-yourself" (BIY) market. Consumers are buying more and more bathroom fixtures and kitchen cabinets themselves and either arranging for someone else to install them, or doing it themselves.

Description

These companies manufacture items for the "do-it-yourself" marketplace: hammers, screwdrivers, sanders, saws, shovels, and rakes, just to name a few.

Characteristics

This industry is influenced by factors that affect both the household product and building materials industries: interest rates, consumer confidence, housing starts, and new product introductions.

Health Care (Diversified)

Outlooks
Relative performance: *Neutral*
Fundamental (STARS): *Positive*

Outlook

The investment outlook for this group will follow closely those of its main components: health care (drugs), hospital management, HMOs, and medical products & supplies.

Description

This industry consists of leading health care product firms that have interests in not only pharmaceuticals, but also hospital management and medical products, and in some cases popular consumer products.

Characteristics

Because of the diverse nature of this group, the factors that influence these companies are similar to those that influence the health care (drugs), hospital management, HMOs, medical products & supplies, and consumer goods

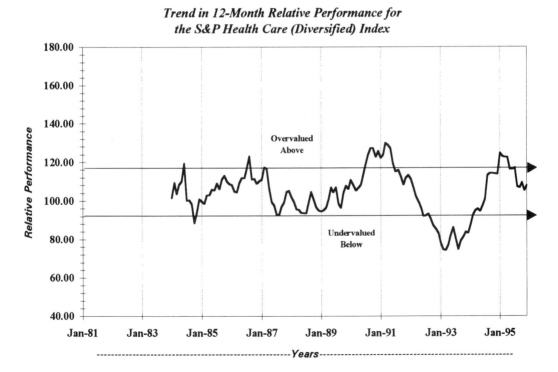

Trend in 12-Month Relative Performance for
the S&P Health Care (Diversified) Index

industries. In particular, such factors include demographic trends, government policies with respect to health care reform and/or legislation, as well as the value of the U.S. dollar, since many of these products are sold internationally.

Health Care (Drugs)

Outlook

Drug stocks should continue to perform well in 1996, although average gains are not likely to match the better than 60% growth seen in 1995. Industry earnings growth is expected to move toward the mid-double digit range, bolstered by improved pricing conditions, rising contributions from a new batch of promising new pharmaceuticals (many of which represent important therapeutic breakthroughs) and more efficient cost structures. Merger and acquisition interest in this sector is also likely to continue, piqued by Upjohn's recent merger with Swedish drugmaker Pharmacia AB and Rhone-Poulenc Rorer's purchase of Fisons PLC. We continue to recommend investments in leading drugmakers with dominant market positions, proven R&D productivity, and strong new drug pipelines.

The regulatory tide has also turned in favor of the pharmaceutical industry. The Republican leadership in Congress is pressuring the FDA for speedier and more efficient review of new drug applications. In addition, the passage of GATT legislation has been a boon for the drug industry by extending drug

Trend in 12-Month Relative Performance for the S&P Health Care (Drugs) Index

patent lives from 17 to 20 years. Proposed cutbacks in the Medicare program would also probably be a net positive since they would force more seniors in HMOs, which typically rely heavily on cost efficient drug therapies. Although the U.S. governmental regulatory situation has improved, drug manufacturers are still having to live with a difficult cost-constrained marketplace in the domestic private sector and governmental controls in international markets. Brand-name drugmakers also face patent expirations on a large list of products and the phase down of important tax credits from manufacturing operations in Puerto Rico.

Despite these negatives, companies with low-cost producer status and strong research and global marketing strengths are expected to perform well in the years ahead. Positive industry fundamentals include the recession-resistant nature of drug products; the aging population; and the cost effectiveness of drugs over more expensive hospital therapies. Restructuring moves should also bolster the margins of many firms. Merger and acquisition activity in this sector is also likely to increase, as companies pool their strengths to compete more effectively in a more price-sensitive marketplace.

Description

The companies in this group create, prepare, and distribute for sale pharmaceutical items to the consumer marketplace.

Characteristics

These issues are typically regarded as defensive plays, with their businesses unaffected by economic fluctuations. Pharmaceutical companies are affected by competitive market shares, the pace of FDA approvals, patent lives, and the strength of R&D pipelines. With most leading producers of drugs deriving substantial revenues abroad, the relative value of the dollar is another important factor. These firms are heavily dependent on R&D, which accounts for nearly 17% of industry sales.

Health Care (HMOs)

Outlook

The outlook for managed care providers is clouded by increased competitive forces which have limited premium rate hikes. In 1995, the S&P HMO Index rose 28.8%, largely as a result of strong performance in the latter portion of the year.

For HMO and other managed care entities, proposals to reshape Medicare and Medicaid present opportunities for both enrollment and profit growth. The debate regarding Medicare/Medicaid reform is ongoing, but it seems likely that beneficiaries will be encouraged to join managed care plans. Medicare HMOs are reimbursed at 95% of the average cost of providing care to patients within a geographic area, and these rates are substantially higher than commercial premiums, while service usage to date has been in-line with that of commercial members. The recent passage of a national 10.1% average Medicare rate increase for 1996 will only partially be offset by additional benefits.

Trend in 12-Month Relative Performance for the S&P Health Care (HMOs) Index

99

Description

Principal providers of health care delivery facilities.

Characteristics

Health care delivery consists of many unrelated fields bound together by common interests in demographics and government and private third-party reimbursement. They are also affected by state and local regulation.

Health Care (Misc.)

Outlooks
Relative performance: *Neutral*
Fundamental (STARS): *Positive*

Outlook

Biotechnology stocks were strong performers in 1995, reflecting renewed investor confidence in both top- and mid-tier segments of the group, positive clinical developments on several experimental biotech products, and heightened takeover interest. Merger speculation is being partly fueled by interest from abroad, as foreign drugmakers eye U.S. biotechnology companies. Mergers and other forms of strategic alliances are also expected among smaller biotech players as a means for them to obtain adequate financing for their R&D projects. While investments in this industry carry an above-average measure of risk, positions in selected firms with promising products should be rewarded over the long term.

On the regulatory front, the industry benefited from the Patent Office's decision to lift the requirement for clinical trials before patents can be issued on new drug and biotech products. The new regulation aided biotech firms to obtain financing on experimental products. Republican leaders in Congress are also pressuring the FDA to speed up its new drug approval process.

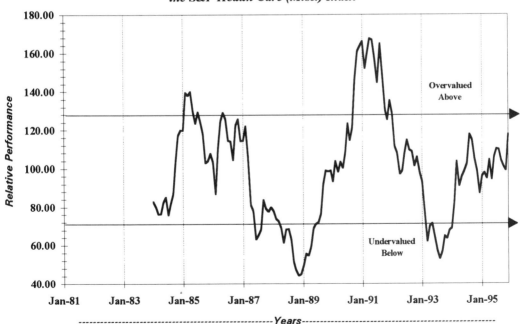

Trend in 12-Month Relative Performance for the S&P Health Care (Misc.) Index

101

Nursing home stocks are likely to drift near term, due to uncertainties associated with proposals to slow the growth of the Medicaid program or change the method by which Medicaid funds are allocated. Government efforts to reshape Medicaid and Medicare will alter the methods of healthcare delivery to the elderly and poor, and forward-thinking nursing home operators are transforming themselves into providers of a full range of cost-effective long-term healthcare, including rehabilitation and subacute care.

Total nursing home revenues are expected to rise by about 12.5% in 1995, to nearly $100 billion. Besides the demographic expansion, revenue growth is being boosted by higher rates, new facilities and an increased number of beds, expanded services and a growing number of companies offering long-term care coverage to their employees. Many nursing home companies are expanding their ancillary service base to include occupational, speech, respiratory and intravenous therapies, while others are branching out into related higher-margined businesses such as subacute care, rehabilitative services, and retirement living facilities. Specialty beds, which are usually paid for by Medicare, can earn a few hundreds dollars a day, as compared with less than $100 a day for a typical nursing home bed.

Description

This group consists of four companies in three unrelated markets: ALZA, which is a leader in the development of controlled release drug delivery systems; AMGEN, a leading biotechnology firm; and Beverly Enterprises and Manor Care, leading nursing home operators.

Characteristics

Biotech firms have successfully commercialized over two dozen new products, with nearly 10 times that number still in clinical trials. However, most biotech firms are still in the developmental stage with their fortunes largely determined by investor perceptions of the relative merits of their R&D pipelines. With future new financings likely to be more difficult to obtain than in the past, strategic alliances between major drug companies and biotech firms are expected to increase.

The most significant risk currently associated with nursing home stocks is their reliance on Medicaid. The program accounts for over 50% of the industry's annual revenues, and proposals to reduce the rate of growth of Medicaid, or to change the way program funds are allocated, could have a severe impact on those companies who are not diversifying their service offerings. Medicare accounts for less than 10% of revenues.

Heavy Duty Trucks & Parts

Outlooks	
Relative performance:	*Positive*
Fundamental (STARS):	*Negative*

Outlook

The outlook for shares of manufacturers of heavy-duty trucks and parts is negative. Heavy-duty truck orders deteriorated through late 1995, and it is clear that the truck cycle is turning down after several years of outstanding demand. While stocks of heavy-duty truck manufacturers and parts have lagged the market, we think they are preparing for another leg down. We rank the truck and engine manufacturers "avoid." Through December 1995, heavy duty truck stocks rose 4%, versus a 34% gain for the S&P 500.

U.S. sales of Class 8 vehicles set a record in 1994 reaching 185,696 units, up 18.2% year over year. We now believe 1995 will go down as another record year with sales of 195,000 heavy-duty trucks (gross vehicle weights exceeding 33,000 lbs). Despite a significant order backlog which should sustain the sales rate through early 1996, we expect sales to deteriorate by mid-year 1996 and result in an overall decline for 1996 to 160,000 units. Prompting the decline in orders is economic weakness and poor results anticipated from motor carriers.

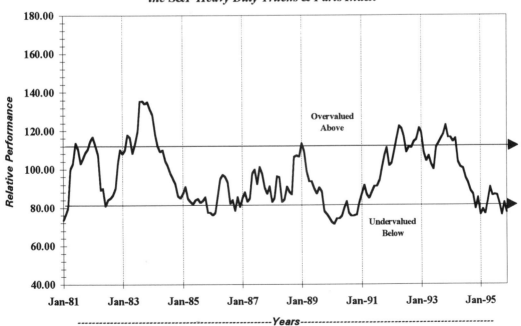

Trend in 12-Month Relative Performance for the S&P Heavy Duty Trucks & Parts Index

103

Recent demand for heavy-duty trucks has far exceeded the growth for freight volumes. This partly reflects the trend to shipping more freight in smaller lots, which results in lower equipment utilization. Also spurring truck orders has been the need to replace aging fleets, as well as attractive prices for new vehicles. Interest rates, which have gyrated wildly in the past two years, appear to have little influence on overall demand. Aiding truck sales are lower maintenance and repair requirements, as well as better gas mileage over the vehicles they replace. Truck sales also are being spurred by the need to curb driver turnover by providing better-appointed vehicles

Longer-term, heavy-duty truck sales may remain sluggish for several years as truckers are increasing their use of rail intermodal service, which will cut sharply into the number of tractors required by long-haul fleet operators and make lighter-weight trucks preferable. Also contributing to the next downturn is the improvement in quality built into the new models being sold.

Description

These companies manufacture, and serve as component suppliers of, vehicles that have a gross weight of over 33,000 pounds (Class 8). These are the big vehicles used for hauling 48- to 50-foot trailers and double trailers. They sometimes are used for off-highway construction purposes. These vehicles are called trucks by the layperson and tractors by the industry.

Characteristics

Sales, earnings, and share prices are influenced by most general economic indicators (GDP, industrial production, and retail sales). In a cascading effect, factory orders drive freight volumes, which influence order rates for trucks and finally move share prices.

Homebuilding

	Outlooks	
	Relative performance:	*Neutral*
	Fundamental (STARS):	*Neutral*

Outlook

The S&P Homebuilding Index rose 41% in 1995, versus a 34% gain in the S&P 500, with most of the Homebuilding Index appreciation related to declining mortgage rate trends since the spring of 1995. However, with the current government budget battle causing nervousness about interest rate prospects, the Homebuilding Index has fallen by 7.3% year to date in 1996 through January 10. Although we can understand the investor apprehension about homebuilding investments, our belief is that the government battle will have little impact on interest rates, and continue to have a favorable investment opinion about homebuilders. Given the current environment of slower economic growth and little inflation pressure, we expect the interest rate picture to remain favorable for a period of time, with the Fed's 1/4 point easings in July and December 1995 accentuating that belief.

After experiencing difficulties through the early part of 1995, homebuilding industry conditions have improved since mortgage rates plunged in the spring. The change in rate trends generated a strong increase in new home sales

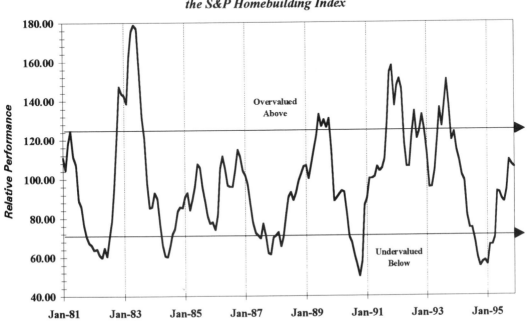

Trend in 12-Month Relative Performance for
the S&P Homebuilding Index

105

between March and July 1995 (on a sequential basis, based on annual seasonally adjusted rates), which remain at a solid level even after three straight monthly declines; the robust annual rate of 785,000 home sales in July would be tough to maintain unless in a boom period. The pickup in demand led to a revival of the homebuilding market, with housing starts rising in four consecutive months between April and July. On the downside, housing starts have fallen somewhat from their 1995 peak in July, reflecting in part sluggish economic growth and the need of builders to temper their enthusiasm a bit, as new home inventories had reached a 5-1/2 year high. However, despite the somewhat negative trends of recent months (although starts gained 5.7% in November on a pickup in the multi-family area), we think they should be viewed as a plateauing of the housing market at higher levels rather than a renewed downtrend.

On the investment front, while the current economic environment should enable shares of most homebuilders to sustain some additional appreciation, our two favorites are U.S. Home and Lennar Corp. Both of those companies have a presence in demographically favorable areas, while U.S. Home should benefit from its focus on becoming a strong niche player in the active adult market and Lennar should be aided by real estate and rental properties investments.

Description

Companies in this industry construct new residential housing, typically called site-built homes (versus mobile homes).

Characteristics

The most important sales, earnings, and share-price influencing indicators for this industry are interest rates, employment trends, and personal spending figures, which then translate themselves into a higher monthly housing starts report; building permits are typically a leading indicator for the industry. As would be expected, sales and earnings are strongest during the prime home-sales periods of the second and third quarters when the weather is the warmest and before the kids start a new school year.

Hospital Management

Outlooks
Relative performance: *Neutral*
Fundamental (STARS): *Neutral*

Outlook

The outlook for the leading for-profit hospital companies remains positive, aided by market penetration, ongoing consolidation and modestly improved utilization trends. During 1995, the S&P Hospital Management Index soared 39.4%, outpacing the 34.1% gain recorded in the S&P 500 Index.

The debate concerning Medicare and Medicaid cutbacks will lead to dramatic changes in the operating environment for hospital companies, as pricing and utilization will come under increased pressure. The industry currently faces overcapacity, which has resulted in a supply/demand imbalance for beds. With increasing competition for scarce resources, hospitals are forced to consolidate in order to negotiate effectively when seeking contracts with HMOs and large insurers. Prospects for individual companies hinge on their relative market position, cost structure, and physician relationships.

Although the U.S. hospital industry will contract under mounting pressure from managed care, leading investor-owned chains should continue to grow. Bolstered by strong management, expansive geographic reach, and

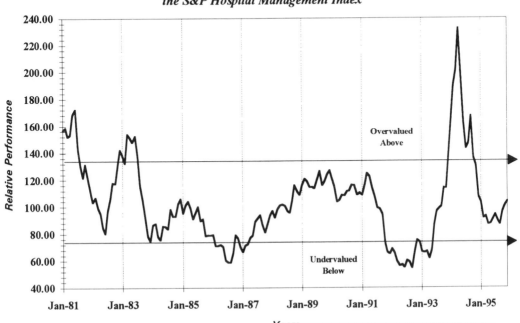

*Trend in 12-Month Relative Performance for
the S&P Hospital Management Index*

economies of scale, these firms should capture the majority of the managed care business and will benefit from the acquisition of their non-profit cousins.

Description

Principal providers of health care delivery facilities include inpatient general hospitals, independent diagnostic units, and psychiatric and rehabilitation facilities.

Characteristics

Health care delivery consists of many unrelated fields bound together by common interests in demographics and government and private third-party reimbursement. They are also affected by state and local regulation.

Hotel-Motel

Outlook

Our overall investment outlook for lodging stocks is positive, as we expect year-ahead operating results to generally be good. Occupancy and room rate levels are being helped by a stronger economy and declines in new construction during the 1990s. For companies looking to expand, we expect further emphasis on conversions of existing properties from other brands. Among the lodging stocks we follow, our current favorites include Prime Hospitality, Host Marriott, Hilton Hotels, and the new ITT Corp., which was spun off as a separate publicly owned stock in December 1995. Investors should keep in mind that some major lodging companies also have significant other operations; for example, Hilton and ITT have large gaming operations.

We are generally less enthused about the prospects for purer-play gaming stocks. With development of new U.S. markets having slowed, we expected that the gaming industry's growth rate during the next few years will be slower than it was between 1992-95. Since 1992, industry growth has

Trend in 12-Month Relative Performance for the S&P Hotel-Motel Index

included the opening of casinos in states such as Mississippi, Louisiana, and Missouri, where water-based gaming facilities are now operating. However, a number of initiatives in other states to expand gaming activity have been turned down. Development prospects for various industry participants are quite speculative, since they are dependent on such factors as legislative approvals, court rulings, and licensing decisions. Other casino-type activity includes gaming facilities on Indian land, and the debut of state lottery games using machines that resemble video slot machines.

Among the major casino companies, Harrah's Entertainment (formerly Promus Cos.) is the farthest along in developing a presence in new U.S. markets. In general, smaller companies have moved faster than the traditional industry leaders in getting new projects open. However, most, if not all, of the major gaming companies have expressed interest in geographic expansion. Currently, our favorite gaming stock is Circus Circus Enterprises. We view the company's new president/CFO as a significant plus, and the shares could be helped by a large stock buyback authorization. We look for long-term earnings to be helped by investments in both existing facilities and new casino/ hotels.

Description

Companies in this industry offer away-from-home lodging establishments, including casino facilities that have affiliated hotel rooms. The customer base for this industry includes both business and recreational travelers.

Characteristics

Factors influencing revenues, earnings, and share prices include consumer confidence and spending; travel costs, such as airline fares; and industry construction levels, as too much construction can create an unfavorable supply/demand situation and lead to discounting. For companies that build and own properties, this is a capital-intensive business, and one in which cash flow may significantly exceed reported earnings, due to noncash depreciation/amortization expenses. However, some companies emphasize franchising, and largely function as service organizations. For hotel operators, this is a labor-intensive industry. Investors seeking major lodging companies without significant gaming operations will find few opportunities other than Marriott International and Prime Hospitality. For investors seeking to focus primarily on gaming, the choices include Aztar, Circus Circus Enterprises, Harrah's Entertainment, Mirage Resorts (formerly Golden Nugget), and Bally Manufacturing.

Household Furn. & Appliances

Outlook

Stocks of appliance manufacturers underperformed the market in 1995 by 45%. Both leading appliance manufacturers, Whirlpool and Maytag, reported subpar returns during 1995, which we attribute to announcements by the Association of Appliance Manufacturers that domestic appliance shipments were down in the first ten months of 1995, year to year, and are likely to decline about 3% below those shipped in 1994 for the full 1995 year. The AHAM expects shipments will increase only slightly in 1996.

Stocks of furniture and floor covering companies slightly underperformed the market 1995. We attribute these stocks subpar performance mainly to lower than expected earnings and losses at many furniture companies during most of 1995, reflecting the inability to pass on higher raw material prices, weak demand for furniture, and a highly promotional retail environment. We believe investor concerns over high consumer debt levels and job layoffs, growing demand for less expensive furniture (which has mostly been fueled by greater offerings of ready-to-assemble furniture), and sated demand for

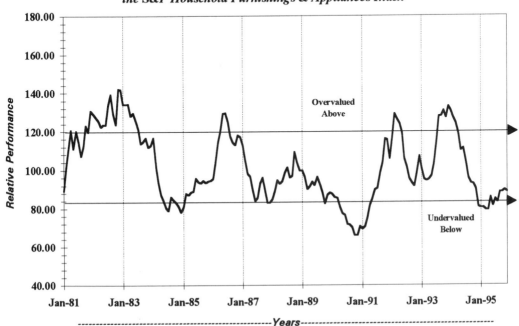

Trend in 12-Month Relative Performance for the S&P Household Furnishings & Appliances Index

111

furniture in 1994 will continue to limit these stocks' appreciation over the near and intermediate term.

The longer-term outlook for furniture and appliance demand is mixed. Demographic trends and predictions that household formations will increase to 106 million in 2000 from 93.3 million in 1994 should create fairly healthy demand. Furniture and appliances suited to more comfortable living could be especially in demand. Less expensive items could also remain a hot seller, reflecting most consumers' efforts to buy value-priced products. However, manufacturers of medium to higher priced furniture could continue to see weak demand, unless they can educate consumers as to the quality vis-à-vis price of their product offerings.

Description

These companies manufacture household items from the floor to the ceiling: carpeting and floor tiles, chairs, sofas, stoves, dishwashers, and lighting fixtures, just to name a few.

Characteristics

The domestic furnishings and appliances industry is influenced by general economic conditions, replacement demand, the housing cycle, and consumer buying patterns. Furnishings and appliances are characterized as being big-ticket, postponable purchases, and are usually bought on credit. The furnishings industry is fragmented, given the numerous styles and price points. An important factor driving appliance sales is the new housing market. While new housing only accounts for 20%-25% of all appliance shipments, each new house has the potential to add four to six new appliances. Housing, which is driven by interest rates and consumer demand, is a critical trigger in determining both upward and downward cycles for appliance shipments. Replacements make up about 70%-80% of all appliance sales. This market is largely driven by existing housing turnover and home renovations. Replacement demand is also fueled by the need to upgrade worn out appliances, which typically have a lifespan of 10-15 years. The appliance industry is more mature and is dominated by five companies—AB Electrolux, General Electric, Maytag, Whirlpool, and Raytheon.

Household Products

Outlooks	
Relative performance:	*Neutral*
Fundamental (STARS):	*Neutral*

Outlook

Household product stocks underperformed the market in December 1995, following positive performances for most months during 1995. Despite December's subpar return, these stocks outperformed the market by 7.3% in 1995. Winning stocks included Procter & Gamble, Colgate-Palmolive and Clorox. We believe these stocks will continue to reward investors for the short and long term. Earnings of household product companies are fairly predictable, and were on target or slightly above investor expectations in the first nine months of 1995. We project above-average earnings growth for the rest of 1995 (which will be announced in late January 1996) and 1996, which should fuel price advances. This industry is well-suited for risk-adverse investors who are focused on a longer-term, buy-and-hold strategy and are looking for above-average price appreciation potential, along with stable yearly increases in dividends.

Internationally, the household products industry is an oligopoly, with Colgate-Palmolive, Procter & Gamble, and Unilever controlling two-thirds

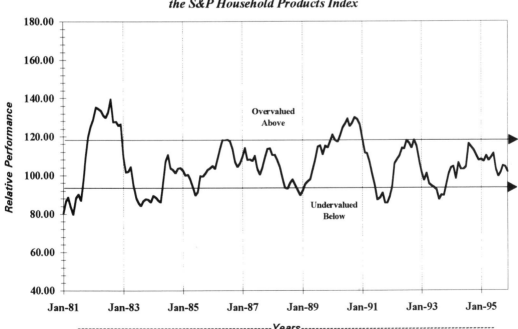

**Trend in 12-Month Relative Performance for
the S&P Household Products Index**

of the global market for these products. Expected growth for household products differs throughout the world. In the U.S., growth is expected to be lackluster, since Americans use more of these products than anyone in the world. Overseas markets offer good growth prospects. Leading companies are boosting their performance by expanding into huge untapped overseas markets, such as Latin America and Southeast Asia, where usage rates are especially low.

We expect the existing market in the U.S. and Europe for soaps and detergents to remain intensely competitive, particularly for brand-name manufacturers that have suffered from increasing demand for cheaper private label products. Although branded products maintain major share, we believe thrifty and value-conscious consumers increasingly are turning to private label products because they are cheaper and often perform nearly as well as branded products. Brand-name manufacturers of products such as bleach and ammonia have always been subject to private label competition, but manufacturers are now faced with increasing competition from private label products including detergents and other household cleaners. As a way to fight back, brand-name competitors are striving to increase their presence on retailers' limited shelf space by offering a stream of new products and variations of old products, as well as investing in making their manufacturing and distribution more efficient.

Description

Companies in this industry manufacture soaps, detergents, and tissue and paper products for the household marketplace.

Characteristics

This industry, while valued for its defensive characteristics, is influenced by interest rates, the housing market, and new-product introductions. Internationally, the household products industry is an oligopoly, with Colgate-Palmolive, Procter & Gamble, and Unilever controlling two-thirds of the worldwide market for these products.

Housewares

Outlooks
Relative performance: *Positive*
Fundamental (STARS): *Neutral*

Outlook

The investment outlook for housewares stocks is at best neutral. The S&P Housewares Index gained only 5.7% in 1995, versus a 34.1% surge in the overall market. Earnings for the third quarter of 1995 for housewares stocks were mixed. As expected, Rubbermaid posted substantially lower year-to-year earnings mainly due to the inability to pass on higher resin costs. Black and Decker and Newell reported higher and "as-expected earnings," while Premark posted higher-than-expected profits. Given these varied results, along with our forecasts that consumer spending is not likely to pick up substantially anytime soon, we have a neutral opinion on this industry as a whole over the near-term. However we do rate both Premark, Newell, and Black and Decker "accumulate." Premark's shareholders should benefit from the upcoming spin-off of the Tupperware division, Newell is slightly undervalued, and Black and Decker is enjoying surging demand for its power tools.

Longer term, we also feel neutral about this industry in the U.S., mainly

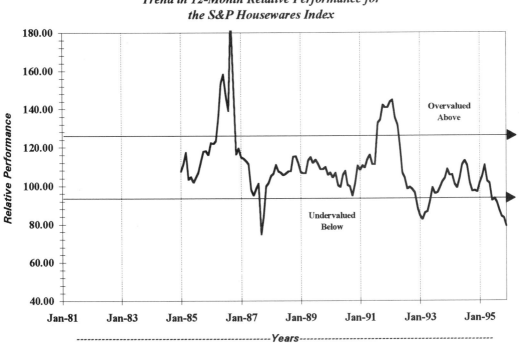

Trend in 12-Month Relative Performance for the S&P Housewares Index

115

given the high saturation levels of housewares in homes. However, we feel there are good growth opportunities for savvy houseware makers, such as those mentioned above. The almost $40 billion housewares industry is very fragmented, providing good opportunities for acquisitions and a quick way to broaden product offerings. As mega-retailers, such as Wal-Mart, have consolidated and grown, they have become more cost-conscious and have sought partnerships with only large houseware suppliers that can supply an enormous amount of inventory on short notice, well-known brands, national advertising, and electronic interchange. Growth opportunities also lie in new product introductions, which currently increase at about 20% a year. Savvy marketing aimed at stimulating more purchases of housewares than are needed (such as having many sets of plates or glasses versus everday goods) should also boost volume.

Outside of the opportunities for houseware companies to grow in the U.S., we feel the most successful houseware companies will be those with increasing overseas exposure. Homes in many overseas markets typically lack many houseware products found in most American homes. Currently, Black and Decker and Premark are those houseware companies with the largest overseas expansion, but Newell and Rubbermaid are now also expanding into foreign markets.

Description

Companies in this industry manufacture such small-ticket items as cookware, beverage glasses, flatware, and small appliances.

Characteristics

This industry is influenced by interest rates, the housing market, and new product introductions. The almost $100 billion housewares industry is very fragmented: the average company has only $15 million in annual sales. New product introductions, as well as new designs, colors, and packaging, are key to stimulating sales in this industry. Total new-product introductions normally increase about 23% a year.

Insurance Brokers

Outlook

Insurance brokerage stocks lagged the broader market in 1995, rising 10.8%, versus a 34.1% advance in the S&P 500. After significantly underperforming the broader market, in the first eight months, the group began picking up steam in late September when Marsh & McLennan Cos. announced an aggressive stock-buyback program. But, the group had a mixed performance in the final quarter, amid less than stellar third-quarter earnings, and ongoing competitive market conditions. Further gains for this group are predicated on a sustained turnaround in property-casualty insurance pricing. Since commission levels are dependent on the level of insurance premiums, the brokers' business tends to track the cyclicality of the underwriters' business.

Despite over seven years of weak pricing and rising loss costs, p-c premium pricing, in the aggregate, remains competitive. After barely recovering from the $20 billion in catastrophe losses during 1992, p-c insurers paid out almost $16 billion in catastrophe claims during 1994. As a result of these losses, property insurance rates have climbed considerably. However,

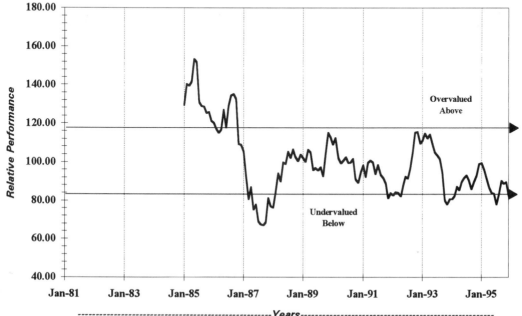

Trend in 12-Month Relative Performance for the S&P Insurance Brokers Index

117

ongoing competitive pricing pressures in most casualty lines will restrain overall written-premium growth. We anticipate written premiums will advance about 6% during 1996. As a means of partially reducing the cyclical nature of their business, many brokers have expanded their focus to include benefits and management consulting, loss-control surveys and analysis, and self-insurance consulting services. Brokers' dependence on fee-based income such as this will likely continue to expand, as they seek to compensate for slowing commercial insurance premium growth and an increasing trend of self-insurance by commercial clients. Benefits consulting is now typically the second-largest source of revenue for brokers. While increased legislative action usually forces clients to seek the specialized services of a human resources expert, for example, further growth in this area will be aided by an economic upturn.

Consolidation is another trend emerging in the insurance brokerage community. The brokerage business is a very competitive, labor-intensive business dependent on strict cost controls to ensure profit margins. As such, smaller regional brokers are consolidating in the hopes of achieving greater economies of scale and wider geographic representation. Larger, publicly held brokers are seeking acquisitions as a means of offsetting slower internal growth.

Definition

These companies act as intermediaries between underwriters and purchasers of insurance. In exchange for placing insurance with a policyholder, the broker receives a commission from the underwriter that is based on the value of the insurance premium.

Characteristics

Insurance brokers derive most of their revenues from commissions earned in the placement of insurance coverage. And since commission levels are dependent on the level of insurance premiums, the brokers' business tends to track the cyclicality of the underwriters' business. As a means of partially reducing the cyclical nature of their business, many brokers have expanded their focus to include benefits and management consulting, loss-control surveys and analysis, and self-insurance consulting services. The fortunes of brokers also are closely tied to the health of the overall economy. And since investment income represents a significant earnings source, rising interest rates (and investment yields) are a positive for brokers.

Investment Banking/Brokerage

Outlooks	
Relative performance:	*Neutral*
Fundamental (STARS):	*Neutral*

Outlook

Investment Banking and Brokerage stocks, as measured by S&P's index, rose 50.1% for 1995, versus a 34.1% rise for the S&P 500. The outperformance primarily reflects record third quarter profits and the broad advance in the stock market averages. As a matter of policy, S&P carries no investment opinions on securities brokers.

Broker profits in 1995's third quarter hit a record level, nearly doubling from second quarter 1995 levels. Wall Street owes its good fortune to the stock market rally and the year-to-date drop in interest rates, which has benefited trading and investment banking revenues. Other contributors are continued strength in mergers and acquisitions and good retail investor demand for equities.

The mega mergers in Europe of Dresdner Bank and Kleinwort Benson, Deutsche Bank and Morgan Grenfell, and Swiss Bank and S. G. Warburg indicate growing competition on the international front. The eventual demise of Glass-Steagall, the depression-era legislation setting forth sharp boundaries

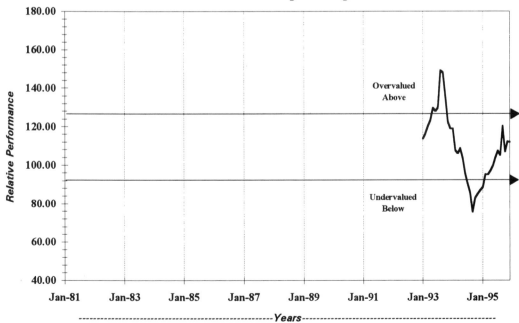

Trend in 12-Month Relative Performance for the S&P Investment Banking/Brokerage Index

between security brokers and commercial banks, could further increase competitive conditions. Two rumored takeover targets in the U. S. are Alex Brown and Lehman Brothers.

Description

These companies are involved in the buying and selling of financial instruments for clients and for themselves. They also raise capital for corporate clients through stock and bond offerings, as well as other commercial finance activities.

Characteristics

The key factors impacting future earnings are investor confidence, equity transaction volume, and the level and direction of long-term and short-term interest rates. While educated guesses can be made, these factors are not predictable. Long-term growth factors include higher savings, favorable demographics, and increased internationalization of markets. The securities industry has been unable to develop a solution to its perennial problem of volatility. Price to tangible book value is a measure investors frequently use to value brokers, because their highly liquid balance sheets can be readily marked to market. The traditional P/E ratio tends to make the stocks look undervalued at market tops and overvalued at market bottoms. Of course, brokerage stocks should be valued on all relevant factors, including earnings stability or volatility, financial strength, size, reliance on trading income, strength of diversified operations, cost structure, and other considerations.

Leisure Time

Outlooks
Relative performance: *Neutral*
Fundamental (STARS): *Neutral*

Outlook

The year-ahead investment prospect for leisure stocks is mixed, partly due to the diverse makeup of the group. In 1995, the S&P Leisure Time Index gained 24%, versus a 34% rise for the S&P 500. With leisure-related stocks, we recommend a selective approach, based on a variety of top-down and company-specific factors. In our coverage universe, our favorite leisure-time stock is motorcycle maker Harley Davidson. Also, we have an "hold" recommendation on the shares of Brunswick Corp, which makes boats and other recreation-related products.

Factors influencing long-term leisure spending include demographics, income levels, and the amount of free time available. Also the presence of two wage earners in many families has boosted household incomes. However, with people often working longer hours, spending patterns are likely to include more long-weekend getaways and greater use of the home as a setting for entertainment.

Between now and the year 2000, the number of Americans between the

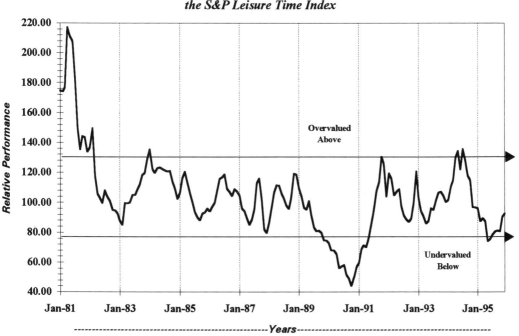

Trend in 12-Month Relative Performance for the S&P Leisure Time Index

ages of 20 and 34 is expected to decline, while the number of 35- to 54-year-olds should rise substantially. This suggests a no-better-than modest growth prospect for pursuits that require vigorous activity, such as skiing and tennis, whereas it portends an improving outlook for such areas as boating and golf, which tend to be favored by middle-aged and older Americans. At least near term, a recent baby boomlet should be favorable to the toy industry and portions of the sporting goods arena. In various consumer areas, well-known brand-names can be helpful in obtaining retail shelf space and attracting customers; also, they offer potential for line extensions. However, further pricing pressure is expected for a number of products, due to competition from private labels and the value consciousness of consumers.

Description

Companies in this industry manufacture products to be used during discretionary nonwork time. Such categories include boating, golfing, skiing, and theme parks. In general, this group excludes the subject areas included in the entertainment and hotel-motel industries.

Characteristics

The primary influencing factors are consumer spending and confidence; demographics, as some industries may be better suited to particular portions of the population (e.g., golfing with people ages 40 to 75); and new products, such as theme park attractions and roller blades.

Life Insurance

	Outlooks
Relative performance:	*Neutral*
Fundamental (STARS):	*Neutral*

Outlook

After underperforming the broader market during 1994, life insurance stocks gained 38.5% year to date through December 27, versus a 34% rise in the S&P 500 during this period. During 1994, the S&P Life Insurance Index tumbled 18.3%, while the S&P 500 declined 1.5%. Though the group has outperformed the broader averages during much of 1995, concerns that eroding consumer credit quality would impact several firms' finance units led to a near-term pullback in the fourth quarter. Nevertheless, over the longer term, some compelling values currently exist, particularly among those insurers that have tailored their product mix and pricing structure to offer a cost-effective line of savings-oriented products to an aging population.

To meet the savings and retirement needs of the public, many life insurers have shifted their mix of business away from so-called traditional life insurance products and toward more investment-oriented types of policies, like universal life and annuities. As a result of this shift, policyholders have absorbed more of the investment risk. While this shift has allowed life insurers to compete

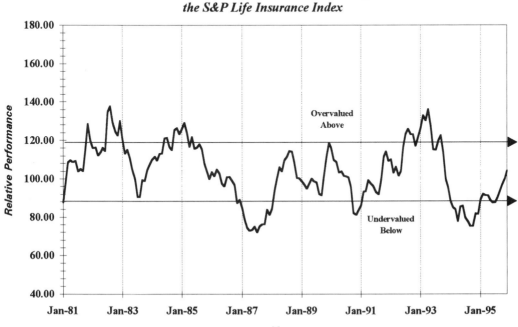

Trend in 12-Month Relative Performance for the S&P Life Insurance Index

123

more effectively with other financial intermediaries, it has also led to a narrowing of life insurers' profit margins. Nevertheless, the annuity business has evolved into one of the fastest growing sectors of the life insurance industry. However, competition here is keen. A recent Supreme Court ruling allowing banks to distribute annuities will provide insurers with an additional distribution channel. But, we believe this ruling also opens the possibility of banks being permitted to underwrite annuities, further blurring the lines that separate the various financial services sectors and increasing the competitive challenge to life insurers.

The largest participants in the life insurance industry are mutual insurance companies, which are insurers that are owned by their policyholders. During the 1980s, many pursued aggressive investment strategies that enabled them to capture market share from the stock companies through more aggressive product pricing. As a result, many saw their capital bases weaken further amid a collapse of the commercial real estate market and tighter regulatory requirements aimed at increasing capital requirements. Thus, an increasing number of mutuals are likely to merge to strengthen their capital bases or convert to a shareholder-owned structure to gain access to the capital markets.

Definition

Life insurance is a contract between a policyholder and an insurer whereby the payment of a stated monetary amount is guaranteed upon the death of the insured. Once merely a means of compensating for the loss of life, life insurance has evolved into an interest-sensitive, estate planning, and asset preservation tool.

Characteristics

Interest rates are perhaps the most significant economic factor affecting the results of life insurers. During periods of declining rates, life insurance profits usually rise, because the rate of interest paid on life insurance policies is adjusted downward more rapidly than the rate of interest earned on investments. Employment, savings, and tax rates also affect the purchase life insurance. Demographic shifts, such as the aging of the baby boomers, also play an important part in the growth potential for this industry.

Machine Tools

Outlooks	
Relative performance:	*Neutral*
Fundamental (STARS):	*Neutral*

Outlook

The S&P Machine Tool Index (which consists of Giddings & Lewis and Cincinnati Milacron) rose 11.3% in 1995, versus a 34% gain for the S&P 500. Through September 28, the index had matched the market, rising a 27%, in line with the 500. But a 14.4% decline in the index in October was caused by a severe drop in shares of Cincinnati Milacron (CMZ) right after the sale of one of its machine tool units. The index should at least track the market in 1996, however, as CMZ recovers from investors' overreaction.

Based upon our 1996 projection of 2.7% growth in real GDP, a 6.0% increase in spending for producer's durable equipment and stronger European economies, we expect that orders will rise again in 1996. Longer term, demand will benefit from the need for modernization and a secular trend toward substituting capital for labor in manufacturing.

According the Association for Manufacturing Technology, machine tool orders for the first 11 months of 1995 rose 8.2%. We expect that the 7% to 8% rate will approximate the rate for all of 1995, down from 1994's torrid

Trend in 12-Month Relative Performance for the S&P Machine Tools Index

125

42%, which was the second largest gain on record. Less rapid economic growth and a slowing auto industry account for the decline from 1994. We project an increase of 4% to 5% for 1996.

Although the outlook for sales and earnings is a little more positive than before, we are maintaining our "hold" rating on Giddings & Lewis (GIDL). Third-quarter earnings of $0.25 versus $0.29 were on target and GIDL expects sequential improvement in 1995's fourth quarter. We currently project earnings of $1.30 in 1996, but are reluctant to upgrade the stock until we are convinced that most of the problems with low-margin jobs are truly over. Longer term, we are positive on GIDL given its strong market position, its potential to grow via acquisitions, and the eventual acceptance into the marketplace of its revolutionary new machine tool, the VARIAX. Following the decline in October to a level where the shares sell at 11 times our 1996 estimate, we upgraded CMZ to "accumulate" from "hold." The sell-off was overdone and creates an opportunity to accumulate the shares at an attractive level. Longer term, CMZ's earnings and profit growth will depend much less on machine tools. Since 1993 the company has been aggressively acquiring non-machine tool businesses.

Definition

Machine tools are power-driven metal working machines that shape or form metal by cutting, pressure, impact, electrical techniques, or a combination of these processes. Machine tool companies also make factory automation systems.

Characteristics

The principal economic factors influencing stock prices in the machine tool industry are the strength in the overall economy, capital spending for the metalworking and automobile industries, and the monthly machine tool orders report. While there is little seasonality to sales and earnings, orders tend to slow in July and August in anticipation of the International Machine Tool Show held every September. Share prices typically are unaffected by this slowdown. The most distinguishing feature of this industry is its very small size relative to other capital goods industries. Total sales are about $5.0 billion, which is less that the annual sales of several large capitalization manufacturers. The index is composed of just two companies, Cincinnati Milacron and Giddings & Lewis.

Machinery (Diversified)

Outlook

Our near-term outlook for the Diversified Machinery group is neutral. After a large gain in share prices early in 1995, the group has retreated vis-à-vis the S&P 500. Our longer-term outlook is positive, however, based on the continued (albeit slower) economic growth and the competitive position these companies hold in the global marketplace. During 1995, the S&P Machinery (Diversified) Index gained 21% versus a 34% rise for the S&P 500. The index had been slightly outperforming the 500 through August, but the announcement by CAT that third-quarter earnings would not match 1994's led to an 8.2% drop in the group in September.

We expect sales and profit growth for companies in the diversified machinery industry to rise again in 1996, but at a lesser rate than in 1995, based on the S&P forecast of real GDP growth of 2.7% for 1996 versus 1995's projected rate of 3.3%. Positive factors include an improvement in commercial real estate, a projected 6.3% increase in aggregate capital expenditures in 1996 (including an 6.0% rise in spending for producer durable

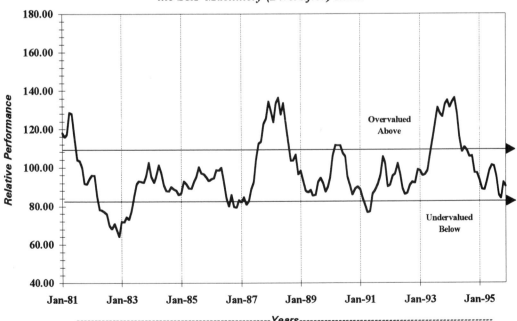

Trend in 12-Month Relative Performance for the S&P Machinery (Diversified) Index

goods), an upturn in aerospace, and greater impact from the highway spending bill. Other positive factors include stable overseas economies and continued strength in both the chemical and pulp and paper industries, as well as a possible upturn in capital spending for the oil and gas industry.

Nearly all of the companies in the index now appear to be fairly priced on a P/E basis. We rate Caterpillar Inc., Deere & Co. and Ingersoll-Rand "hold" based upon price and valuation. None of these issues is seriously overvalued on a P/E basis, but there is little upside potential after large price gains earlier in the year. We rate Harnischfeger Industries (HPH) "accumulate" based upon our expectation for accelerating sales and earnings. Also, we believe that HPH's earnings will not peak until 1997 at the earliest versus a possible earnings peak for the other companies in the index in 1996. Recently, the shares have been very weak due to HPH's takeover of UK-based Dobson Park. However, we believe this is just a temporary setback and don't think that HPH has overpaid for the acquisition. While the stock has been strong lately, we continue to rate Briggs & Stratton (BGG) "avoid" based our forecast for lower sales and earnings in fiscal 1996 (ending June 1996). Comparisons for fiscal 1996's first half will be particularly difficult.

Description

The S&P Machinery (Diversified) Index consists mostly of companies that manufacture heavy equipment for the agriculture and construction industries.

Characteristics

The principal factors affecting stock prices in this industry group are interest rates, housing starts, and automobile sales. Sales and earnings for these companies usually decline in the third quarter due to vacation schedules and planned maintenance.

Major Regional Banks

Outlooks

Relative performance: *Negative*

Fundamental (STARS): *Neutral*

Outlook

Earnings for most regional banks in the third quarter of 1995 continued to be propelled by a rising level of interest-earning assets (reflecting healthy loan demand) and reduced credit costs (made possible by improved asset quality). Bank stocks were one of the best performing groups in 1995, with a 52% rise in the S&P Major Regional Banks Index, easily outpacing the 34% gain in the S&P 500. Overall industry conditions for banks are favorable, despite our expectation of a slower economic environment (but with still healthy loan growth), flat to declining interest rates, low inflation, and credit quality that remains above historical averages.

Net-interest margins in the first nine months of 1995 were below year-earlier levels, mostly reflecting a higher cost of funds and competitive pressures that have kept down yields on loans. To reduce margin pressure, banks have been attempting to alter their mix of earning assets toward higher-yielding sectors, particularly credit cards and other consumer lending areas. However, the rate of delinquencies in those areas is generally higher, which

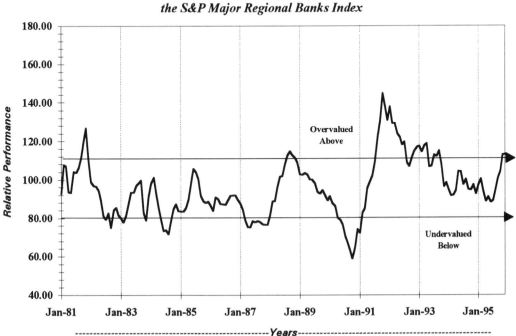

Trend in 12-Month Relative Performance for the S&P Major Regional Banks Index

129

could put some pressure on banks to begin bolstering loan-loss reserves. Still, we expect regional banks to continue reaping the benefits of historically low credit costs. Put another way, reserves in most cases remain more than adequate, and loan-loss provisioning, despite the expected increase, should not be much of a drag on profits. Bank earnings over the next few quarters should also benefit from continued efficiency gains and further consolidations.

Looking further ahead, the potential for reduced economic growth later in 1996 remains a concern. As such, investors would be wise to focus on banks whose regional service territories could withstand slower economic activity but still post respectable loan growth. For this reason, banks in the Southeast and Midwest, such as NationsBank, First Union, and First Bank System, look especially attractive. We also favor banks, such as Bank of New York, that have been able to widen net-interest margins despite higher interest rates over the past year through smart asset/liability management. Bank merger activity is also expected to continue, which has the speculative effect of propping up share prices in anticipation of acquisitions. The torrid pace of multi-billion dollar deals in 1995, however, will likely subside.

Description

These banks are distributors of capital by acting as lending sources to businesses in the form of commercial loans, as well as consumer debt through credit cards. Their lending and deposit bases tend to be concentrated in regional areas.

Characteristics

Revenues, earnings, and share prices are affected by (1) interest rates, as higher rates tend to dampen loan growth whereas lower rates spur growth— higher rates also adversely affect financing spreads by narrowing the difference (profit margin) between the rate at which money is borrowed and lent; (2) inflationary expectations (CPI), since increasing prices may cause consumers to defer purchases; and (3) employment trends, for an increase in the number of people working usually causes loan demand to rise. These institutions also are affected by the health of the regional economies.

Manufactured Housing

	Outlooks
Relative performance:	*Neutral*
Fundamental (STARS):	*Neutral*

Outlook

The Manufactured Housing Index (composed solely of Fleetwood Enterprises since Skyline Corp. was switched to the SmallCap 600 in mid-July) has performed erratically in 1995. After registering declines for several months, the Manufactured Housing Index rose 17% in November, boosting it to a 23% year to date gain through November 30, but still below the 32% rise in the S&P 500. However, the performance of the index has not reflected any particular volatility in the manufactured home industry. Rather, the down period was related to two Fleetwood announcements about weak motor home sales, while the November gain was related to a stronger than expected earnings report (on manufactured housing gains). It should be noted that companies with no exposure to the recreational vehicle (RV) market, such as Clayton Homes and Oakwood Homes, have had strong stock performances in 1995.

In forecasting upcoming results of manufactured homebuilders, the two factors most important in their performance, a strong level of consumer

Trend in 12-Month Relative Performance for the S&P Manufactured Housing Index

131

confidence and favorable employment trends, are mixed. Although economic uncertainty has caused the consumer confidence index to fall at certain points in 1995, it still remained at a favorable 101.4 after the latest reading. On the other hand, employment trends have been negative during much of the year, with job creation levels slowing and initial unemployment claims exceeding expectations. With the two major factors probably offsetting, other influences are likely to determine the industry's direction in upcoming periods. Although the generally modest prices of manufactured homes make the industry less sensitive to interest rate trends than conventional homebuilders, the downturn in long-term rates since the spring of 1995 should nonetheless prove helpful in boosting top line growth. Also, when adding growing consumer acceptance of factory-built homes into the equation, it leads us to believe industry output should remain on the upswing into 1996. However, volume gains are likely to fall below the 20% rise in 1994, given the more difficult economic environment.

As mentioned before, many manufactured home producers also make recreational vehicles, such as motor homes and travel trailers. With discretionary spending generally slowing in a moderating economy, we anticipate ongoing difficulties in the RV area in upcoming periods, and believe that builders with no exposure to the RV market will continue to be the best investments in the group.

Definition

Manufactured homes are structures built in a factory and transported to a home site. These structures are frequently referred to as mobile homes. Most producers also make recreational vehicles (trailers and motor homes).

Characteristics

There is an old saying in the industry that a manufactured home is bought by the newly wed and the nearly dead. This implies that manufactured homes are sold on a cost basis and that demographics also play a key role as most manufactured homes are sold to cost-conscious newlyweds and pensioners in the Sunbelt region of the United States. Also important are consumer confidence and employment trends. Interest rates are probably the dominant role in share-price performance, even though manufactured housing sales are not as sensitive to increasing rates as is the conventional housing market, since the change in monthly payments is so much smaller for any given change in rates. Investors still regard these companies as interest-sensitive issues.

Manufacturing (Diversified)

Outlooks

Relative performance: *Neutral*

Fundamental (STARS): *Neutral*

Outlook

Given the recent run of numbers, there is little doubt that the economy is slowing down. And while the outlook may not be as bright as it was a few months ago, it is not that grim either. We do not foresee a recession in 1996. On the other hand, we don't see much chance of renewed robust growth in the next few quarters. And if growth does suddenly reappear, it could be followed close behind by the Fed.

Capital spending slowed during the second half of 1995, and housing gains flattened out. Until we get a further decline in intermediate and long-term interest rates, we will not see renewed gains in housing. And while projected gains in capital spending are mixed, a slowing economy is not a good sign for business investment.

Specifically, S&P Economics projects annualized GDP growth of 2.8% for 1995 and 2.4% for 1996. Industrial production is forecast to grow 2.8% and 2.5% in 1995 and 1996, with capacity utilization expected to have peaked in the first quarter of 1995. Capital spending should surge 12.7% in

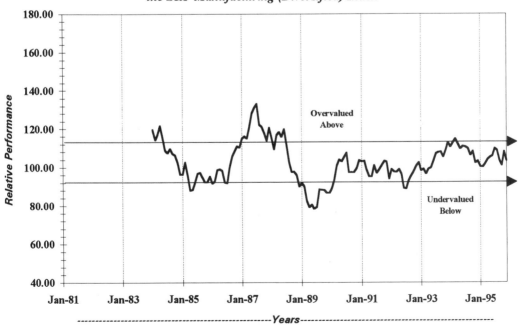

Trend in 12-Month Relative Performance for the S&P Manufacturing (Diversified) Index

133

1995 and 4.1% in 1996. Finally, the yield on the 30-year Treasury bond is likely to remain around 6.0% for the remainder of the first half of 1996.

Description

This industry consists of a variety of companies that offer a broad array of products and services to the industrial and consumer marketplaces.

Characteristics

The companies within this industry are less likely to be affected by sector-specific events than they are by the direction of macroeconomic components: GDP growth, industrial production, consumer confidence, interest rates, imports and exports, and the value of the U.S. dollar.

Medical Products & Supplies

Outlooks	
Relative performance:	*Negative*
Fundamental (STARS):	*Positive*

Outlook

Medical supply stocks should continue to perform well over the near term, reflecting credible earnings showings and investor recognition of the group's defensive, non-cyclical characteristics. Industry sales and earnings are benefiting from improved demand in key hospital markets, foreign expansion and new products. However, the gains are expected to be less than the high double-digit growth rates of several years ago, as pricing remains tough in the present managed-care oriented, cost-constrained health care environment. Companies with dominant positions in growing markets, which are also able to successfully develop and market new cost-effective products, should continue to post the best performances in this group.

The growth of managed care in the private sector, with its emphasis on cost efficiency, has engendered more conscientious buying patterns by hospitals, especially for "big ticket" items, such as multi-million dollar electronic imaging systems. Tighter reimbursement and restrictions on certain surgical procedures have also had a negative impact on industry sales. In

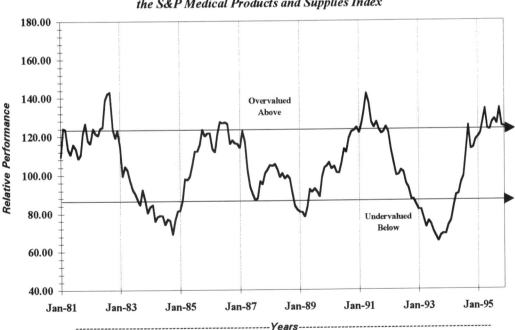

Trend in 12-Month Relative Performance for the S&P Medical Products and Supplies Index

135

addition, producers have been hurt by greater regulatory scrutiny of medical devices by the FDA, which has resulted in increased costs and delays in new-product approvals. However, the overall regulatory environment has improved somewhat with the present Republican leadership in Congress.

Largely in response to a tougher and more competitive marketplace, merger and acquisition activity has increased in this sector, as producers seek business combinations to compete more effectively and reduce costs. The most recent major combination is Johnson & Johnson's planned acquisition of Cordis, a leading maker of angioplasty and angiographic equipment, for stock valued at about $1.8 billion. Further consolidations in the medical device industry are anticipated in the coming years.

Positive longer-term fundamentals include the nation's insistence on quality health care; the swelling ranks of the elderly (principal consumers of medical products); and rising R&D outlays, which should spawn a steady flow of new diagnostic and therapeutic products in the future. Niche-oriented companies focusing on successful specialty products, particularly in the high-technology sector, should outperform the industry average.

Description

This industry manufacturers more than 130,000 different items that range from ordinary gauze pads to sophisticated diagnostic machines. The Commerce Department divides the industry into five broad product classifications: surgical appliances and supplies, surgical and medical instruments, electromedical equipment, x-ray apparatus and tubes, and dental equipment and supplies.

Characteristics

These issues are typically regarded as defensive plays, with their businesses unaffected by economic fluctuations. Medical products and supplies companies are affected by competitive market shares, the pace of FDA approvals, patent lives, and the strength of R&D pipelines. With most leading companies deriving substantial revenues abroad, the relative value of the dollar is another important factor.

Metals (Misc.)

Outlook

This index is dominated by copper companies. We see the copper group outperforming the S&P 500 in 1996, as investors correct valuations that have discounted a worst-case copper-price scenario. With earnings multiples for many copper issues some 40%-50% below that for the S&P 500, the group could launch a substantial rally even against a backdrop of flat earnings. The stocks of copper companies displayed a firm tone toward the end of 1995, bolstered by the proposed $1.8 billion acquisition of Magma Copper by Australia's Broken Hill Proprietary Co. The merger would make BHP the world's largest producer at 800,000 tons and give it reserves of 26 million tons. The 30% premium BHP offered for Magma initially sparked buying in other copper stocks but later inspired a sell off as some viewed the deal as a sign of a market top.

The price of the red metal rallied up to $1.40/lb. in December before sliding back $0.10/lb. as the December contract expired. Although the rally fell short of the $1.47/lb. high in July, we are convinced that, in view of the

Trend in 12-Month Relative Performance for the S&P Metals (Misc.) Index

Years

137

tight supply situation, the anticipated price erosion may be shallower than many investors believe. In late-December, the Comex spot price for copper was $1.31/lb. up from its a 12-month low of $1.21/lb. set in October. Backwardation of future prices continue to point to lower prices for 1996. On December 20, the December 1996 copper contract was priced 13.5% below the December 1995 contract. However, with inventories very low, we doubt if copper prices for 1996 will average more than $0.15/lb. below current levels.

World copper consumption for 1996 is projected at 11.5 million tons, up about 3.6% from 11.1 million tons in 1995. Meanwhile production continues to lag behind consumption. Production for 1995 is likely to fall short of consumption by some 310,000 tons in 1995. This compares against a 278,000-ton consumption deficit in 1994. To bridge this gap in supply and demand, copper stocks have been drawn down. At the end of September, copper stocks at the London Metal Exchange and COMEX aggregated 189,000 tons, which was off nearly 75% from the 700,000 tons reached in late 1993. The copper supply deficit should narrow dramatically in 1996 to perhaps 25,000 tons as new production comes on line and existing properties are expanded. Chile, the world's largest copper miner, will produce some 2.5 million metric tons in 1995, up from 1994's 2.22 million, reflecting the start up of the new Zaldivar mine in June.

Description

This industry consists of companies engaged primarily in the mining and production of copper and, to a lesser extent, nickel, lead, and zinc.

Characteristics

Since copper demand is a function of business activity, one should consider the economic outlooks for the world's major copper consumers: the United States, Japan, Europe, and newly industrialized Asian countries. Another influencing factor is the demand from such end markets as autos, building/ construction, computers, and telecommunications industries. Lead is used mainly in automotive batteries, comprising 63% of Western world demand.

Miscellaneous

Outlooks
Relative performance: *Positive*
Fundamental (STARS): *Neutral*

Outlook

Given the recent run of numbers, there is little doubt that the economy is slowing down. And while the outlook may not be as bright as it was a few months ago, it is not that grim either. We do not foresee a recession in 1996. On the other hand, we don't see much chance of renewed robust growth in the next few quarters. And if growth does suddenly reappear, it could be followed close behind by the Fed.

Capital spending slowed during the second half of 1995, and housing gains flattened out. Until we get a further decline in intermediate and long-term interest rates, we will not see renewed gains in housing. And while projected gains in capital spending are mixed, a slowing economy is not a good sign for business investment.

Specifically, S&P Economics projects annualized GDP growth of 2.8% for 1995 and 2.4% for 1996. Industrial production is forecast to grow 2.8% and 2.5% in 1995 and 1996, with capacity utilization expected to have peaked in the first quarter of 1995. Capital spending should surge 12.7% in

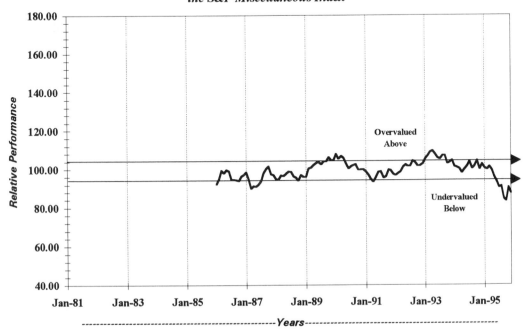

Trend in 12-Month Relative Performance for the S&P Miscellaneous Index

139

1995 and 4.1% in 1996. Finally, the yield on the 30-year Treasury bond is likely to remain around 6.0% for the remainder of the first half of 1996.

Description

This industry consists of a variety of companies that offer a broad array of products and services to the industrial and consumer marketplaces.

Characteristics

The companies within this industry are less likely to be affected by sector-specific events than they are by the direction of macroeconomic components: GDP growth, industrial production, consumer confidence, interest rates, imports and exports, and the value of the U.S. dollar.

Money Center Banks

Outlooks	
Relative performance:	*Neutral*
Fundamental (STARS):	*Positive*

Outlook

After rising nearly nonstop in the first ten months of 1995, bank stock prices eased somewhat in the last two months on concerns over credit quality given sluggish economic conditions. Even so, the group easily outpaced the broader market in 1995, with the S&P Money Center Banks Index up 58%, versus a 34% rise for the S&P 500 Index. We remain positive on the group for the near term, as modest loan growth, continued strong credit quality, and cost-control measures propel earnings. Initial fourth-quarter earnings reports have been encouraging, and the group is expected to outperform over the next several months. The intermediate term has also brightened now that it appears the Fed's efforts to restrain inflation have succeeded and short-term interest rates could be in for a further decline.

Loan growth continues at a healthy pace. And while pressure remains on the net interest margin, reflecting both higher rates in effect this year than last and continued competitive pressures, there have been respectable gains in net interest income. Some money center banks have begun to focus on their

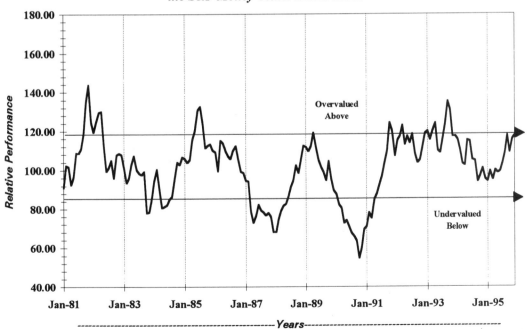

Trend in 12-Month Relative Performance for
the S&P Money Center Banks Index

more profitable consumer businesses, such as credit cards and other variable-rate lending, where the outlook for loan growth is particularly strong. It is difficult to talk about the bank industry without mentioning consolidation. The recent Chase/Chemical merger announcement has brought renewed attention to the group's revenue growth objectives and could place additional emphasis on the need for efficiency improvements, since the new Chase has set lofty performance goals for itself that may become the new standard going forward.

The December 1995 lowering of interest rates by the Federal Reserve also bodes well for the longer term for this interest-sensitive group. While loan growth has slowed somewhat from the strong pace of 1994, loan spreads should widen going forward in a flat to declining interest rate environment. However, credit quality remains a concern given dampened economic activity, and loan-loss provisions could creep up with expanding loan portfolios. In any case, investors should continue to focus on banks able to weather the challenging environment ahead. Our favorite in the group remains Citicorp, whose far-reaching global presence should allow it to produce strong results despite volatile economic and capital market conditions. Also favored is BankAmerica given its renewed focus on middle-market commercial lending.

Description

These banks are large distributors of capital by acting as lending sources to businesses in the form of commercial loans, as well as to consumers through credit cards, mortgages, and personal loans. These banks also engage in securities and currency trading and tend to be located in major metropolitan areas.

Characteristics

Revenues, earnings, and share prices are affected by (1) interest rates, as higher rates tend to dampen loan growth whereas lower rates spur growth; (2) inflationary expectations (CPI), since increasing prices may cause consumers to defer purchases; and (3) employment trends, for an increase in the number of people working usually causes loan demand to rise.

Multi-Line Insurance

Outlooks	
Relative performance:	*Neutral*
Fundamental (STARS):	*Positive*

Outlook

Multi-line insurance stocks outperformed the broader market in 1995, rising 47%, while the S&P 500 advanced 34%. During 1994, the Multi-line Index rose 3.5%, while the S&P 500 declined 1.5%. Much of the near-term activity reflects company-specific events, including pending and rumored restructuring moves at Aetna and Cigna, and strength in shares of AIG. Longer term, the dynamics of this sector will be marked by a radical change in operating strategy. Realizing that the market rewards focused, niche insurers with higher multiples, many multi-lines are rethinking their strategy of attempting to service all markets with all types of coverage. Hence, the pullback from selected lines already underway will likely accelerate.

Many multi-line insurers invested aggressively in commercial real estate and mortgage loans to help fund their large-case pension business. Write-offs of these investments amid a collapsed commercial real estate market plagued the multi-lines during the last several years. Now, some insurers are capitalizing on the signs of life that are emerging in parts of the commercial

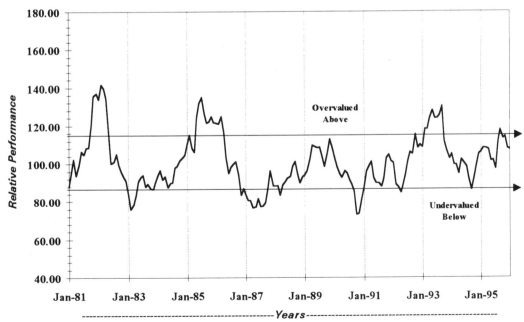

Trend in 12-Month Relative Performance for the S&P Multi-Line Index

real estate market, and are selling off some of their holdings. The bulk of multi-line insurers' profits tends to come from providing some form of health insurance coverage. Against a backdrop of escalating healthcare costs and ever-increasing cost shifting on the part of the government, health insurance providers have turned to managed care vehicles, such as health maintenance organizations (HMOs) and preferred-provider organizations (PPOs) to help their clients manage health care expenses. However, establishing HMO/ PPO networks is very capital intensive, and many multi-line insurers have yet to achieve adequate returns from their investment. A consolidation of the managed care sector is likely, as small- to mid-size players decide they do not have the means to achieve a critical mass in managed care.

Though a Republican-controlled Congress will not likely assign a very high priority to health care reform, a growing cost consciousness on the part of the purchasers of health care will lead to a continuation of the shift to managed care from traditional indemnity (or fee for service) health care coverage. While managed care providers will see their premium volume grow, only the most cost-efficient providers will thrive in an environment that will likely be extremely price-competitive.

Description

Multi-line insurers underwrite an array of life, health, and property-casualty (p-c) insurance products for both consumers and businesses. These insurers also have a fairly large presence in the managed care arena. Still others have diversified into other financial services, such as securities brokerage and asset management.

Characteristics

The demand for insurance is a function of economic growth, inflation rates, and the need to protect assets. The supply curve for insurance is interest-sensitive. When interest rates rise, the supply of insurance also rises, as insurers are willing to provide more insurance at the same price since each premium dollar will generate a higher return. As a result, competition increases and prices decline until additional demand is reduced or until it becomes unprofitable to provide coverage and insurers withdraw from the market.

Natural Gas

Outlooks	
Relative performance:	*Neutral*
Fundamental (STARS):	*Positive*

Outlook

In 1995 the S&P Natural Gas Index rose 37%, versus a 34% gain in the S&P 500 Index. Near-term fundamentals for gas demand make us optimistic, since growth in the domestic economy is boosting gas sales, and overhanging supply caused by mild winter weather in early 1995 is being absorbed by higher demand caused by cooler than normal temperatures. Rising interest rates in 1994 sent investors in gas utilities fleeing. However, the Fed recently made the second in what we expect to be a series of interest rate cuts. Meanwhile, the commodity characteristics of gas utility stocks have become more pronounced, since distributors now are responsible for the inventory of natural gas. Falling prices did cause producers to "shut-in" gas in 1995, when production became uneconomic. In turn, throughput volumes of natural gas, the bread and butter for pipelines, dropped. We believe the near-term bodes well for pipeline stocks, since gas volumes are likely to pick up on stronger demand.

Cold weather in early 1996 is leading to higher gas volumes for most

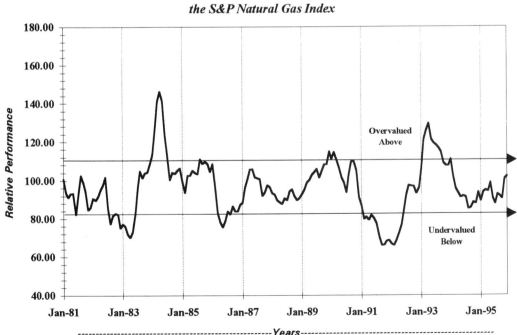

Trend in 12-Month Relative Performance for the S&P Natural Gas Index

145

pipelines. However, gas volumes continue to be restricted by increased electric generation at several nuclear power plants, as well as cheap imports from Canada. The gas industry has retooled itself to meet heightened competition. The traditional transportation business has been separated from service activities. Pipelines now offer storage, hub and gathering services, as well as marketing and hedging services. The pipeline has become a common carrier, and transportation volumes provide nominal margins. With pipeline companies offering unique services, their investment prospects differ and we are recommending a small group of well-positioned companies.

Natural gas prices averaged $1.83 per million Btu in 1994. For 1995, gas prices averaged $1.80, due mainly to mild winter weather in the crucial Mid-Atlantic and Midwest regions. However, we forecast a rise in average prices for 1996 to $1.85. A favorable interest rate environment will impact drawdown rates in the near term, and we note that storage levels as of early January were below year-ago levels. Over the long-term, anticipated growth in electricity cogeneration, driven by improvements in gas turbine design, should buoy the shares.

Description

A distributor is a local gas utility that receives natural gas from a natural gas pipeline and in turn transports and/or sells it to the industrial or residential end user. A pipeline is a tubular structure that brings natural gas from the producing areas to the local natural gas utility or large-volume end user.

Characteristics

The restructuring of the gas industry resulted from FERC Order 636 which was implemented in late 1993. Order 636 shifted the merchant function from gas pipeline companies to gas distributors. Gas pipelines no longer buy gas, inventory gas, and sell it on demand. Rather, the inventory function has shifted to gas distributors who are generally permitted to include in their customer rates the costs of gas inventory. As gas distributors built inventories, pipeline companies increased their inventory capacity through the construction of new pipelines and also gathering and hub facilities.

Prices for natural gas stocks are affected by growth in the economy, interest rates, and natural gas prices. The performance of the overall economy is a good indicator for growth in gas demand, as industrial production and housing starts will offer an idea as to the direction and magnitude of demand from the industrial and residential end users, respectively. Interest rates play a key role for these stocks as investors regard them as dividend plays.

Office Equipment & Supplies

Outlook

In 1995, the S&P Office Equipment & Supplies Index outpaced the S&P 500's 34% rise with a 38% gain. During 1994, the index declined 0.5% (due to concerns about product-refocusing efforts at Pitney Bowes and Xerox), versus a 1.5% fall in the S&P 500. Our near-term investment outlook is still favorable, reflecting steady, although less robust, economic growth. Longer-term demand should be propelled by improving global economies, technological advances, and increasing affordability of equipment.

Pitney Bowes and Xerox have both seen their share prices rise sharply in 1995, after they came under selling pressure in the second half of 1994. These companies are well-positioned for growth, as borne out by strong results so far in 1995. Pitney Bowes has taken recent steps to focus on its core strengths of preparing, delivering, tracking, and storing packages, letters and other materials. Top line growth should continue, driven primarily by increased rental and facilities management revenues. International mailing operations should also contribute to increased revenues. The company

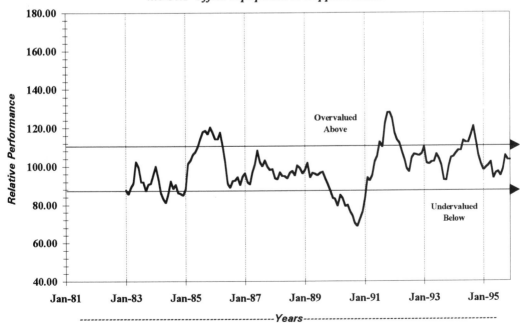

Trend in 12-Month Relative Performance for the S&P Office Equipment & Supplies Index

147

reported an 21% EPS increase during the first nine months on favorable revenue comparisons. Xerox, meanwhile, has divested operations that are not directly related to its core document-processing business and realigned its sales force. The company recently announced a realignment designed to increase efficiency, eliminate a top tier of management, and accelerate growth and productivity. During 1995's first nine months, the company reported sharply higher net income on double-digit revenue growth. Xerox should continue to benefit from improving worldwide economies, new product introductions, strong demand for digital products, color copiers and printers, and a growing facilities management business. Cost-cutting efforts should lead to double-digit earnings growth and additional share appreciation.

The outlook for the business forms segment is mixed. While the U.S. economy continues to grow, this segment is undergoing structural changes as companies position themselves for the electronic age. This is underscored by the recent $1.35 billion hostile offer by Moore Corp. for fellow forms maker Wallace Computer Services. Also, Moore recently signed an agreement to sell its retail/franchise operation in Europe in order to focus on its key businesses of forms and print management, labels, and customer communication services.

Description

Office equipment includes photocopiers, facsimile systems, mailing and shipping systems, business supplies, and business forms.

Characteristics

The key factor influencing the office equipment industry is the general strength of U.S. businesses, although foreign markets, most notably Japan and Europe, also play a role in the overall success of these firms. Some economic indicators we use to gauge the overall strength of an economy include capital spending trends by businesses, the general direction of interest rates, and employment trends.

Oil & Gas Drilling

Outlook

We are optimistic about prospects for a number of drillers, due to climbing day rates and increased utilization figures, which owe much to increased energy consumption worldwide. Oil prices in 1994 averaged $17.16 a barrel, down from $18.49 a bbl. in 1993. For 1996, our forecast calls for a slight drop to $18.30 from 1995's average of $18.40. We began recommending U.S.-based driller Global Marine in May 1995. We believe the shares of Global Marine will rise still further, as investors focus on favorable long-term domestic and foreign gas prospects, and a rig fleet which ranks among the industry's most modern. Excess offshore drilling rig counts are forecast to decline over the next several years, and semi-submersible rigs capable of drilling in deep water will be in high demand, and we expect to see a number of long-term contracts signed in coming months.

Drilling activity in the U.S. had been firm during the past few years. With the downturn in natural gas prices in 1994, the domestic rig count fell. We forecast the number of domestic gas rigs will climb in 1996. As of mid-

Trend in 12-Month Relative Performance for the S&P Oil & Gas Drilling Index

149

December, the Hughes Christensen domestic rig count showed 773 rigs in operation, down from 827 units in the year-earlier period. Long-term prospects for domestic natural gas drilling remain favorable, due to projected growth in gas consumption. Overseas, exploration projects are directed more toward oil. The international rig count stands at 764, up from 735 a year ago; rig utilization is also rising, mainly due to higher oil prices observed year to date in 1995, and increased demand from the growing economies of non-OECD Europe, and the Pacific Rim. Though oil prices are forecast to be stable, the foreign rig count should move higher near term. Drilling activity has been strong in Latin America where Argentina, Columbia, and Venezuela have been encouraging investment in the oil sector. We expect Mexico to emerge as an important drilling market because of its vast hydrocarbon potential in the Gulf of Mexico. A pickup in North Sea output is also forecast, as a number of fields in the U.K.'s West of Shetlands sector come on line.

Untapped gas reserves, industry outsourcing, and increased demand from the Pacific Rim will benefit this group's performance. Successful drilling firms, able to access hydrocarbons under difficult climatic and environmental conditions, will command the highest day rates for their services.

Definition

Contract drilling companies rent their rigs and related crews to exploration companies. Rigs are utilized in both onshore and offshore locations. Rigs are rented or contracted out on a daily basis and the fee is referred to as the day rate.

Characteristics

Earnings and equity prices for companies within the energy sector are affected by the same four factors: commodity prices (oil and gas); the value of the U.S. dollar, since the commodity itself is traded in U.S. dollars worldwide (a strong dollar is good for equity prices, whereas a weak dollar is not); refined product margins (e.g., the difference between crude oil and gasoline); and volumes, or the amount of product sold. Among all of the industries within the energy sector, drillers are the most sensitive to oil and natural gas prices. Higher oil and natural gas prices increase spending for oil and gas exploration. Greater exploration spending increases the demand for drilling rigs and leads to higher day rates. The principal measurement of domestic drilling activity is the Baker Hughes rig count, while the primary overseas index is the Hughes Christensen international rig count.

Oil - Domestic Integrated

Outlook

Domestic integrated oil stocks continued to rise in 1995, as a result of somewhat higher oil prices and the expansion of chemical markets. However, oil supplies continued to grow faster than demand, and Iraq will likely return to world oil markets in 1996. We believe that a pickup in natural gas prices that is underway and continued improvement in downstream margins will offset somewhat weaker chemical earnings. We anticipate the group will continue to show gains, though valuations based on trailing earnings are excessive, and the yield on S&P's Domestic Oil Index is near a five-year low. We expect the price of benchmark West Texas Intermediate (WTI) crude oil to average $18.10 a bbl. for 1995, rising to $18.30 in 1996. Natural gas prices, battered by higher storage levels, experienced a pickup in late 1995, after falling precipitously due to a warm winter in the early part of 1995. We expect gas prices to have averaged $1.60 in 1995, rising to $1.75 in 1996. Moreover, a recovery in refined product markets, which were shaken by the introduction of reformulated gasoline (RFG), will likely take place by

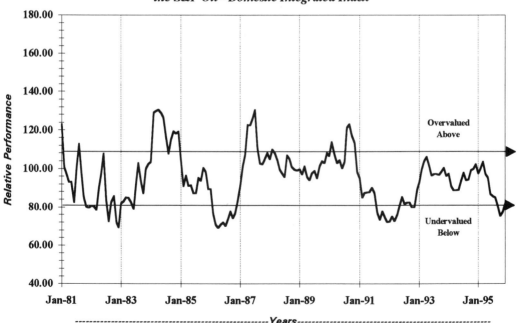

Trend in 12-Month Relative Performance for
the S&P Oil - Domestic Integrated Index

mid-1996. We are recommending selected refiners and marketers, and are giving the domestic oil group a market weighting.

The current price per barrel of West Texas Intermediate oil of $18.90 seems reasonable to us, given relatively high (2.4%) demand growth we forecast for 1996. We expect to see an average 1996 oil price of $18.30 a bbl. However, North Sea production, especially from Norway, is surging while Latin American and Pacific Rim output is on the upswing. But political uncertainty in Russia will undermine near-term production plans there.

Heavy involvement in U.S. natural gas production will benefit domestic integrated oil stocks. Although natural gas markets in 1994 were weak, lower than expected storage levels in November bode well, and the long-term demand outlook is more favorable than that for oil. Moreover, reserves as a percentage of production have been dropping steadily. Natural gas is environmentally benign and priced at a discount to crude oil. Technological advances now make identification of gas reserves less costly, allowing companies to undertake exploration projects not previously viewed as economically feasible. We are also optimistic about refiners with modern asset bases in Europe, where antiquated refining networks are commonplace.

Definition

Domestic oil companies engage in exploration and production (also called "upstream" activities), as well as refining, marketing, and chemicals ("downstream"). Integrated means upstream activities are coordinated to downstream operations. Domestic oil firms differ from international oil companies in that the refining, marketing, and chemical businesses are for the most part contained within the United States. However, the exploration and production operations are located in both domestic and overseas oil and natural gas provinces.

Characteristics

Domestic refined product fundamentals are a function of crude oil costs, refined product prices, and sales of refined products; the principal cost is crude oil, the prices of which are a volatile combination of worldwide production and consumption. The primary U.S. refined product is gasoline. The price is mostly determined in highly competitive local markets. Other refined products include diesel fuel, home heating oil, jet fuel, and petrochemicals. Domestic integrated oil companies, like international oil firms, have constructed diversified oil, natural gas, and refined product portfolios designed to limit market fluctuations while exploiting economic opportunities.

Oil - Exploration & Production

Outlook

Oil and gas exploration stocks have rebounded, in spite of lower cash flow and earnings that have accompanied falling average domestic natural gas prices. Crude oil prices have been stable recently, however, amidst uncertainty over Iraq and climbing demand. In October 1995, we upgraded Louisiana Land & Exploration to an "accumulate," based on our belief that long-term earnings growth will result from a new development strategy. However, we recommend the group only to the aggressive investor who can withstand the volatility of corporate earnings which are influenced by crude oil and natural gas prices. The possibility of major oil and gas discoveries in the Gulf of Mexico, Alaska, the Ivory Coast, the North Sea, Asia, and the former Soviet Union will likely convince investors that current valuation levels are reasonable. We also anticipate the group will benefit from further industry consolidation as leveraged players, like debt-laden Maxus, are forced to seek deep-pocket partners.

Average oil prices, as measured by the U.S. light sweet futures contract,

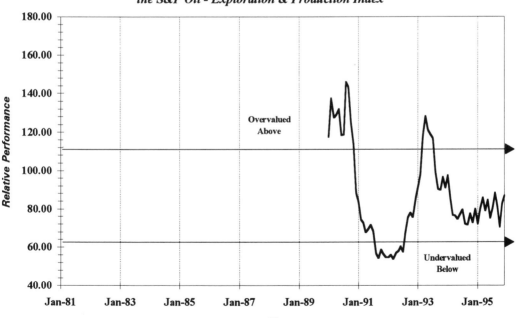

Trend in 12-Month Relative Performance for the S&P Oil - Exploration & Production Index

153

declined from 1990 through 1994. In 1990, triggered by Iraq's invasion of Kuwait, oil prices peaked and averaged $24.40 a barrel. Average prices in 1994, were $17.16 a bbl. In 1996, we expect oil prices to average $18.30 a bbl., down only slightly from the average of $18.40 during 1995, since we believe Iraq's intransigence will preclude their return to full-scale production prior to mid-1996. Worldwide oil production has increased, owing to greater output from the North Sea, Latin America, and the Pacific Rim, as well as other non-OPEC (Organization of Petroleum Exporting Countries) sources. However, demand for petroleum products is growing quite rapidly when compared with the past 20 years. Therefore, much will hinge on whether OPEC's production discipline is maintained, as member states vie for increased production quotas.

Longer term, the outlook for natural gas markets is more favorable than for crude oil, as gas replaces oil in industrial, commercial, residential, and utility applications. New technologies, including seismic evaluation, horizontal drilling, directional drilling, enhanced oil recovery, and the development of more efficient drill bits and mud motors have all helped finding and development costs to fall over the past several years, and we expect this trend to continue.

Definition

Exploration and production companies search for crude oil and natural gas (hydrocarbons) worldwide.

Characteristics

Exploration and production companies generally have not integrated or diversified their operations with petroleum refining and marketing because of the significant costs associated with manufacturing and distribution. As a result, exploration and production fundamentals are highly leveraged to the price of crude oil. Exploration firms will diversify, or limit their sensitivity to crude oil prices through natural gas. Natural gas fundamentals differ from oil fundamentals in so much as oil is a world commodity and pricing is relatively homogeneous, whereas natural gas is a regional commodity and pricing is a function of local market conditions. Because of favorable domestic natural gas fundamentals, exploration and production companies are shifting their development focus to gas.

Oil - International Integrated

Outlooks	
Relative performance:	*Neutral*
Fundamental (STARS):	*Neutral*

Outlook

Investors in integrated oil stocks found 1995 rewarding. Third-quarter earnings reports largely exceeded expectations, due to an expansion in chemical profits, higher oil prices, and the impact of pervasive cost-cutting programs. The near-term outlook for petrochemicals is negative, though we are anticipating a modest recovery in refined-product markets, which have been bolstered by demand for gasoline that has significantly exceeded analyst's expectations. Stabilizing gasoline markets seem to have finally shrugged off the dumping of large quantities of reformulated gasoline (RFG). The group is trading at a slight discount to the S&P 500 multiple. We expect oil prices to remain stable near $18 over the next three quarters, while natural gas prices are expected to taper off from recent highs. As a result, we are giving international integrated oil equities a market weighting.

We are optimistic about the current environment for refining and marketing operations, since demand for gasoline in the U.S. and Europe has been particularly strong, and gasoline prices at the pump have been sticky.

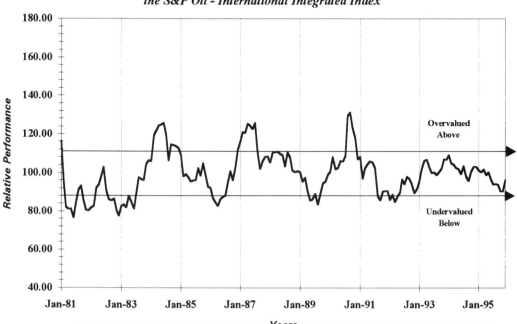

Trend in 12-Month Relative Performance for the S&P Oil - International Integrated Index

Turning to the upstream, oil prices had been declining since 1991, amidst the expansion of non-OPEC production. We estimate oil prices will average $18.10 a bbl. in 1995, rising to $18.30 in 1996, up from 1994's $17.16. We expect OPEC to enforce production discipline in 1996. At the same time, oil exports from Russia may be undermined by political uncertainty. However, increased capital spending budgets have spurred production in the North Sea, the Gulf of Mexico, Latin America and the Pacific Rim. Output has been accelerating, particularly from the North Sea and South America. We believe Iraq's eventual return to world oil markets will lead to only a temporary downturn in oil prices, since markets have already factored in this increase in supply.

Both Europe and Japan are gradually emerging from recession and demand for petroleum products will remain essentially flat through 1996, leading to oversupplied markets, while U.S. demand should improve moderately. Oil companies will focus on natural gas reserves, and shift their capital spending to Pacific Rim and Latin American nations, where growth opportunities exceed those of the mature Western economies.

Description

International integrated oil firms, like domestic integrated companies, are vertically integrated oil companies, engaging in exploration and production activities, as well as refining and marketing; they also produce chemicals in principal world markets. Historically, the two leading international oil companies were Standard Oil and Shell. The heirs to Standard Oil are Exxon, Mobil, Amoco and Chevron. Shell by most measures is the world's largest publicly held oil company. Privately held oil companies have as much impact and influence on world oil markets as publicly held firms. Most notable among the private oil companies is Aramco, the Arabian American Oil Co., which is entirely owned by the Kingdom of Saudi Arabia. Aramco is the largest of the 12-member oil consortium, OPEC (the Organization of Petroleum Exporting Countries).

Characteristics

Integrated oil companies build diversified portfolios of oil, natural gas, and refined-product properties that limit the volatility of any one factor. Global oil markets are also highly sensitive and perhaps hinged upon geopolitics.

Oil Well Equipment & Services

Outlooks	
Relative performance:	*Neutral*
Fundamental (STARS):	*Positive*

Outlook

Oil service equities continue to rise on improved industry fundamentals, and the likelihood of further increases in capital spending by the major integrated oil companies. We now recommend an over-weighting for the oil services group, and view selected companies as poised to benefit from increased worldwide demand for petroleum products and natural gas, as well as a stable oil price outlook. We recently upgraded Halliburton to "buy" from "accumulate" and Schlumberger and Dresser Industries to "accumulate" from "hold." Exposure to strong North Sea, Gulf of Mexico, and South American exploration areas and an aggressive approach to new technology should result in double-digit earnings growth over the next several years for each company.

We have lowered our forecast for average oil prices in 1995 to $18.30 a bbl., on reports that worldwide supplies appear to be rising faster than demand in the near term. The likelihood that Iraq will not be allowed to resume production until mid-1996, coupled with a U.S. ban on Iranian oil

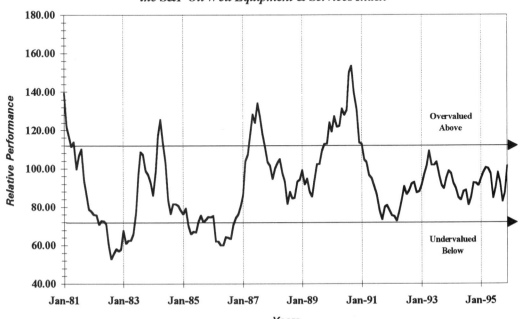

Trend in 12-Month Relative Performance for the S&P Oil Well Equipment & Services Index

157

sales abroad by U.S. domiciled oil companies, shook oil markets in early 1995. OPEC, in November, maintained its production quota, and seems focused on curtailing member quota violations. Meanwhile, domestic natural gas prices are up sharply on lower-than-anticipated storage levels. In Europe, excess supply has led to a gas "bubble." The Hughes Christensen international rig count as of December showed 773 rigs in operation, down from 827 rigs in the year-earlier period. We expect the Hughes Christensen count to trend higher in the near term as a result of lower extraction costs on a per barrel of oil equivalent basis. Superior companies will command higher prices and margins with the development of proprietary products and services in such areas as seismic and logging services and directional drilling.

Worldwide energy needs are a factor of growth in the mature economies, as well as the speed with which developing nations accept technological progress. Increased demand from the Pacific Rim and Latin America bode well for the group, since incremental demand increases from the U.S. and Europe over the next several years are not expected to be significant. Within the industrialized countries, a growing realization that natural gas provides an environmentally benign form of fuel that is more economical than oil will result in its substitution for other types of fuel in industrial applications.

Description

Oil service companies develop technologically sophisticated equipment, products, and services used in exploration and production of oil and natural gas. During drilling and production, the geology surrounding a well must be evaluated for changes. Wireline tools are utilized to detect the geological changes. Seismic evaluations, or shoots, amass data for geophysical scientists who assess the information for potential oil and natural gas deposits. Onshore vibrating equipment or offshore sonic equipment is used to send or shoot waves into the geology. The waves rebound and are recovered by data processing units that compile the seismic information. Once a potential oil and natural gas deposit is identified and an oil company commits to developing the field, a well is drilled.

Characteristics

As mentioned earlier, oil company earnings and equity valuations are a function of the price of commodities, the value of the dollar, refined product margins, and volumes. Each oil company has a unique sensitivity to these factors. Just like oil and gas drillers, oil service fundamentals are highly sensitive to oil and natural gas prices.

Paper & Forest Products

Outlooks	
Relative performance:	*Positive*
Fundamental (STARS):	*Neutral*

Outlook

The S&P Paper and Forest Products Index sharply underperformed the broader market in 1995, posting only a 7.4% gain versus a 34.1% rise in the S&P 500. The two components of the index experienced opposite performances for much of the period, with most firms with predominant operations in paper enjoying significant stock appreciation and those stressing wood products not faring as well. However, with moderating economic conditions and inventory buildups causing worries about a possible cyclical peak in the paper industry, shares of paper companies have recently undergone a correction. On the other hand, although easing credit and a revival of the homebuilding market would seem likely to boost the stock performance of wood predominant firms (opposite conditions started the downtrend in early 1994), oversupply has contributed to a continued disappointing sector stock performance.

Following a boom in the late 1980s, the paper industry experienced some very difficult conditions for a number of years until the recent upturn.

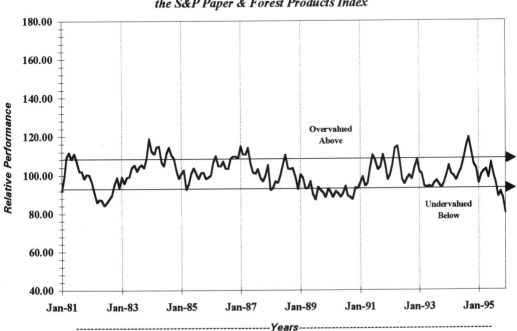

Trend in 12-Month Relative Performance for the S&P Paper & Forest Products Index

159

The initiation of the uptrend was largely related to economic recoveries in both the U.S. and Europe. With little capacity expansion undertaken in the industry in recent periods, as firms learned from their greater-than-necessary additions near the late 1980's cyclical peak, steep price rises for most paper products accompanied the shipment gains. These very favorable trends enabled most paper companies to experience strong earnings gains in recent periods. However, as the fall of 1995 arrived, operating conditions started to deteriorate for paper manufacturers. Interestingly, the industry's troubles could be largely attributed to its own self-defeating efforts to make up for all of its down years, as customers were driven to stockpile inventory in efforts to beat the next in a series of almost incessant price hikes.

With a large portion of wood demand coming from the housing industry, the homebuilding market's period of sluggishness weakened demand and pricing for wood products. However, although trends have grown much more favorable in homebuilding, market conditions remain difficult for wood products. The troubles are related to oversupply generated by excess timber production, which has been stimulated by wood chip demand in pulp and paper markets. With a moderating paper industry now demanding less wood chips, lumber production should slow, with the supply/demand situation finally achieving a balance.

Description

This industry produces both paper and wood products. There are many types of paper, from newsprint to wrapping paper. Wood products consist mainly of lumber, plywood, and building panels.

Characteristics

Most paper and forest products companies are integrated from the tree to the customer. And since the highest value end use of the larger trees is lumber, most companies have large wood products operations. Although the paper and wood products markets are both highly cyclical, their cycles are often at variance, giving some protection to earnings. The most cyclical paper companies are those that primarily produce undifferentiated commodity paper products such as newsprint, linerboard, and market pulp. Companies that produce specialty papers tend to have much more stable earnings. Although most paper products are sold under long-term contracts, prices vary widely depending upon industry conditions, most notably upon the capacity utilization rate. Any excess capacity in the industry quickly translates into lower prices, and tight markets lead to rapidly rising prices.

Personal Loans

Outlook

The investment outlook for the personal loans industry is positive because of the favorable impact on profit margins from projected lower interest rates. Toward the end of 1995, yields on short-term government bills were 5.20%, up from 3.63% in September 1993, but down from 7.75% in January 1995. The yield on long-term government bonds was 6.04%, down from 8.18% in November 1994 but up from 5.87% in October 1993. We anticipate that short-term rates and long-term rates will decline through mid-1996. The slope of the yield curve (gap between the typically higher yield on 30-year bonds and lower-yielding 3-month Treasury bills) is an important determinant of financing spreads (the return on assets less the related cost of funds) for many financial firms. S&P projects the yield curve to widen slightly by mid-1996.

A healthy economy is generally favorable for financial firms, in that it stimulates borrowing and leads to reduced credit losses. In a recession, borrowing slackens and credit losses rise. The U.S. Gross Domestic Product

Trend in 12-Month Relative Performance for the S&P Personal Loans Index

161

(GDP) grew at a 4.2% rate in the third quarter of 1995, and we project growth at 2.1% for the fourth quarter, 2.9% for the first quarter of 1996, and 2.7% for the second quarter of 1996.

Most financial businesses are characterized by low returns on assets and shareholders equity resulting from intensely competitive and highly cyclical industry conditions and few barriers to entry. There are, however, a handful of well-capitalized high return, growth companies in the universe. The market consistently values certain financial firms at modest P/E ratios because they are by their very nature highly leveraged and perceived to carry a high level of credit risk, although actual losses in many instances are modest.

Description

This group is composed of a broad array of consumer-oriented financial service companies, offering, among other things, credit cards, and mortgages.

Characteristics

The level and direction of interest rates is a key determinant of this industry's profitability. In addition, the slope of the yield curve (gap between the typically higher yield on 30-year bonds and lower-yielding 3-month Treasury bills) is an important determinant of financing spreads (the return on assets less the related cost of funds) for many financial firms. Other influencing factors include the level of unemployment, which correlates to the number of loan defaults, and the outlook for the stock and bond markets, as two components of this index are investment firms.

Photography/Imaging

Outlooks	
Relative performance:	*Neutral*
Fundamental (STARS):	*Neutral*

Outlook

Our investment outlook for the photography stocks we cover is neutral. We have an "accumulate" opinion on Eastman Kodak, but this is offset by an "avoid" opinion on Polaroid, which recently indicated that fourth quarter 1995 earnings would be weak. With Eastman Kodak, we have increased our earnings estimates for full-year 1995 and 1996, and look for the stock to get some support from an authorization for the company to repurchase up to $1 billion of its common stock.

The conventional U.S. consumer photo industry is very mature, since most households already own a camera. Factors that should affect spending include consumer confidence, and related vacation travel. Also, the growing presence of camcorders -- portable video cameras that enable users to see moving images almost immediately -- has inevitably crimped the growth of still photography. Long term, U.S. photography companies are likely to have growth opportunities from overseas markets and from development of improved camera and processing systems.

Trend in 12-Month Relative Performance for
the S&P Photography/Imaging Index

163

In the past decade, U.S. photo activity has been stimulated by the development and proliferation of relatively easy-to-use 35-millimeter cameras, as well as quick-service photofinishing outlets. Recently, one of the fastest-growing segments has been single-use, pocket-size cameras, selling for $6 to $20. These cameras offer convenience for consumers who have forgotten to bring their more expensive, permanent equipment or did not feel like carrying a larger camera.

The debut of Kodak's Photo CD, which integrates conventional photography with televisions and computers, has not become a hot item with consumers. Much of the initial demand is likely from government and corporate users. Photo CD allows home users and businesses to create electronic libraries of relatively high-quality still photographs for viewing on a TV or computer screen. Potential capabilities of Photo CD are expected to include manipulation of images and combining pictures with graphics and sound. With Photo CD, consumers would take 24 pictures with a 35-millimeter camera, and the images could then be transferred to a disk capable of storing about 100 images.

Description

This group is involved in the reproduction of visual images, including both silver halide (traditional photography) or electronically created images. Activities may include both recreational (e.g., vacation photos) and business applications (e.g., office copier machines).

Characteristics

The factors that influence sales, earnings, and share prices include demographics, as the high birth rate in recent years should be favorable for picture taking; consumer confidence and personal income trends, which affect travel patterns, since lots of photos are taken during vacation; and finally the introduction of new technology and products, since the convenience of disposable cameras has likely stimulated picture taking during the past few years. While the U.S. consumer film (noninstant) market is dominated by Eastman Kodak, and Polaroid dominates instant photography, the industry is moving toward more electronic imaging.

Pollution Control

Outlook

The S&P Pollution Control Index was among the worse performing groups in 1995, rising an anemic 11.8%, while the S&P 500 advanced 34.1%. The group had performed well through July, but growing evidence of a slowdown in landfill volumes, flat tipping rates, and sliding prices for recycled materials gave investors a case of the jitters. Third-quarter results showed no change in this trend. With several quality companies now trading below the market multiple, we have upgraded our opinion of the group. Taking a longer view of industry prospects, there remains considerable room for industry consolidation. As this occurs and Subtitle D regulations push out small landfill operators, prices will advance. We also see favorable growth opportunities for companies serving the municipal wastewater treatment industry.

The solid waste group's profits in 1995 have benefited from higher volumes and modest price increases, as well as contributions from acquisitions. Pricing has been aided by the passage of the Subtitle D regulations in 1993, which set higher landfill standards and forced the closure

Trend in 12-Month Relative Performance for the S&P Pollution Control Index

165

of those that fail to comply. We expect more industry consolidation as major companies gobble up smaller operators and even mergers between large companies. Near term, we anticipate some slippage in prices for recycled paper products, which tripled in 1995. The long-term outlook for the group is positive, with earnings growth driven from acquisitions and volume increases, partly offset by waste minimization and recycling.

In the hazardous waste area, waste production by the chemical industry has slowed to a snail's pace in recent years. This largely reflects a sharp jump in the industry's spending on pollution abatement: some $5.7 billion was spent in 1994, up 25% from $4.3 billion in 1993. Consequently, wastes and emissions from the chemical industry have slid, causing headaches for hazardous waste management firms. Clouding the longer-term outlook is the likelihood that the Republican-controlled Congress will delay or loosen requirements for environmental regulations and be less aggressive toward new legislation. In the air pollution control area, activity remains light as customers have delayed taking actions as they evaluate compliance options and the enforcement framework related to the Clean Air Act.

Description

Pollution control refers primarily to the collection, treatment, and disposal of wastes, which are commonly categorized as solid, hazardous, and nonhazardous. Treatments and disposal methods range from landfilling to incineration. Other major areas are recycling, remediation (the clean up of contaminated sites), air and water quality control, and waste-to-energy. The term "environmental control" has become the common industry title.

Characteristics

The three economic factors that influence industry stock prices are industrial production, as more wastes are generated in good economic times; capital spending, as the level of spending by companies on site remediation projects and air and water pollution control equipment is directly related to capital spending budgets of those corporations; and, finally, construction activity, as more wastes are generated when construction activity picks up. The industry is also regulation driven. Two pieces of legislation are the major factors that contribute to the industry's growth: the Resource Conservation and Recovery Act (RCRA), which regulates the treatment of current and future hazardous wastes; and the Comprehensive Environmental Response, Compensation and Liability Act (CERCLA), or Superfund, which established a fund to finance the cleanup of sites that were abandoned prior to 1976.

Property-Casualty Insurance

Outlooks
Relative performance: *Neutral*
Fundamental (STARS): *Positive*

Outlook

After outperforming the broader market in 1994, the S&P Property Casualty Index gained 34% in the year ended December 31, 1995, the same pace as the S&P 500. Investors recently began to focus on this group's previously depressed valuations. Despite a near-term outlook that will likely remain highly competitive (and lead to modest written premium growth), opportunities exist for a handful of companies due to an expected industry shakeout.

Results in the first nine months of 1995 were mixed, as mild first-quarter weather was offset by the second-quarter's hail and wind storms that most severely affected regional and personal lines insurers. For many insurers, however, year-over-year comparisons were aided by the absence of 1994's Northridge earthquake losses. Net written premiums inched up 3.3%, year to year, as growth in property lines offset ongoing price competition in most casualty lines. Underwriting losses narrowed to $5.7 billion from $16.2 billion amid lower catastrophe losses. As a result, the combined loss, expense, and dividend ratio improved to 105.4% for the nine months ended September

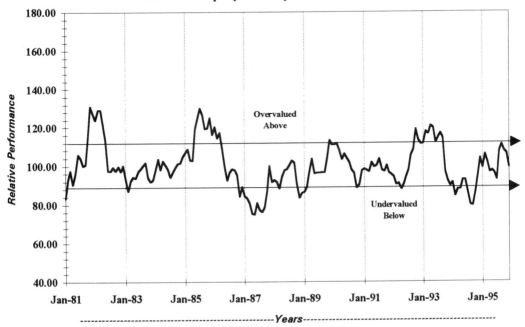

Trend in 12-Month Relative Performance for the S&P Property-Casualty Insurance Index

30, 1995, versus 110.0% in the year-earlier period. The robust securities markets helped produce $3.7 billion in investment gains, compared with $1.7 billion in the 1994 interim. As a result, net income surged to about $14.7 billion in the first nine months of 1995, from $4.8 billion.

Consequently, industry surplus (or capital) jumped 16%, year to year, ending the first nine months of 1995 at $220.8 billion, versus $190.7 billion in the 1994 interim. For the 12 months ended June 30, 1995, the net premiums written to surplus ratio (an indicator of underwriting capacity) equaled about 1.2:1, versus a "typical" leverage ratio of about 2:1. Much of this cushion could evaporate if catastrophe losses continue at their record pace, if the stock and bond markets retreat, or if some heretofore inadequately reserved insurers fully account for their potential environmental claims. Unlike the last cycle turn in the mid-1980s that was driven by an acute shortage of liability coverage, this recovery (albeit modest) will likely be paced by stronger property lines pricing. We estimate full year 1995 net written premiums will come in about 4% higher, to $260 billion, and up about 5.8% to $275 billion during 1996. This compares with written premium growth rates of 3.4% in 1994 and 5.7% in 1993.

Description

Property insurance protects the physical property of the insured from loss due to theft or physical damage. Casualty insurance primarily protects the insured against legal liability that might arise from injuries and/or damage to others. Many casualty insurers also write surety insurance, which protects the insured against financial loss caused by the acts of others. The markets comprise two major segments: personal and commercial.

Characteristics

The demand for insurance is a function of economic growth, inflation rates, and the need to protect assets. The supply curve for insurance is interest-sensitive. When interest rates rise, the supply of insurance also rises as insurers are willing to provide more insurance at the same price since each premium dollar will generate a higher return. As a result, competition increases, and prices decline until additional demand is reduced or until it becomes unprofitable to provide coverage and insurers withdraw from the market. Even though weather-related catastrophe losses can occur at all times of the year, the storm-prone quarters are the first (winter storms) and third (hurricanes).

Publishing

	Outlooks
Relative performance:	*Neutral*
Fundamental (STARS):	*Neutral*

Outlook

Publishing stocks, by and large, will probably do no better than keep pace with the overall market during the next several months. Although revenues are advancing, investors will remain leery of magazine stocks until still-escalating coated paper prices begin to subside. Book publishers can look forward to softening paper costs ahead, but modest unit sales growth.

The fortunes of publishers are largely driven by sales (circulation), advertising revenues (where applicable), and variable cost items such as personnel, paper, ink, and postage. We expect consumer magazine advertising revenues in 1996 to advance faster than the 12% rise we estimate for 1995. Circulation revenues probably rose less than 3% in 1995, the gain largely the result of higher cover prices. Single-copy sales have trended downward for over a decade, while growth in the number of subscriptions has slowed.

On the cost side, modest wage increases, staff reductions, and trimmed-down benefit packages will help to keep personnel expenses down. Paper

Trend in 12-Month Relative Performance for the S&P Publishing Index

cost increases, under 5% for most of 1994, took off late in that year. Double-digit price increases for uncoated paper (books and newspapers) and for coated paper (magazines) became the norm in 1995, after several years of depressed prices. A common refrain in third-quarter 1995 earnings releases was that paper costs had risen more than 50% in the past year. Postage rate hikes of roughly 10%-14% are also being felt. In spite of pressured margins, profits should rise for book and magazine publishers.

The dollar value of publishers' book sales are projected to rise no more than 3% in 1996 after an estimated rise of roughly 7% in 1995. Unit sales are expected to rise fractionally, 0.4%, in 1996, compared to 2.8% in 1995. Publishers generally agree that 1996 will be an off year in most school textbook adoption schedules, and sales will be further hurt by weak school and library funding. Concerns about consumer confidence and rising cover prices are also dampening factors for 1996. In addition to educational texts, soft unit sales are likely in six segments: juvenile hard and soft covers; book club hard and soft covers; mail order; and business. The adult trade segment is expected to show respectable growth. Religious book sales, the smallest category, should continue to advance at very strong double-digit rates.

Description

These companies publish books and magazines.

Characteristics

Book publishers' revenues are affected primarily by changes in the overall economy, consumer spending patterns, and demographic trends. Magazine revenues and earnings are directly affected by advertising expenditures and circulation; they are indirectly affected by growth in the economy. Profitability for both categories is also greatly affected by paper and postage costs, which together can account for some 25% of total expenses.

Publishing (Newspapers)

Outlooks	
Relative performance:	*Neutral*
Fundamental (STARS):	*Neutral*

Outlook

Newspaper publishing stocks are expected to perform about in line with the general market in the months ahead. Public statements in December from industry sources that newsprint prices have probably peaked provided only a small lift to the stocks. The market's sluggish reaction reflected the general belief that newsprint prices have peaked but are not likely to decline before late 1996. In addition to newsprint's impact, investors are concerned about the general sluggishness in newspaper advertising linage. Some publishers are being squeezed, while operating conditions for others are considerably more positive. Thus, each publisher should be evaluated on its own merits, with consideration given to operating conditions in each newspaper market and the relative contribution from other media businesses owned.

The slowdown in newspaper advertising growth has been very uneven across the U.S. On the whole, we see total ad linage being flat in 1996. Announcements of advertising rate increases effective as of January 1996 have clustered around 7%-8%. We are tentatively projecting a 6% gain in

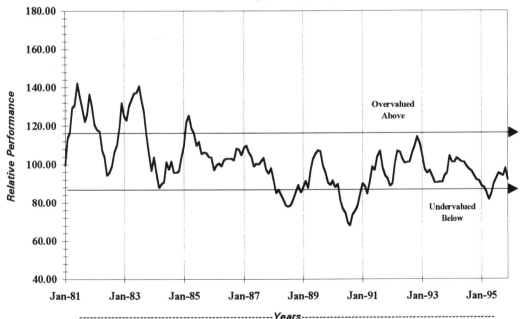

Trend in 12-Month Relative Performance for the S&P Publishing (Newspapers) Index

171

total advertising in 1996. For 1995, we estimate that classified advertising rose 4.5%. Retail advertising, which accounts for over 50% of total newspaper advertising, probably gained 7.0%. National advertising is thought to have risen 7.7%.

Daily newspaper circulation has been in a downturn since 1987, due to attrition in afternoon and evening editions and an ongoing decline in readership. Sunday circulation, in an uptrend since 1987, also began to weaken beginning in 1994. Although hefty cover and subscription price hikes are among the major reasons for the sluggishness, the aggressive pricing has kept circulation revenues rising modestly for most publishers.

Given the growing evidence that newsprint supply and demand are back in balance, price hikes of 5% per metric ton announced in the fall of 1995, that were slated to take effect in early 1996, will probably be rescinded. Newspapers have cut back on usage through cuts in editions and page size, reduced circulation, and other measures. No significant additions to newsprint production capacity are expected within the next several years, nor are any significant labor disruptions likely. Newsprint prices are expected to stabilize in 1996 after having advanced an estimated 50% in 1995.

Description

These companies publish newspapers, as well as hold interests in other forms of media and entertainment.

Characteristics

Newspaper revenues and earnings are directly affected by advertising expenditures and circulation, and are indirectly affected by growth in the economy. Personnel and newsprint are the major cost factors in a newspaper's operation. Newsprint pricing fluctuations directly impact margins.

Railroads

	Outlooks
Relative performance:	*Neutral*
Fundamental (STARS):	*Positive*

Outlook

Rail issues, which were among the strongest sectors in 1995, are expected to continue to outperform the market in 1996, albeit to a lesser degree. For 1996 we expect a continued favorable economic climate plus stronger coal shipments, thanks to cooler weather, to drive earnings and stocks to higher levels. Additionally, takeover rumors and deals may surface involving eastern and midwestern lines. Finally, the profit performance at the recently created Burlington Northern Santa Fe could exceed current modest expectations if merger benefits come through sooner than anticipated. For all of 1995, the S&P Rail Index was up 42.9%, compared with a 34.1% gain for the S&P 500.

Although the economy perked up in the third quarter, the soft landing has not yet given way to a renewed business acceleration. Rail traffic in 1995's fourth quarter continued to ratchet down toward low single-digit levels, but the weaker groups, intermodal and lumber have become invigorated. Grain traffic, which advanced nearly 15% in 1995 may be flat

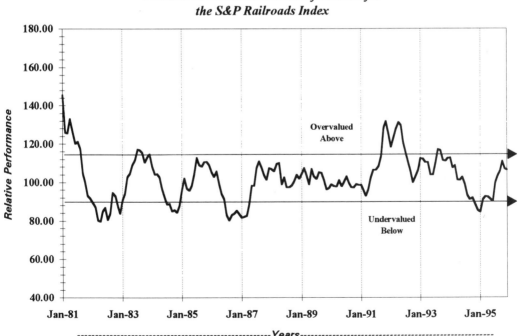

Trend in 12-Month Relative Performance for the S&P Railroads Index

173

in 1996 due to smaller corn and soybean harvests. More than offsetting will be increased coal shipments as cold weather in December and January helped burn off excess utility inventories which will require restocking. Operating margins in 1996 will continue to benefit from the application of technology to boost productivity, more efficient utilization of equipment, and merger-related savings. With pressure from shippers to pass through cost savings, rail rates are expected to slip 0.2% in 1996 following an estimated 0.1% drop in 1995. For 1996 we project a 3.2% increase in traffic to 1,300 billion ton-miles, following the 4.9% gain anticipated for 1995. Operating profits in 1996 are projected to rise 8.6% to $6.47 billion from the $5.96 billion estimated for 1995. Our 1996 profit estimate may have to be revised later on should savings from the Burlington/Santa Fe merger be realized sooner than anticipated.

The industry's rejuvenation reflects several favorable developments. Thanks to deregulation, costs are being recovered in a timely manner. The popularity of coal since the 1970s has provided rails with steadily increasing and profitable long-haul traffic. The industry's improved cash flow enabled it to buy out redundant workers and lift productivity through capital investment. Driver shortages in the trucking industry is helping rails gain market share as motor carriers increase their use of rail piggyback.

Description

Railroads are primarily freight carriers (specializing in bulk commodities) that own and operate their own private rights of way.

Characteristics

The share prices of railroad companies are affected by the condition of the economy, exports, and the weather. Rail traffic, as measured by the product of tonnage and distance moved, tends to move in tandem with industrial production. With coal traffic now accounting for nearly half of the volume, weather patterns and the state of the export market can have an important bearing on rail traffic. Grain shipments are influenced by unpredictable overseas demand.

Restaurants

Outlook

Our overall near-term investment outlook for restaurant, or food-service, stocks is neutral. We are concerned about weakness in comparable-unit sales in recent months, and the prospect of some wage-cost pressure from a tighter labor market. During 1995, the S&P Restaurants Index rose 48.9% versus a 34.1% gain for the S&P 500.

In the past several years, restaurant industry profitability has generally been supported by an absence of significant food cost pressure. With such cost trends looking favorable, restaurant operators have been able to seek volume increases through lower menu prices and increased marketing efforts. Competitive conditions have led to an increased industry emphasis on offering "value" to consumers. In part, this has meant an emphasis on lower-priced menu items, and in some cases, has resulted in lower prices for either single offerings or combinations of products. Near term, we expect restaurant operators to face some pressure from labor costs, but we look for overall increases in food costs to be relatively modest. The industry's value emphasis

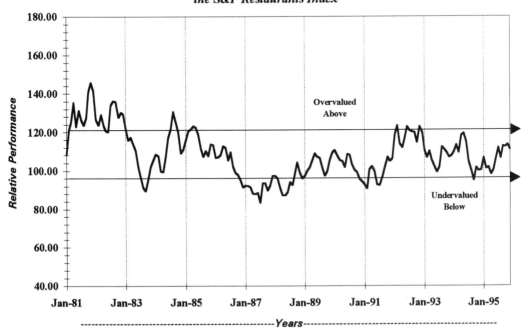

Trend in 12-Month Relative Performance for the S&P Restaurants Index

175

is likely to continue. Other major industry themes will include an emphasis on lowering development costs of new restaurants. Reducing the cost of new units can both boost companies' return on investment and better enable them to enter smaller markets.

During the past two decades, an increasing portion of U.S. food dollars has gone to eating out. With a greater percentage of people working, particularly women, there has been less time available for at-home food preparation. Demographics will likely have a significant impact on future restaurant spending as well. As consumers get older, they are more likely to move away from fast-food outlets toward mid-scale restaurants.

Among restaurant companies, there can be sizable variations in how well their operations are doing. Overall sales growth typically comes from three factors: the opening of new units, higher contributions from older restaurants, and acquisitions. Often, a good way to judge a business's overall health is to look at year-to-year sales comparisons among outlets that were open in both periods, particularly with menu price increases excluded.

Description

These companies are basically food-service establishments located away from consumers' homes, offering both on-premise consumption of food and takeout service.

Characteristics

Influencing factors on revenues, earnings, and share prices include consumer spending and confidence; disposable income; cost pressures, such as commodities/food and labor (both direct wages and benefits); and individual restaurant unit sales comparisons. Among restaurant companies, there can be sizable variations in how well their operations are doing. Overall sales growth typically comes from three factors: the opening of new units, higher contributions from older restaurants, and acquisitions. Often, a good way to judge a business's overall health is to look at year-to-year sales comparisons among outlets that were open in both periods, particularly with menu price increases excluded.

Retail (Department Stores)

Outlooks

Relative performance: *Positive*
Fundamental (STARS): *Neutral*

Outlook

We remain neutral on department stores for the near term, but we are more sanguine over the longer term as the consolidation in retailing strengthens the market position of the strong department store chains. The industry is now so concentrated that department store sales are in the hands of a few major chains. These chains have lowered their operating expenses by consolidating divisions, eliminated back office staff and merging operations. This has enabled department stores to lower prices over the past few years and regain market share. Although a highly promotional atmosphere will remain through much of 1996, as a number of troubled companies run sales to boost earnings, the picture brightens in the second half as comparisons get easier. The outlook gets even brighter by 1997 as the marginal players in retailing fade away.

Retail sales in 1996 should not be as much of a struggle as in 1995. We anticipate that spending in the first half will be somewhat subdued. Employment and income gains should be moderate.

Consumers, having greatly expanded their use of credit cards, will pay

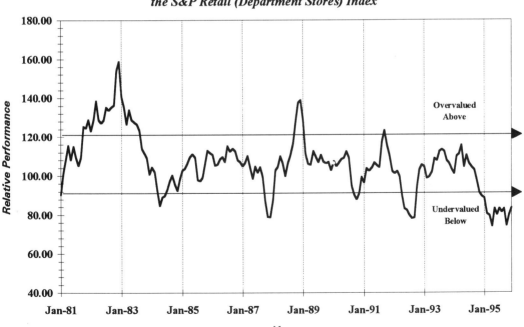

Trend in 12-Month Relative Performance for the S&P Retail (Department Stores) Index

177

down their high household debt levels. The demographics of an older consumer, who is saddled with mortgage and tuition payments, as well as saving for retirement around the corner, is hardly interested in the next "hot" fashion trend. Pent-up demand could boost apparel sales modestly this year, but the consumer of the 90's is practical and value conscious. In addition, the trend toward casual clothing means that there is a greater versatility of usage; a much narrower wardrobe can suffice. With price an overriding issue and a plethora of retail outlets to choose from, consumers are in the driver's seat. Lower inventories and cost-cutting measures to increase productivity will continue to be a means of increasing earnings.

Apparel sales will get a boost in the second half from easy comparisons and pent-up demand. But home goods, such a sheets and towels, will outperform apparel. Electronics will have the highest rates of growth but most department store chains have abandoned this category of merchandise in favor of higher margin categories, such as apparel. Earnings are projected to rise around 12% in 1996. S&P projects consumer consumption to increase 3.4% in 1996, consisting of a 5.8% rise in consumer durables, a 2.7% advance in consumer non-durables, and a 3.0% gain in consumer services.

Description

These stores sell products allocated to particular departments, ranging from apparel to home furnishings. Some stores may be regional in nature, such as The Broadway, or national in scope, such as J.C. Penney.

Characteristics

The retail industry is directed by the factors that influence consumer spending: consumer confidence, disposable income, and job growth. Industry progress can be monitored through the monthly retail sales report.

Retail (Drug Stores)

Outlooks	
Relative performance:	*Neutral*
Fundamental (STARS):	*Positive*

Outlook

Retail drug store stocks outpaced the market in 1995, rising 40.2%, versus a 34.1% gain for the S&P 500. The industry continues to experience strong sales volume; during the first 11 months of 1995, sales at large chain drug stores (at least 100 stores) gained 9.1%. Prescription and over-the-counter drug sales also advanced at a healthy pace. Chains are consolidating in order to boost their earnings. Our investment outlook is positive for the group as a slight pickup in drug price inflation, combined with continued efforts to control costs, should allow chain drug stores the ability to report higher earnings.

Sales continue to be buoyed by: consumers' fundamental interest in health and personal care; an aging population; the increased number of drugs coming off patent to more readily available over-the-counter (OTC) status; and an increasing use of drug therapies as an alternative to hospitalization. The baby boomer generation, in particular, is taking health matters into their own hands by adhering to vitamin therapies and home diagnostic testing. The long-term demographics of an aging society indicate prescription usage increases.

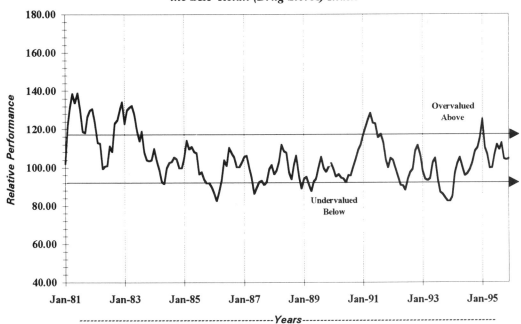

Trend in 12-Month Relative Performance for the S&P Retail (Drug Stores) Index

179

Margins continue to be pressured by third-party payment plans, reflecting the increased enrollment in managed care plans. To offset this, the big chains are gobbling up the smaller ones in order to achieve the economies of scale necessary to operate profitably.

The competition has also recognized the longer-term pluses of this industry. Supermarkets (combination food/drug stores) and discount store operators have added pharmacies and beefed up their assortments of health and beauty aids departments (H&BA). Clearly, this has stiffened the competitive landscape. The combination of sharper pricing by the competition, increased low-margin, third-party payment plans, and lower drug-price inflation is forcing chains to focus on generating more aggressive growth in their core businesses and finding ways to broaden into specialized areas. The challenge imposed by these competitors will, no doubt, intensify over time. As a result, the industry is fashioning a more proprietary identity based on comprehensive selections of basic H&BA items and OTC products and in-and-out shopping convenience. In addition, capital investments in retail technology and distribution efficiencies to keep costs in line have become a priority. As a result, we anticipate continued earnings growth of about 10% to 12% over the next few years, reflecting the strong underlying fundamentals of the industry.

Description

Retail drug chains are large drugstores that sell prescription drugs, over-the-counter products, and general merchandise.

Characteristics

Drug chains are regarded as more defensive than other stocks, as they are less susceptible to fluctuations in the growth of the economy than are other industries; one doesn't stop getting sick just because times are good or bad. Revenues can be influenced, however, by the rate of inflation, disposable income, and demographics.

Retail (Food Chains)

Outlook

The outlook for supermarket chains remains bright. During 1995, the Retail Food Chain Index rose 26% versus a 34% gain in the S&P 500. Growth in the economy has slowed and interest in these more defensive stocks has been renewed. Consumer spending for food should continue to show only modest gains, but operators are developing new merchandising techniques and controlling expenses to improve overall profitability.

The lowering of operating costs has become the key to success for supermarkets in the 1990s. By and large, they have been successful at balancing the pressures for immediate cost containment against the challenge to increase productivity over the longer term. Better inventory management and more efficient distribution have become important factors in this effort. Companies are strengthening their merchandising and marketing efforts, and are investing in technology systems for accounting, ordering, receiving, and scheduling. In this business, where fixed costs are high but profit margins are razor thin, weak sales gains can translate into sharp profit declines as

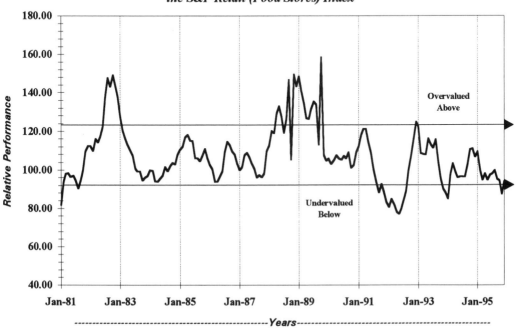

Trend in 12-Month Relative Performance for the S&P Retail (Food Stores) Index

181

was seen last year. In short, chains are sharpening their prices, adding value, and attempting to build on their unique strengths. The goal has been to position the supermarket as the consummate convenience retailer -- a provider of one-stop shopping. In addition, they are strengthening their value/price image by adding an array of private label products. These can sell at some 20% below branded goods and bring in heftier margins than branded goods.

Supermarket operators are wily competitors, and we believe that the industry is rising to the occasion with sales and earnings in an uptrend which will continue in 1995 and 1996. We anticipate earnings gains in the 12% to 15% range, on average, for many major chains. Also, the consolidation in the warehouse club industry has slowed the building of clubs. Although supermarkets have not yet been declared the victors in their struggle to maintain market share against warehouse clubs and discounters, they are increasingly holding their own. But competition will remain tough. Always a new threat on the horizon, supercenters that sell food and general merchandise are being rolled out by Wal-Mart and Kmart. Over time, these powerhouse retailers could pose the next threat to traditional grocery stores, on a market-by-market basis.

Description

Retail food chains vary from supermarkets to convenience stores. Some establishments offer a large array of food products, whereas others offer a smaller, more focused assortment.

Characteristics

Food chains are regarded as more defensive than other stocks, as they are less susceptible to fluctuations in the growth of the economy than are other industries. Whether times are good or bad, one has to eat. Revenues can be influenced, however, by the rate of inflation, disposable income, and consumer confidence. The supermarket industry is a highly competitive, volume-driven business, which operates on low markup. Profits are made by increasing volume and reducing costs. Since the industry is labor intensive, efforts to cut costs include an emphasis on computer technology and taking a hard line on union negotiations.

Retail (General Merchandise)

Outlooks	
Relative performance:	*Positive*
Fundamental (STARS):	*Neutral*

Outlook

The near-term investment outlook for general merchandise retailers is neutral. We anticipate continued weak consumer spending and pricing pressures to continue into the first few months of 1996. An excess of retail square footage overhangs the industry. Value pricing is still the order of the day. Pricing pressures will be exacerbated by a number of regional disounters in bankruptcy. We also continue to see the consumer favoring home furnishings and more durable items, such as appliances and electronics, over apparel purchases. In 1995, the General Merchandise Index rose only 10.5% versus the S&P 500's gain of 34.1%.

The lackluster consumer spending picture reflects broad discontent, and we would not be surprised to see consumer confidence sink further. Growth in nominal wages is slow. The number of job layoffs that hit the front pages of the newspaper weekly have left many Americans concerned about their futures. The well-educated, well-healed 30% of the population, the baby boomers, are aging. This has resulted in a shift in priorities from shopping

Trend in 12-Month Relative Performance for the S&P Retail (General Merchandise) Index

183

and spending to saving for retirement, paying college tuition, and the like. With the economy slowing we see little reason to be optimistic about a strong rebound in retail sales in 1996. S&P projects consumer consumption to increase 3.4% in 1996, consisting of a 5.9% rise in consumer durables, a 2.7% advance in consumer non-durables, and a 3.0% gain in consumer services.

The longer-term investment outlook for general merchandise retailers is neutral. Because of the highly competitive nature of retailing today, retailers are being forced to make cost cutting a top priority. Major chains are eliminating redundancies and closing underperforming stores. Modest sales growth expectations, due to the proliferation of a value-conscious consumer, have forced retailers to trim inventories and invest in cost-cutting technology to boost productivity. Investments in technology have helped many chains obtain better information about sales trends, which enables them to keep less merchandise in stock. And costs have been brought in line with sales growth. But there is no pricing power in this industry and too many stores. Over time we anticipate that there will be a reduction in retail square footage as companies close stores; this should create a better balance between supply and demand.

Description

These are stores that sell a variety of items, from apparel to household products to consumer electronics.

Characteristics

The retail industry is directed by the factors that influence consumer spending: consumer confidence, disposable income, and job growth. Industry progress can be monitored through the monthly retail sales report.

Retail (Specialty)

Outlooks
Relative performance: *Positive*
Fundamental (STARS): *Neutral*

Outlook

The near-term outlook for specialty retailers is neutral. Apparel sales continue to be weak as Americans focus on durable goods: electronics, computers, and other products for the home. Purchases have been geared toward utilitarian and longer-lasting items. During 1995, the Retail-Specialty Index fell 3.6, while the S&P 500 rose 34%.

We think retail sales will slowly pick up as 1996 progresses, but competition will remain keen and the country overstored. Consumer's uncertainty, reflected in erratically slower buying behavior, should continue to characterize purchasing patterns in the first half of 1996. Slow growth in real incomes, high consumer debt levels, and satiated pent-up demand should keep consumer spending modest. Apparel sales have remained weak and price competition should continue to characterize the first half, but easy comparisons could boost apparel retailers profitability in the second half of 1996.

Longer term, we see a widening gap between the winners and the losers

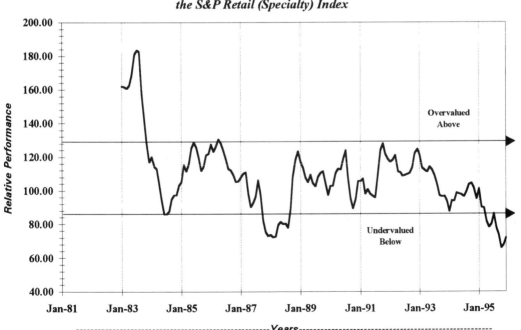

Trend in 12-Month Relative Performance for the S&P Retail (Specialty) Index

185

in retailing. Despite sharper competition from the department stores, as they lower prices to regain some lost market share, specialty stores will continue to have strong appeal. This fragmentation of the marketplace has become a blight on mass-market retailing. As a result, becoming a specialist helps to establish a clear and unique identity in the mind of the consumer. But the apparel sector is clearly overstored. We have seen the number of companies in bankruptcy increase in 1995, and we anticipate more in 1996. Also, apparel specialty retailers are slowing their store expansion programs because of the excess apparel square footage in the U.S.

Description

These are stores that sell a narrow product assortment. While department stores and general merchandisers provide breadth of assortment, specialty retailers, dubbed "category killers," thrive on offering enormous selection in a single-product category at unbeatable prices. Large outlets or superstores, such as Circuit City, Toys "R" Us, and Home Depot, are gobbling up market share from "Mom and Pop" stores that cannot compete on price and assortment. Quick and convenient shopping add to the appeal of these specialty stores; they truly are customer friendly.

Characteristics

The retail industry is directed by the factors that influence consumer spending: consumer confidence, disposable income, and job growth. Monthly results for the industry can be monitored through the retail sales report.

Retail (Specialty-Apparel)

Outlooks	
Relative performance:	*Neutral*
Fundamental (STARS):	*Neutral*

Outlook

The near-term outlook for specialty retailers is neutral. Apparel sales continue to be weak as Americans focus on durable goods: electronics, computers, and other products for the home. Purchases have been geared toward utilitarian and longer-lasting items. Retail-Specialty Apparel Index gained only 7.8% in 1995, while the S&P 500 rose 34%.

We think retail sales will slowly pick up as 1996 progresses, but competition will remain keen and the country overstored. Consumer's uncertainty, reflected in erratically slower buying behavior, should continue to characterize purchasing patterns in the first half of 1996. Slow growth in real incomes, high consumer debt levels, and satiated pent-up demand should keep consumer spending modest. Apparel sales have remained weak and price competition should continue to characterize the first half, but easy comparisons could boost apparel retailers profitability in the second half of 1996.

Longer term, we see a widening gap between the winners and the losers

Trend in 12-Month Relative Performance for the S&P Retail (Specialty-Apparel) Index

187

in retailing. Despite sharper competition from the department stores, as they lower prices to regain some lost market share, specialty stores will continue to have strong appeal. This fragmentation of the marketplace has become a blight on mass-market retailing. As a result, becoming a specialist helps to establish a clear and unique identity in the mind of the consumer. But the apparel sector is clearly overstored. We have seen the number of companies in bankruptcy increase in 1995, and we anticipate more in 1996. Also, apparel specialty retailers are slowing their store expansion programs because of the excess apparel square footage in the U.S.

Description

These are stores that sell a variety of apparel items for men, women, and children through outlets and catalogs. While department stores and general merchandisers provide breadth of assortment, specialty retailers, dubbed "category killers," thrive on offering enormous selection in a single-product category at unbeatable prices. Large chains, such as The Gap, are gobbling up market share from "Mom and Pop" stores that cannot compete on price and assortment. Quick and convenient shopping add to the appeal of these stores.

Characteristics

The retail industry is directed by the factors that influence consumer spending: consumer confidence, disposable income, and job growth. Monthly results for the industry can be monitored through the retail sales report.

Savings & Loans

Outlooks

Relative performance: *Neutral*

Fundamental (STARS): *Positive*

Outlook

Savings & Loans issues have outperformed the overall market in 1995 for three reasons. First, the year-to-date drop in interest rates implied wider margins and gains in mortgage lending volume, both of which benefit earnings. Second, widespread expectations for massive consolidation pushed up the prices of takeover candidates. And third, the industry's excellent asset quality has reassured investors that they no longer need to fear large loan write-offs. The investment outlook for the industry as a whole is positive, although some issues are fairly valued following this year's big run up.

At the end of November 1995, the average publicly traded thrift sold at a price-to-book-value ratio of 107%, up from 80% at December 31, 1993. The industry also sold, on average, at a P/E ratio on trailing 12 months earnings per share of 14.6, up from the P/E of 10.5 at December 31, 1993.

We still believe that long-term industry consolidation will be a major theme for investors. Reasons to expect a big pickup in takeovers include: interstate banking, a large supply of companies up for sale, the industry's

Trend in 12-Month Relative Performance for the S&P Savings & Loans Index

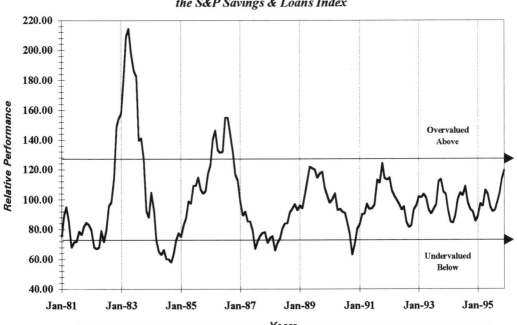

189

need to rationalize its cost structure, a number of well-capitalized suitor banks, and limited internal growth opportunities.

Absent other factors, thrift stocks generally trade on interest rates. S&P projects that both long- and short-term interest rates will continue to decline until mid-1996. Under this scenario, interest rate spreads would widen considerably, providing a welcome boost to the bottom line, since spread or net interest income is a major determinant of profits. Lower rates would also increase the profits that S&Ls obtain from selling loans and mortgage-backed securities, but the market never valued income obtained from this source very highly.

The general perception that S&Ls are not investment grade is outmoded. Since 1989, the industry has rebuilt its capital considerably, and on an aggregate basis may now even be overcapitalized. The industry reported 19 consecutive quarters of profits through September 1995. We believe it will also be in the black for the December 1995 quarter.

Description

The nation's savings and loan industry, which is highly fragmented, offers a variety of transaction and savings products that fund the issuance of long-term fixed- and adjustable-rate mortgages.

Characteristics

S&Ls compete with banks, mortgage bankers, credit unions, and other financial institutions in making home mortgage loans and in accepting retail deposits. This commodity-like nature of the business results in weak profits for most participants. The level and direction of interest rates is a key determinant of this industry's profitability. In addition, the slope of the yield curve (the gap between the typically higher yield on 30-year bonds and lower-yielding 3-month Treasury bills) is an important determinant of financing spreads (the return on assets less the related cost of funds) for many financial firms. Other influencing factors include the level of unemployment, which correlates to the number of loan defaults and mortgage foreclosures, and housing prices, which also affect the volume of mortgages written and the losses from foreclosure resale.

Shoes

Outlooks
Relative performance: *Neutral*
Fundamental (STARS): *Negative*

Outlook

The S&P Shoe Index outperformed the market in December 1995, causing it to perform nearly as well as the S&P 500 did for the entire year. However, we attribute the S&P Shoe Index's surprising return solely to NIKE's spectacular rise. Like apparel, consumer spending on footwear in general remains lackluster and is expected to remain that way into the foreseeable future. Indeed, many shoe stocks in the S&P Shoe Index saw their stock prices erode severely in 1995 due to poor and uncertain earnings growth. In contrast, NIKE's stock price practically doubled in 1995 on positive earnings surprises, strong orders, and a two-for-one stock split that was effected in late October. While we are negative on the group as a whole, we recommend that investors accumulate NIKE. We also like Reebok, on the premise that the company will return to a profit growth mode in 1996.

Shoes are divided into two categories: athletic footwear and non-rubber shoes. Domestic wholesale shipments of athletic footwear totaled about $6.5 billion in 1994, according to the trade publication *Sporting Goods*

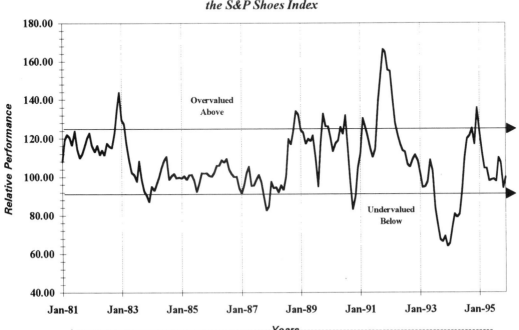

Trend in 12-Month Relative Performance for the S&P Shoes Index

Intelligence, and volume is growing about 2% annually. We think many consumers are not wearing athletic footwear for casual purposes as much as they did in the 1980s, when the market exploded. Instead, they are increasingly wearing non-rubber shoes. Nevertheless, athletic footwear leaders, Reebok and NIKE, are benefiting from increased share, higher athletic apparel sales, and new product introductions in high growth areas including hiking boots and walking shoes. Overseas expansion, however, is providing these athletic footwear makers with the greatest growth. The international market is valued at about $12 billion, and according to many industry pundits, is as untapped for athletic footwear as the U.S. was in the 1970s and 1980s.

Despite the fact that non-athletic footwear has become more popular over the past few years, demand is in a slump. Domestic producers are suffering from cheap imports and increased demand for less-profitable, moderately priced shoes. Domestic producers are doing what they can to fight back, including stepping up their marketing, introducing new styles, closing domestic factories, and increasing less-expensive overseas sourcing. But, until strong overall consumer demand returns for apparel and shoes, we do not expect non-athletic footwear makers to report significant earnings gains.

Description

Shoe companies manufacture athletic footwear and non-rubber shoes.

Characteristics

This industry is cyclical and is dependent on consumer spending patterns. Share prices are subject to movements in consumer confidence and spending, interest rates, and disposable income.

Specialized Services

Outlooks	
Relative performance:	*Neutral*
Fundamental (STARS):	*Positive*

Outlook

Our investment outlook for the business or commercial services group, which often fill needs for labor-intensive tasks, is positive.

We expect users of many business services to be cautious about adding large numbers of full-time, or relatively permanent, employees to their own staffs. By using service firms, instead, to fill needs, companies can help keep overhead down and add to their nimbleness in responding to business conditions. Increasingly, large corporations are providing on-site locations for temporary service firms, which facilitates the management of staffing needs. Going forward, companies providing temporary employees should benefit from situations where business conditions have improved, but not enough to stimulate sizable additions to more permanent personnel levels. In general, there is strong secular growth for providers of temporary service employees; however, they are still susceptible to cyclical downturns in economic conditions.

Besides helping companies keep overhead costs low, a service firm also

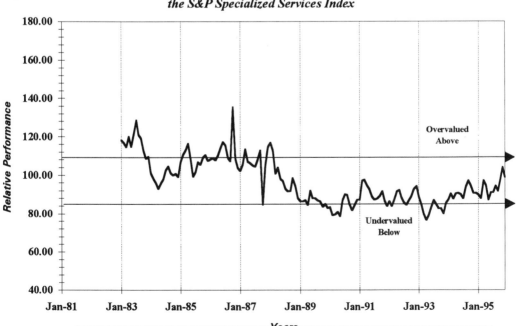

Trend in 12-Month Relative Performance for the S&P Specialized Services Index

193

may be more experienced in certain functions, such as telephone marketing. At least initially, the cash outlay of using a service firm to perform a task may be less than it would be if a company sought to develop and provide the same function in-house. Service firms may have economies of scale that their customers do not, particularly if the customers are small businesses.

With the unemployment rate having moved lower, we expect that wage pressure on service businesses will increase somewhat in the year ahead. However, with the Republicans now controlling Congress, the passage of a sweeping national health care reform plan is dead, which eases the prospect that benefit costs for some employers could rise significantly.

A projected decline in the population of young adults in the next several years may add to the difficulty in attracting and retaining employees for these relatively low-paying jobs. However, longer-term wage pressures could be moderated as employers turn to older people to fill more positions, and some people use service jobs for second-income or temporary situations.

Description

Specialized service companies perform labor-intensive tasks for companies or households that choose not to maintain a full-time staff to perform these services. These services may range from temporary office help to lawn care.

Characteristics

The factors that influence the earnings and equity prices for these firms include (1) growth in the overall economy; (2) business and consumer confidence, as seen through the consumer confidence surveys and spending by advertising agencies; and (3) labor costs/capacity utilization, since companies will be less willing to hire full-time employees to perform these tasks during the early phase of an economic recovery as orders are just beginning to increase. Even with rising sales, companies can help keep overhead down and add to their nimbleness in responding to business conditions by using service firms to fill needs. Besides helping companies keep overhead costs low, a service firm also may be more experienced in certain functions, such as telephone marketing. Also, service firms may have economies of scale that their customers do not have, particularly if the customers are small businesses.

Specialty Printing

Outlooks

Relative performance: *Neutral*
Fundamental (STARS): *Neutral*

Outlook

The year-ahead investment outlook for this small, yet diverse, group is neutral. Deluxe Corp. is the largest U.S. concern engaged principally in printing bank checks. It also produces deposit tickets; makes computer forms and related products; provides software and services to financial institutions; and is a direct marketer of selected consumer products. A secular slowing in the check printing demand is being countered by strong growth in newer businesses, augmented by acquisitions. A small improvement in operating margins is anticipated in 1996, aided by significant operating economies and an expected slowing in startup and acquisition spending.

R. R. Donnelley & Sons is the largest commercial printer in the United States and produces catalogs, tabloids, directories, computer documentation, and other printed material. Sales and earnings are benefiting from strong marketing and business expansion efforts, improving business trends, and several publications.

John Harland is a leading supplier of checks, business documents, and

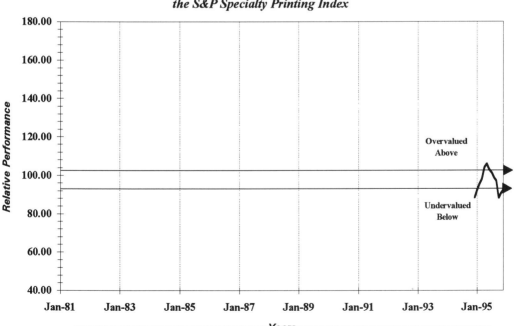

Trend in 12-Month Relative Performance for the S&P Specialty Printing Index

forms to the financial industry. The company is continuing to take measures to counter a fundamental softening in check sales. These acquisitions include acquisitions, plant closings, faster growth in noncheck businesses, and efficiency measures. An aggressive stock repurchase program is also continuing. The dividend was increased for the forty-first consecutive year in 1994.

Description

Companies in one of the newer industries within the S&P 500 print financial documents and personal checks, as well as directories and catalogs. Component companies are Deluxe Corp., R.R. Donnelley & Sons, and J.H. Harland.

Characteristics

These companies are influenced by interest rates, advertising spending trends, and paper prices.

Steel

Outlooks

Relative performance: *Positive*
Fundamental (STARS): *Positive*

Outlook

The S&P Steel Index fell 8.4% in 1995, versus a gain of 34% for the S&P 500, continuing the underperformance recorded for 1994 when steel shares fell 3.6% while the 500 declined 1.5%. Several times during 1995, the index recorded double-digit declines. However, following a firming in carbon flat roll prices in late 1995, the index recovered toward year end. The group should recover in 1996 from 1995's deeply oversold levels as money managers look for groups of stocks that have reasonable fundamentals and have not participated in 1995's advance. Beyond 1996, however, the outlook is less favorable, due to a projected cyclical downturn in auto sales and the addition of some 7 to 10 million tons of carbon flat roll minimill capacity between 1996 and 2000.

Based upon the S&P forecast for real GDP growth of 2.7% in 1996, coupled with a lower level of imports and inventory rebuilding by service centers, shipments, prices, and operating profit per ton should increase from 1995's levels. Assuming only small increases in raw material costs and lower

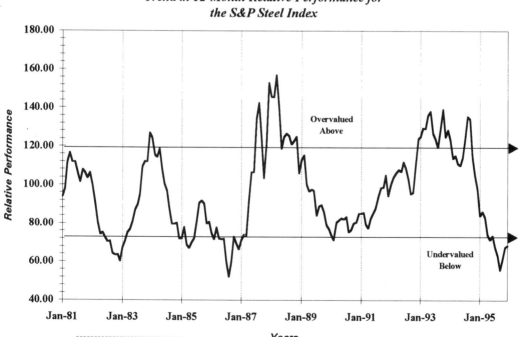

Trend in 12-Month Relative Performance for the S&P Steel Index

interest expense, earnings should also rise. Lower imports and inventory rebuilding will be critical to lifting both prices and profits in 1996. Minimill profits will improve from 1995's levels on rising volume and higher prices. However, gains could be limited by higher scrap costs. Specialty steelmakers should be able to achieve higher profits in 1996 as a result of a lower level of imports, higher prices, and only moderate increases in raw material costs.

We expect demand for stainless flat roll to stabilize and then move higher as service centers rebuild inventories and the economy strengthens. We also believe that carbon flat prices may be near bottom and the steel stocks are attractive based on expectation of better pricing and profits in 1996.

Description

There are two types of steel companies: integrated and minimills. Integrated steel companies are vertically integrated and transform iron ore, limestone, and coal into carbon flat roll steel. Minimills are not vertically integrated and use scrap steel to manufacture their output. Steel from both types of companies is used in the manufacture of durable goods such as cars, appliances, and a host of other products.

Characteristics

The steel industry's health is closely linked to the growth in the overall economy. Therefore, such economic variables as interest rates, currency fluctuations, capital spending, and expenditures for consumer durables are important for the demand for steel. However, the strength or weakness of certain key industries such as autos and construction, as well the level of steel imports, can have a profound impact on industry shipments. Although shipments generally track the movements in the economy, sales and earnings tend to be more volatile. Sales and earnings for steel companies generally decline in the third quarter of every year due to seasonally lower auto production.

Telecom. (Long Distance)

Outlooks	
Relative performance:	*Neutral*
Fundamental (STARS):	*Neutral*

Outlook

The S&P telecommunications group lagged the overall market in 1995 on expectations that pro-competitive federal legislation would soon be enacted. It was passed in early 1996, and, in our opinion, positions the Baby Bells more favorably than the long distance carriers. One reason is the economics of long distance service. A Bell company seeking to buy long-distance capacity can play AT&T, MCI Communications, and Sprint against one another to get the best wholesale price, or could even go to a smaller provider such as WorldCom.

Conversely, the long distance providers have less choice in the local market. For the most part, the Bell's huge presence in the local market means that the long distance carriers will need to rely heavily on that local phone company. Therefore, long distance companies are likely to receive smaller wholesale discounts from the Bells than vice versa.

Overall long-distance calling volume growth has slowed in recent years as industry pricing trends have stabilized. The top carriers instituted price

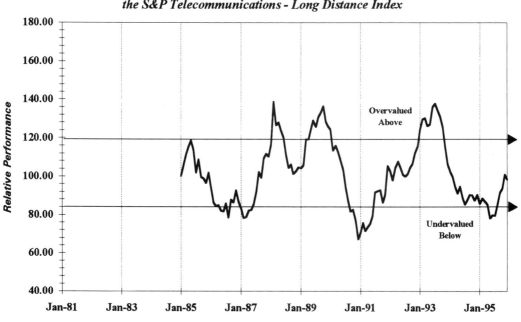

*Trend in 12-Month Relative Performance for
the S&P Telecommunications - Long Distance Index*

increases in 1994, but 1995 saw a return to selective price discounting. Both MCI and Sprint implemented discount plans in an effort to turn back AT&T's gains in market share. We do not believe overall prices will decline significantly during 1996, although sharp discounting may continue in certain segments of the market; annual calling volume growth is seen in the 6% to 7% range for the foreseeable future. The major carriers are working to stimulate volume growth and round out service offerings by entering new markets. Aggressive moves to tap into demand for global advanced services by multinational corporations are likely to help rein in the high costs of international calling and contribute to stronger volume growth.

The top carriers are also accelerating efforts to tap into the rapidly growing wireless market and encourage incremental usage growth of their own networks. AT&T took the lead with its acquisition of McCaw Cellular, while Sprint has formed a wireless venture with major cable operators, which participated in last year's PCS (personal communications services) auctions. However, MCI believes it can participate in the wireless market through a reseller strategy and is focusing some incremental capital expenditures on entering the local telephone market. In addition to revenue growth, wireless and local ventures could also contribute to faster earnings growth by offering an alternative to the local telephone company in hooking up long-haul calls; charges to access the local network account for the bulk of the carriers' costs.

Description

Sometimes called interexchange carriers, these companies provide the transmission services for the long-haul portion of long-distance calls. However, they must rely on local operators for both the originating and terminating connection to customers.

Characteristics

The factors that influence share prices include GDP growth, as economic growth correlates with growth in demand for telephone services; inflation, since inflation rates are typically factored into regulators' formulas for determining local carriers' rates, which will impact long-distance carriers' costs to connect to local networks; inflation, through its impact on interest rates, also affects the carriers' cost of capital; and finally regulatory policy. The industry is dominated by three national carriers but includes several hundred smaller carriers which operate regional networks or resell capacity leased from network-based carriers.

Telephones

Outlooks
Relative performance: *Neutral*
Fundamental (STARS): *Neutral*

Outlook

The new telecommunications law was passed in early 1996, and, in our opinion, positions the Baby Bells more favorably than the long distance carriers. One reason is the economics of long distance service. A Bell company seeking to buy long-distance capacity can play AT&T, MCI Communications, and Sprint against one another to get the best wholesale price, or could even go to a smaller provider such as WorldCom.

Conversely, the long distance providers have less choice in the local market. For the most part, the Bell's huge presence in the local market means that the long distance carriers will need to rely heavily on that local phone company. Therefore, long distance companies are likely to receive smaller wholesale discounts from the Bells than vice versa

Over the longer term, the outlook is mixed as the inevitable increase in competition and the opening of new market opportunities offer both risks and rewards. Those companies with corporate strategies that have prepared

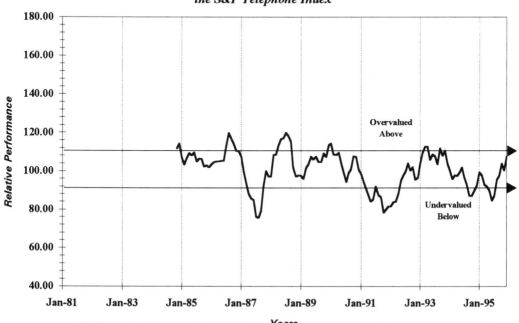

Trend in 12-Month Relative Performance for the S&P Telephone Index

them for the more competitive environment are likely to outperform the group and the market averages over time.

In the event of a market downturn, the group's above-average yields should provide support, as well as contribute to adequate total returns. However, the group's attractiveness as a yield play is diminishing as the companies look to redeploy resources to long-term growth opportunities rather than growing dividends at a rapid pace. The companies are facing a limited window of opportunity for investments in international telephone company privatizations and wireless spectrum licenses.

The telephone companies have also benefited from a court ruling overturning an FCC decision requiring the telcos to allow competitors to bring their equipment onto telco premises to interconnect with the telcos' switching equipment. The court ruling will make it harder for alternative telephone service providers to compete for other than private line services. But the telcos are also taking advantage of regulators' efforts to open the local markets by seeking to provide competitive telephone service within sister companies' operating territories.

Description

Sometimes referred to as local exchange carriers, these companies provide basic local telephone service, including dial tone and access to interexchange carriers for long-distance calls. Most of these companies also have significant cellular telephone service operations and related international telecommunications investments.

Characteristics

Economic growth correlates with growth in demand for phone services, specifically impacting growth in access lines and minutes of use. Because most local phone companies are regional, regional GDP growth is more significant than national GDP growth. Inflation impacts the local phone companies both through the impact on prices to customers and through the impact on interest rates. These companies typically have heavy capital expenditures, so higher interest rates, and therefore cost of capital, have an adverse impact on earnings. The industry is heavily regulated and protected from competition by the high cost of installing a phone network. The industry is divided into two major camps: the seven Bell regional holding companies (RHCs) and the more than 1000 "independent" local companies.

Textiles

Outlooks
Relative performance: *Positive*
Fundamental (STARS): *Negative*

Outlook

Stocks of apparel companies underperformed the market in 1995, as consumers seem disinterested in buying clothing, which especially proved true during the holiday season as indicated by weak preliminary sales data. We feel this less than buoyant desire to buy clothes reflects the lack of any fashion trend and too much "sameness" in many of the stores, as well as high debt levels and uncertain job outlooks. We also think changing demographics are hurting apparel sales. The population is aging (and gaining weight, which tends to make buying apparel an unappealing task), and as such prefers to stay at home and dress comfortably in moderately-priced apparel. In addition, consumers continue to spend heavily on household items and computer-related products. As such, our near-term and intermediate-term investment outlook for the apparel industry is negative.

There are some apparel companies that we like, however. Liz Claiborne now appears to be more focused on consumer market research and providing an appropriate clothing mix. We also like Kellwood, which is not in the

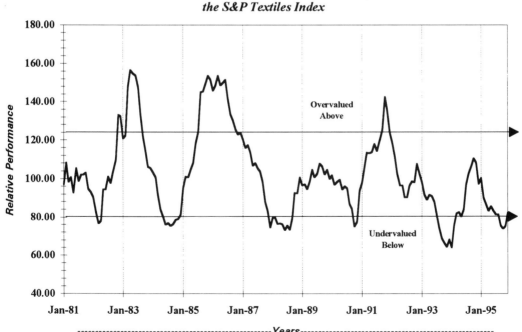

Trend in 12-Month Relative Performance for the S&P Textiles Index

S&P 500, and produces moderately priced, brand-name apparel that is sold through a variety of fast-growing retail formats, such as catalogs, mass merchandisers, and discounters. Kellwood has been especially successful selling the Kathie Lee Gifford apparel line through Wal-Mart. We expect this trend will continue as mass merchandisers and discounters step up their apparel offerings.

Demand for home textile products (37% of all textiles) should rise only slightly in 1996, following a strong 8.1% increase in home textile sales in 1994. Demand for apparel fabrics (38%) will be equally disappointing in 1995 and 1996, as we do not expect consumers to step-up expenditures on apparel anytime soon. Demographics and changing consumer attitudes should continue to limit apparel expenditures. In addition, imports of apparel and apparel textiles still plague domestic manufacturers of apparel fabrics. With the passage of the General Agreement on Tariffs and Trade (GATT) in late 1993, we assume these imports will continue to increase at a high level. On the bright side, demand for industrial fabrics (25%) has picked up.

Longer term, we feel consumer demand for apparel should pick up, mainly due to pent-up demand. It is unlikely, however, that demand will ever equal that in the 1980s when annual growth averaged 7.4%. Some leading apparel manufacturers could also benefit from the passage of NAFTA. Not only does this agreement create a huge new market for apparel manufacturers, but it also will enable manufacturers to give retailers shorter lead times by sourcing production in Mexico instead of the Far East.

Description

The major markets served by textile manufacturers are home furnishings (37% of all textiles), apparel fabrics (38%), and industrial fabrics (25%).

Characteristics

This industry is highly cyclical and is dependent on consumer spending patterns. Each cycle usually precedes an economic downturn by 6 to 12 months. The industry remains one of the most fragmented, with the majority of the players being small and privately held. Share prices are subject to movements in consumer confidence and spending, interest rates, and housing starts.

Tobacco

Outlook

The S&P Tobacco group rose nearly 50% in 1995, outperforming the S&P 500 by a wide margin. Driving the sector's performance was principally the strong performance in the shares of Philip Morris (MO), which climbed 57%. MO's surge reflected the company's recent strong earnings momentum and investor beliefs of a somewhat easing regulatory environment in light of the new Republican-controlled Congress. Also, the current slow economy has helped the performance of these historically defensive issues. In spite of the tobacco industry's well above-average business risks, we remain mildly bullish on the sector's near-term fortunes due to the aforementioned factors, and for their relatively low valuations and high dividend yields.

Tobacco company earnings in 1995's first nine months were mixed for the nation's two largest companies. Philip Morris' global tobacco profits surged 16% on sharp U.S. market share gains for best-selling Marlboro and continued rapid growth abroad. RJR Nabisco's RJ Reynolds unit, meanwhile, recorded a 4% profit dip for its global tobacco business, owing

Trend in 12-Month Relative Performance for the S&P Tobacco Index

205

primarily to further weakness in its aging Winston and Salem brands, and lower cigarette exports. In May, these companies put through an approximate 3% price increase, which should help boost profits going forward. Longer-term earnings progress will rely heavily on selling price increases and international expansion due to the steadily shrinking size (1%-3% unit decline per annum) of the U.S. market.

U.S. cigarette companies have over the years pursued an aggressive expansion strategy both geographically and operationally in order to help alleviate their dependence upon a highly profitable, but also highly controversial business in the U.S. The actions were also an attempt to boost the valuations of their stocks, as investors have not in the past assigned generous price-earnings multiples to tobacco companies due to their greater perceived investment risk. Cigarette companies have recently taken action: In December 1994, American Brands sold its beleaguered American Tobacco unit to British-based B.A.T. Industries. In January 1995, RJR Nabisco Holdings (RN) sold a 19.5% stake in its food business, and signaled that a total split from tobacco could be effected in 1997. Recent pressure by disgruntled RN shareholders may force a total split even sooner.

Description

This group includes cigarette manufacturers, tobacco traders, dealers, and non-smoking tobacco products.

Characteristics

As defensive issues (those with earnings that are not generally tied to the overall health of the economy), any economic indicator that points to economic weakness will influence these issues favorably as it makes them more attractive to investors than the economically sensitive industries. Such indicators would include interest rates, consumer sentiment, and personal income growth. Investors should realize, however, that these issues respond much more to legislative actions, as they impact cigarette demand.

Toys

Outlooks
Relative performance: *Neutral*
Fundamental (STARS): *Positive*

Outlook

Toy stocks have just emerged from the period between the release of the seasonally strong third-quarter earnings and the end of the year when they consistently underperform the market. Prior to this period, we lowered our investment opinion on Tyco Toys to "accumulate" from "buy" despite our belief that a takeover of the company could be imminent. Our continuing "accumulate" recommendations on Mattel and Hasbro reflect our belief that these stocks represent solid long-term value. Mattel's multiple remains reasonable for a consumer products company with its record of consistent growth. Hasbro appears poised for a turnaround in 1996 with a revamped management structure and a rejuvenated product line.

Third-quarter earnings reports from the major toy companies were mildly disappointing. Mattel reported the best results of the major companies with earnings per share increasing to $0.67 from $0.58 on a 13% increase in sales. Hasbro saw earnings per share dip to $0.72 from the year earlier $0.85, which included an $0.08 a share gain. Sales were 3.8% higher. Tyco

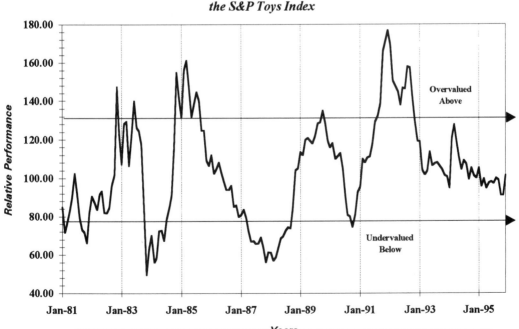

Trend in 12-Month Relative Performance for the S&P Toys Index

Toys managed to return to modest profitability, but sales were 6.1% lower.

However, we anticipated a strong fourth quarter, which has become increasingly important in recent years with a shift to just-in-time inventory. Softness in video games, due to the introduction of relatively expensive new systems that are unlikely to become truly mass market products, should make for a less competitive environment.

SLM International, which filed for bankruptcy in late October, made news in mid-July with the sale of substantially all of the assets of its Buddy L subsidiaries to Empire of Carolina, Inc. Buddy L had revenues of approximately $150 million in 1993. The sale of Buddy L continued a long string of acquisitions in the toy industry in recent years as companies have sought to acquire companies whose brands were undermanaged. In late February 1995, Hasbro announced that it had purchased the Super Soaker line of water guns from the Larami group of companies. In the half dozen years prior to 1995, a wide number of other toy companies have been acquired, including Revell-Monogram, Kransco, Fisher-Price, Tonka, Universal Matchbox, View-Master Ideal Group, Coleco, and Kenner Parker Toys.

Description

Toys are dolls, male action figures, board games, and other products of amusement for children. (Toys for grownups are found in the entertainment and leisure time industries.)

Characteristics

The share prices of toy companies are affected by consumer confidence and spending, as well as disposable income. Individual companies' fortunes are affected by the acceptance of new products. Share prices in general demonstrate strength leading up to the mid-February industry toy fair where new products are unveiled. These issues also show strength in late October when seasonally strong third-quarter earnings are reported. (Toy manufacturers sell their products to toy retailers in the third quarter, whereas the toy retailers show strongest earnings in the fourth quarter.)

Transportation (Misc.)

Outlooks

Relative performance: *Neutral*

Fundamental (STARS): *Neutral*

Outlook

Shipments and profits for the air cargo industry are expected to suffer from the blizzard that hit the Northeast this past winter. Accordingly, air cargo stocks were off during the first few weeks of the year. The slow start in 1996 follows a disappointing 1995 when most companies in the group underperformed the S&P 500. Share appreciation in the first half of that year was partially given back after industry statistics showed a trend of diminishing traffic growth. In November 1995, domestic freight and express traffic for the largest U.S. carriers rose just 2.2%, lowering year-to-date gains to 4.2%. A similar downturn was seen in the international sector. Although international traffic began the year up almost 22%, November saw a decline of 2.0%.

In 1995, domestic revenue gains were hampered by competitive pricing practices. However, there are indications that the pricing pressures may be starting to abate. The relief will come not a bit too soon given that the slowing U.S. economy will likely add to yield pressures. As economic growth eases,

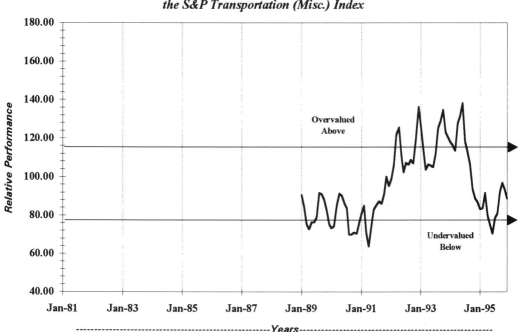

Trend in 12-Month Relative Performance for the S&P Transportation (Misc.) Index

shippers increasingly turn toward less-expensive services. In the air express segment in particular, there is a growing preference for lower-priced second-day delivery, relative to overnight next-day delivery. Some cargo carriers are attempting to return to a more profitable sales mix by offering new classes of priority services or by offering shipping-related services. In addition, a focus on controlling costs and improving technical services to customers should be effective in mitigating the domestic price cutting effects.

Air freight traffic surged during much of the 1980s. FAA statistics show gains ranging from 14% to 19% for the domestic industry in the 1985-89 period. The air express sector was primarily responsible for this strong growth. Although the early 1990s were affected by the recession, domestic express rebounded strongly in both 1993 and 1994. For 1995, express traffic growth was more subdued. Further moderation is expected for 1996.

The truck leasing segment of this industry should closely mirror the outlook for the heavy-duty trucking/truckers industries, which are both less than favorable as investors have shied away from these groups because of concerns with the longevity of the economic expansion. In addition, a growing glut of used vehicles by 1995 also will cause a shift in the decision process away from new trucks, either purchased or leased.

Description

This group includes truck leasing and air freight companies. Truck lessors provide vehicles under an operating lease and include a variety of services, including maintenance, licensing, fuel, and tax reporting. Air cargo companies may operate aircraft or purchase air cargo space to move documents, packages, or heavy cargo.

Characteristics

Both groups are influenced by general economic trends, such as industrial output, retail sales, and fuel costs.

Trucking

Outlook

Trucking stocks rebounded sharply late in 1995 after touching a four-year low in October. Propelling the S&P Trucking Index higher was the decision by Roadway Services to pull the plug on its two-year old air freight unit while Consolidated Freightways benefited from takeover rumors. Investors also are heartened by apparent unity among less-than-truckload (LTL) carriers to boost rates January 1996. Despite the group's healthier tone, the industry's fundamental picture remains gloomy. While this rally indicates a change in investor psychology, since trucking stocks are early cycle plays, we think the current action is premature. A sustainable advance will require several tests, and ironically, more evidence that the economy has turned down

The truckload (TL) segment, the industry's largest, is expected to undergo a major consolidation over the next few years reflecting driver and capital shortages and competition from rail intermodal. Truckers overexpanded their fleets through 1994 and are now paying the piper with weak rates and

Trend in 12-Month Relative Performance for
the S&P Truckers Index

211

bankruptcy. In December Burlington Motor Holdings, one of the nation's top 10 TL carriers filed for bankruptcy. Burlington overexpanded and was overleveraged. TL carriers' margins are under pressure. Though fuel costs in November were 1.0% below year-earlier levels, rates are down nearly 2%, year to year, and labor costs are up as truckers try to attract and retain drivers.

LTL carriage, which includes about 25 major players plus about a hundred minor firms, is a much smaller market than the truckload segment. The outlook for this segment is not positive either. Rates have been flat for several years. The industry rallied behind Roadway Express' proposed 5.8% hike for January 1, 1996, but we believe the bulk of this increase will be discounted away within a couple of months. Margins are under pressure as long-haul carriers reposition themselves to handle more of the faster growing regional freight. Accordingly, national lines are bypassing their consolidation centers to expedite shipments and in the process trashing equipment utilization rates. We expect to see more consolidation in the LTL segment near term. Illustrating this trend was the announced acquisition of Transus' LTL business by TNT Freightways, the merger of ANR Freight and Advance Transportation in November and the bankruptcy of Willig Freight Lines in October.

Description

The for-hire trucking industry is divided among two broad lines: full truckload carriers (TL) and less-than-truckload (LTL) companies. Each of the nearly 50,000 trucking firms hauls freight interstate over public roadways. Most companies own both the tractors and trailers used to perform their services.

Characteristics

Truckload carriers operate with few economies of scale and face considerable competition from railroads for shipments exceeding 750 miles. Increasingly, larger TL carriers have formed partnerships with railroads to feed them shipments for their piggyback services. LTL carriage, which includes about 25 major players plus a few hundred minor firms, is a much smaller market than the truckload segment. These issues are considered early cycle performers and will tend to rally once the economy, in particular industrial production, has bottomed. These stocks are also sensitive to changes in interest rates and, obviously, the price of oil.

4

Buy, Sell, and Hold Recommendations

This chapter is made up of a "buy, sell, and hold" listing of more than 1,000 companies arranged alphabetically by industry. The data for each company are as they stood on December 29, 1995, and include ticker symbol, share price, fiscal-year ending, sales/revenues, projected 5-year EPS (earnings per share) growth rate, 1995 EPS, 1996 EPS, P/E (on estimated 1996 earnings), dividend yield, S&P common stock and dividend rank, and STARS.

The S&P common stock and dividend rank is an appraisal of the growth and stability of earnings and dividends over the past 10 years: **A+ = Highest; A = High; A- = Above average; B+ = Average; B = Below average; B- = Low; C = Lowest; D = In reorganization; and NR = Not ranked.** Quality rankings are not intended to predict stock price movements.

STARS stands for S&P's **St**ock **A**ppreciation **R**anking **S**ystem. STARS evaluates the investment potential of the stocks it covers, with emphasis on performance over a 6- to 12-month period: **5 STARS = Buy** (expected to be among the best performing stocks); **4 STARS = Accumulate** (expected to be an above-average performer, relative to the S&P 500); **3 STARS = Hold** (expected to be an average performer); **2 STARS = Avoid** (below-average expectations, relative to the S&P 500); **1 STAR = Sell** (expected to be among the worst performers in all industries). Those investors who wish to keep abreast of STARS changes on a weekly basis (as well as periodic performance measures versus the market) should subscribe to Standard & Poor's weekly investment advisory newsletter *The Outlook*.

The footnotes for the letter codes found in the table are as follows:

e — Estimate.
f — Pro forma.
g — Fully diluted.
i — Foreign currency.
o — Combined earnings.
p — Preliminary.
s — Before tax-loss carryforward.
w — Excluding extraordinary income.
x — Including extraordinary income.
y — Excluding extraordinary charge.
z — Including extraordinary charge.
BE — Breakeven.
EUR — Estimate under review.
NE — No estimate.
NM — Not meaningful.
NR — Not ranked.

Earnings for fiscal years ending March 31 or earlier are shown in the column of the preceding calendar year.

Industry / Company	Ticker	12/95 Price	F-Y End	Rev. ($)	5-Yr. EPS Gr.(%)	EPS 1995	EPS 1996	P/E 1996	Yld. (%)	Com. Stk. Rank	STARS 5=Buy 1=Sell
Aerospace/Defense											
AAR Corp	AIR	22	MY	451	11	0.66	0.85 e	26	2.1	B+	3
Boeing Co	BA	78	DC	21,924	13	1.25 e	2.70 e	29	1.2	A-	4
Genl Dynamics	GD	59	DC	3,058	5	3.85 e	4.00 e	15	2.5	B	4
Genl Motors Cl H	GMH	49	DC	14,099	9	2.75 e	2.95 e	17	1.8	B+	4
Lockheed Martin	LMT	79	DC	22,906	8	5.00 e	5.50 e	14	1.7	NR	3
McDonnell Douglas	MD	92	DC	13,176	12	6.00 e	6.75 e	14	0.8	B+	5
Northrop Grumman	NOC	64	DC	6,711	8	4.90 e	5.70 e	11	2.5	B-	3
OEA Inc	OEA	30	JL	129	24	1.04	1.30 e	23	0.8	B+	4
Precision Castparts	PCP	40	MR	436	13	1.85 e	2.11 e	19	0.6	A-	4
Raytheon Co	RTN	47	DC	10,013	9	3.20 e	3.52 e	13	1.5	A+	4
Rockwell Intl	ROK	53	SP	12,981	10	3.42	3.85 e	14	2.1	A-	5
Sundstrand Corp	SNS	70	DC	1,373	11	2.30 e	4.35 e	16	1.7	B	3
Teleflex Inc	TFX	41	DC	813	14	2.70 e	3.05 e	13	1.5	A+	4
Thiokol Corp	TKC	34	JE	957	6	2.78 y	3.00 e	11	2	NR	3
United Technologies	UTX	95	DC	21,197	11	5.70 e	6.45 e	15	2.3	B	3
Watkins-Johnson	WJ	44	DC	333	18	3.40 e	4.00 e	11	1	B	4
Whittaker Corp	WKR	22	OC	159	21	0.82 p	1.45 e	15	Nil	NR	5
Airlines											
Alaska Air Group	ALK	16	DC	1,316	9	1.00 e	2.00 e	8	Nil	C	3
AMR Corp	AMR	74	DC	16,137	11	7.00 e	8.00 e	9	Nil	C	3
Atlantic So'east Air	ASAI	22	DC	312	12	1.60 e	1.80 e	12	1.5	B+	3
British Airways ADS	BAB	73	MR	11,699	17	7.00 e	7.01 e	10	2.9	NR	4
Comair Holdings	COMR	27	MR	361	17	1.85 e	1.85 e	15	1	A-	4
Contl Airlines B	CAI.B	44	DC	5,670	5	6.20 e	5.50 e	8	Nil	NR	4
Delta Air Lines	DAL	74	JE	12,194	9	4.07 w	7.50 e	10	0.2	B-	5
KLM Royal Dutch Air	KLM	35	MR	5,966	7	3.50 e	4.36 e	8	Nil	NR	3
Northwest Airlines A	NWAC	51	DC	9,143	6	4.00 e	4.25 e	12	Nil	NR	3
Southwest Airlines	LUV	23	DC	2,592	16	1.20 e	1.60 e	14	0.1	B+	4
UAL Corp	UAL	179	DC	13,950	10	27.00 e	25.00 e	7	Nil	C	4
USAir Group	U	13	DC	6,997	7	0.50 e	-1.00 e	NM	Nil	C	2
ValuJet Airlines	VJET	25	DC	134	18	1.20 e	1.50 e	17	Nil	NR	4
Aluminum											
Alcan Aluminium Ltd	AL	31	DC	8,325	7	2.70 e	4.00 e	8	1.9	B-	3
Alumax Inc	AMX	31	DC	2,755	8	4.95 e	4.50 e	7	Nil	NR	3
Aluminum Co of Amer	AA	53	DC	9,904	22	4.75 e	6.00 e	9	1.7	B-	3
Reynolds Metals	RLM	57	DC	6,013	8	5.60 e	7.50 e	8	2.4	B-	3
Auto Parts											
Arvin Indus	ARV	17	DC	2,040	10	0.70 e	1.10 e	15	4.6	B-	2
Breed Technologies	BDT	19	JE	401	0	2.30	2.35 e	8	1	NR	2
Collins & Aikman	CKC	7	JA	1,536	10	1.35 e	1.50 e	4	Nil	NR	3
Cooper Tire & Rubber	CTB	25	DC	1,403	12	1.35 e	1.65 e	15	1.2	A	4
Echlin Inc	ECH	37	AU	2,718	16	2.60	3.00 e	12	2.2	A-	4
Exide Corp	EX	46	MR	1,199	20	1.85 e	2.75 e	17	0.1	NR	2
Federal-Mogul	FMO	20	DC	1,896	11	1.20 e	1.35 e	15	2.4	B-	3
Genuine Parts	GPC	41	DC	4,858	10	2.50 e	2.75 e	15	3	A+	3
Goodyear Tire & Rub	GT	45	DC	12,288	10	4.00 e	4.50 e	10	2.2	B	5
Magna Intl Cl A	MGA	43	JL	4,513	16	5.20 i	5.15 ei	8	Nil	B	3
Mark IV Industries	IV	20	FB	1,603	15	1.55 e	1.80 e	11	0.6	B+	3
Modine Mfg	MODI	24	MR	913	14	2.40 e	2.65 e	9	2.5	A	3
Monro Muffler Brake	MNRO	14	MR	109	15	1.10 e	1.40 e	10	Nil	NR	4
Orbital Engine ADS	OE	7	JE	17	NE	-0.14	0.35 e	19	Nil	NR	5
Simpson Indus	SMPS	9	DC	357	14	0.85 e	0.90 e	10	4.4	B+	2
SPX Corp	SPW	16	DC	1,093	11	0.60 e	1.60 e	10	2.5	B-	5
Superior Indus Intl	SUP	26	DC	457	16	1.75 e	2.30 e	11	0.7	A	5
TBC Corp	TBCC	9	DC	552	9	0.67 e	0.75 e	12	Nil	B+	3
TRW Inc	TRW	78	DC	9,087	11	6.50 e	7.25 e	11	2.8	B+	4

Industry / Company	Ticker	12/95 Price	F-Y End	Rev. ($)	5-Yr. EPS Gr.(%)	EPS 1995	EPS 1996	P/E 1996	Yld. (%)	Com. Stk. Rank	STARS 5=Buy 1=Sell
Automobiles											
Chrysler Corp	C	55	DC	52,224	8	4.30 e	6.00 e	9	4.3	B-	3
Ford Motor	F	29	DC	128,439	7	4.25 e	4.50 e	6	4.8	B-	3
Genl Motors	GM	53	DC	154,951	7	6.75 e	7.50 e	7	2.2	B-	3
Beverages (Alcoholic)											
Anheuser-Busch Cos	BUD	67	DC	12,054	9	4.10 e	4.50 e	15	2.6	A+	3
Brown-Forman Cl B	BF.B	37	AP	1,420	10	2.15 o	2.35 e	16	2.8	A	3
Coors (Adolph)Cl B	ACCOB	22	DC	1,663	8	1.10 e	1.20 e	18	2.2	B-	2
Redhook Ale Brewery	HOOK	26	DC	15	35	0.57 e	0.70 e	37	Nil	NR	3
Seagram Co. Ltd	VO	35	JA	6,399	6	0.63 e	1.45 e	24	1.7	A-	3
Beverages (Soft Drinks)											
Coca-Cola Co	KO	74	DC	16,172	17	2.37 e	2.85 e	26	1.1	A+	5
Coca-Cola Enterprises	CCE	27	DC	6,011	17	0.60 e	0.75 e	36	0.1	B-	5
PepsiCo Inc	PEP	56	DC	28,472	14	2.45 e	2.80 e	20	1.4	A+	4
Whitman Corp	WH	23	DC	2,659	12	1.30 e	1.45 e	16	1.6	B	4
Broadcast Media											
Argyle Television Cl A	ARGL	18	DC	69	NE	-0.35 e	0.05 e	350	Nil	NR	4
British Sky Broadcstg ADS	BSY	38	JE	1,237	22	0.83	1.40 e	27	0.8	NR	3
Cablevision Sys Cl A	CVC	54	DC	837	10	-13.00 e	-10.50 e	NM	Nil	C	4
Capital Cities/ABC	CCB	123	DC	6,379	13	5.00 e	5.80 e	21	0.1	A	4
Chris-Craft Indus	CCN	43	DC	481	-9	0.90 e	0.70 e	62	Nil	B-	3
Comcast Cl A Spl(nonvtg)	CMCSK	18	DC	1,375	15	-0.35 e	-0.20 e	NM	0.4	B-	4
Gaylord Entertainment Cl A	GET	28	DC	688	15	0.73 e	1.60 e	17	1.1	NR	3
TCA Cable TV	TCAT	28	OC	136	15	1.25 e	1.65 e	17	2	A-	4
Tele-Communic A TCI	TCOMA	20	DC	4,936	17	0.05 e	0.25 e	80	Nil	NR	4
Turner Broadcast Cl B	TBS.B	26	DC	2,908	22	0.40 e	0.60 e	43	0.2	B-	3
U S West Media Group	UMG	19	DC	1,908	NE	0.20 e	0.30 e	63	Nil	NR	4
Building Materials											
Centex Construction Prod	CXP	14	MR	194	20	1.45 e	1.50 e	10	Nil	NR	3
Masco Corp	MAS	31	DC	4,468	13	1.75 e	2.15 e	15	2.4	B	3
Owens-Corning	OCF	45	DC	3,351	12	4.50 e	5.00 e	9	Nil	B-	4
Sherwin-Williams	SHW	41	DC	3,100	10	2.30 e	2.65 e	15	1.5	A	3
USG Corp	USG	30	DC	2,290	11	-0.15 e	0.35 e	86	Nil	NR	4
Vulcan Materials	VMC	58	DC	1,253	18	4.95 e	5.80 e	10	2.5	A-	4
York International	YRK	47	DC	2,422	13	2.79 e	3.35 e	14	0.5	NR	4
Chemicals											
Air Products & Chem	APD	53	SP	3,865	12	3.29	3.60 e	15	1.9	A	4
ARCO Chemical	RCM	49	DC	3,423	10	5.10 e	5.00 e	10	5.7	NR	3
Cabot Corp	CBT	54	SP	1,830	18	4.35 p	4.75 e	11	1.3	B+	4
Dow Chemical	DOW	70	DC	20,015	9	7.30 e	8.50 e	8	4.2	B	5
duPont(EI)deNemours	DD	70	DC	39,333	11	5.78 e	6.50 e	11	2.9	B+	3
Eastman Chemical	EMN	62	DC	4,329	10	6.75 e	7.00 e	9	2.6	NR	4
First Mississippi	FRM	27	JE	643	24	2.80	3.25 e	8	1.5	B	4
Freeport McMoRan(New)	FTX	37	DC	1,982	10	-1.12 e	2.40 e	15	0.9	NR	3
Geon Co	GON	24	DC	1,209	5	1.30 e	2.75 e	9	2	NR	3
Georgia Gulf Corp	GGC	31	DC	955	9	4.72 e	4.50 e	7	1	NR	3
Goodrich (B.F.)	GR	68	DC	2,199	25	4.35 e	4.05 e	17	3.2	B-	2
Hercules, Inc	HPC	56	DC	2,821	16	2.80 e	3.15 e	18	1.6	B	3
IMC Global	IGL	41	JE	1,924	7	2.15 y	2.75 e	15	0.7	NR	3
Imperial Chem Ind ADR	ICI	47	DC	14,323	9	4.75 e	5.50 e	9	4.1	B+	3
Lyondell Petrochem	LYO	23	DC	3,857	9	5.12 e	4.00 e	6	3.9	NR	4
Monsanto Co	MTC	123	DC	8,272	11	6.40 e	7.00 e	18	2.2	A-	4
Olin Corp	OLN	74	DC	2,658	10	5.70 e	6.25 e	12	3.2	B	4
Potash Corp Saskatchewan	POT	71	DC	614	16	3.65 e	5.60 e	13	Nil	NR	4
Praxair Inc	PX	34	DC	2,711	14	1.80 e	2.00 e	17	0.9	NR	4
Rohm & Haas	ROH	64	DC	3,534	10	4.10 e	5.00 e	13	2.5	B+	3

Industry / Company	Ticker	12/95 Price	F-Y End	Rev. ($)	5-Yr. EPS Gr.(%)	EPS 1995	EPS 1996	P/E 1996	Yld. (%)	Com. Stk. Rank	STARS 5=Buy 1=Sell
Scotts Co Cl A	SMG	19	SP	733	12	1.11 p	1.45 e	13	Nil	NR	3
Sealed Air	SEE	28	DC	519	16	1.20 e	1.45 e	19	Nil	A-	4
Sterling Chemicals	STX	8	SP	1,030	NE	2.76 y	1.75 e	5	Nil	NR	3
Terra Industries	TRA	14	DC	1,666	21	2.00 e	2.10 e	7	0.8	B-	3
Union Carbide	UK	38	DC	4,865	10	6.30 e	5.50 e	7	2	NR	4
Vigoro Corp	VGR	62	DC	804	8	3.65 e	4.45 e	14	1.4	NR	3
Wellman Inc	WLM	23	DC	936	14	2.44 e	2.55 e	9	1.2	B+	3
Witco Corp	WIT	29	DC	2,225	11	2.45 e	2.30 e	13	3.8	B	4

Chemicals   (Diversified)

Avery Dennison Corp	AVY	50	DC	2,857	13	2.65 e	3.00 e	17	2.3	B+	4
Engelhard Corp	EC	22	DC	2,386	23	0.97 e	1.15 e	19	1.6	B	2
FMC Corp	FMC	68	DC	4,011	10	5.80 e	6.50 e	10	Nil	B	3
PPG Indus	PPG	46	DC	6,331	12	3.80 e	4.00 e	11	2.6	A-	4

Chemicals   (Specialty)

Albemarle Corp	ALB	19	DC	1,081	15	1.00 e	1.00 e	19	1.1	NR	3
Betz Laboratories	BTL	41	DC	708	10	2.60 e	2.85 e	14	3.6	A	3
Crompton & Knowles	CNK	13	DC	590	11	0.90 e	1.05 e	13	4	A+	2
Ethyl Corp	EY	12	DC	1,174	11	0.75 e	0.95 e	13	4	NR	3
Ferro Corp	FOE	23	DC	1,194	10	1.70 e	2.10 e	11	2.3	B+	3
Fuller (HB)	FULL	35	NV	1,097	10	2.22 e	2.45 e	14	1.8	B+	3
Grace (W.R.)	GRA	59	DC	5,093	10	1.68 e	3.00 e	20	0.8	B-	5
Great Lakes Chemical	GLK	72	DC	2,111	11	4.50 e	5.00 e	14	0.6	A+	4
Hanna (M.A.)Co	MAH	28	DC	1,719	17	1.83 e	1.90 e	15	2	B	3
Loctite Corp	LOC	48	DC	704	14	2.60 e	3.10 e	15	2.1	A	3
Lubrizol Corp	LZ	28	DC	1,599	10	2.38 e	2.20 e	13	3.4	B+	3
Morton International	MII	36	JE	3,326	13	1.96	2.20 e	16	1.4	B+	4
Nalco Chemical	NLC	30	DC	1,346	10	2.15 e	2.40 e	13	3.3	A	3
RPM, Inc	RPOW	17	MY	1,017	13	0.86	0.92 e	18	2.9	A+	3
Schulman (A.)	SHLM	23	AU	1,027	13	1.43	1.40 e	16	1.5	A	3
Sigma-Aldrich	SIAL	50	DC	851	13	2.65 e	2.90 e	17	0.8	A+	3

Communications   Equipment   Manufacturers

ADC Telecommunications	ADCT	37	OC	586	22	0.94 p	1.14 e	32	Nil	B	4
cisco Systems	CSCO	75	JL	1,979	33	1.52	2.55 e	29	Nil	B	4
DSC Communications	DIGI	37	DC	1,003	23	1.75 e	2.35 e	16	Nil	B	5
Dynatech Corp	DYTC	17	MR	489	16	0.75 e	1.55 e	11	Nil	B	5
ECI Telecom Ltd	ECILF	23	DC	385	23	1.17 e	1.43 e	16	0.5	NR	4
Ericsson(LM)Tel B ADR	ERICY	20	DC	11,051	18	0.85 e	1.05 e	19	0.8	NR	4
Newbridge Networks	NN	41	AP	801	21	2.31 i	2.20 ei	19	Nil	NR	4
Northern Telecom Ltd	NT	43	DC	8,874	13	1.90 e	2.35 e	18	1	B	4
QUALCOMM Inc	QCOM	43	SP	387	38	0.53 p	0.70 e	61	Nil	NR	2
Scientific-Atlanta	SFA	15	JE	1,147	19	0.83	0.55 e	27	0.4	B+	4
StrataCom Inc	STRM	74	DC	154	30	1.30 e	1.60 e	46	Nil	NR	4
Tellabs, Inc	TLAB	37	DC	494	24	1.20 e	1.50 e	25	Nil	B	3

Computer   Software   &   Services

Adobe Systems	ADBE	62	NV	598	25	2.05 e	2.50 e	25	0.3	B	3
America Online	AMER	38	JE	394	43	-0.49	0.18 e	208	Nil	NR	2
Autodesk, Inc	ACAD	34	JA	455	15	2.05 e	2.40 e	14	0.7	B+	4
Automatic Data Proc	AUD	74	JE	2,894	13	2.77	3.20 e	23	1	A+	4
Banyan Systems	BNYN	10	DC	150	20	-0.55 e	0.15 e	68	Nil	NR	4
BMC Software	BMCS	43	MR	345	21	2.35 e	2.70 e	16	Nil	B+	4
Borland Intl	BORL	17	MR	254	15	0.40 e	0.70 e	24	Nil	C	3
Broderbund Software	BROD	61	AU	172	27	1.72	2.20 e	28	Nil	NR	3
Cadence Design Sys	CDN	42	DC	429	16	1.25 e	1.55 e	27	Nil	B	3
Ceridian Corp	CEN	41	DC	916	18	1.75 e	2.15 e	19	Nil	C	3
Cheyenne Software	CYE	26	JE	128	21	0.97	1.10 e	24	Nil	B-	5
Comdisco, Inc	CDO	23	SP	2,240	12	1.73	1.97 e	11	1.2	B	5
Computer Assoc Intl	CA	57	MR	2,623	17	-0.50 e	3.35 e	17	0.2	B+	5

Industry / Company	Ticker	12/95 Price	F-Y End	Rev. ($)	5-Yr. EPS Gr.(%)	EPS 1995	EPS 1996	P/E 1996	Yld. (%)	Com. Stk. Rank	STARS 5=Buy 1=Sell
Computer Sciences	CSC	70	MR	3,373	17	2.50 e	2.95 e	24	Nil	B+	3
Continuum Co	CNU	40	MR	324	18	1.65 e	2.00 e	20	Nil	B	3
DST Systems	DST	29	DC	402	21	0.83 e	1.00 e	29	Nil	NR	4
Electronic Arts	ERTS	26	MR	493	19	1.05 e	1.30 e	20	Nil	B+	4
First Data	FDC	67	DC	1,652	19	2.25 e	2.73 e	24	0.1	NR	2
Genl Motors Cl E	GME	52	DC	10,052	15	1.95 e	2.25 e	23	1	A+	4
Harbinger Corp	HRBC	23	DC	16	25	0.30 e	0.70 e	33	Nil	NR	4
Informix Corp	IFMX	30	DC	469	29	0.70 e	0.85 e	35	Nil	B	4
Mercury Interactive	MERQ	18	DC	23	50	0.29 e	0.85 e	21	Nil	NR	4
Microsoft Corp	MSFT	88	JE	5,937	21	2.32	3.25 e	27	Nil	B+	4
NetManage Inc	NETM	23	DC	62	40	0.70 e	1.00 e	23	Nil	NR	4
Netscape Communications	NSCP	139	DC	0	75	-0.02 e	0.30 e	463	Nil	NR	2
Novell Inc	NOVL	14	OC	2,041	17	0.90 p	1.10 e	13	Nil	B+	4
Oracle Corp	ORCL	42	MY	2,967	31	1.00	1.35 e	31	Nil	B	5
Parametric Technology	PMTC	67	SP	394	23	1.20	2.20 e	30	Nil	NR	4
PLATINUM technology	PLAT	18	DC	96	30	-0.31 e	1.15 e	16	Nil	NR	4
Policy Mgmt Systems	PMS	48	DC	493	17	2.40 e	2.90 e	16	Nil	C	3
Progress Software	PRGS	38	NV	139	22	1.40 e	1.75 e	21	Nil	NR	4
Seer Tech	SEER	13	SP	117	25	0.45 p	0.80 e	16	Nil	NR	4
Shared Medical Sys	SMED	54	DC	551	12	1.70 e	1.90 e	29	1.5	B+	3
Sierra On-Line	SIER	29	MR	83	25	0.50 e	1.05 e	27	Nil	C	2
Sterling Software	SSW	62	SP	588	23	0.39	3.45 e	18	Nil	B-	5
Structural Dynamics Res	SDRC	29	DC	168	17	0.45 e	0.75 e	39	Nil	C	3
Sybase Inc	SYBS	36	DC	694	26	-0.20 e	1.00 e	36	Nil	NR	3
Symantec Corp	SYMC	23	MR	335	17	0.45 e	1.40 e	17	Nil	C	3
Trans. Sys Architects A	TSAI	34	SP	115	NE	0.57 py	1.05 e	32	Nil	NR	4

Computer Systems

Industry / Company	Ticker	12/95 Price	F-Y End	Rev. ($)	5-Yr. EPS Gr.(%)	EPS 1995	EPS 1996	P/E 1996	Yld. (%)	Com. Stk. Rank	STARS 5=Buy 1=Sell
3Com Corp	COMS	47	MY	1,295	28	0.86	1.40 e	33	Nil	B-	5
Adaptec Inc	ADPT	41	MR	466	22	2.10 e	3.30 e	12	Nil	B	5
Amdahl Corp	AMH	9	DC	1,639	4	0.91 e	1.00 e	9	Nil	C	3
Amer Power Conversion	APCC	10	DC	378	22	0.79 e	0.95 e	10	Nil	B	2
Apple Computer	AAPL	32	SP	11,062	9	3.45	1.50 e	21	1.5	B+	2
Artisoft Inc	ASFT	6	JE	84	NE	-0.41	0.25 e	25	Nil	NR	3
AST Research	ASTA	9	JE	2,468	12	-3.07	-3.65 e	NM	Nil	C	2
Bay Networks	BNET	41	JE	1,342	26	0.73	1.46 e	28	Nil	NR	4
C-Cube Microsystems	CUBE	63	DC	45	NE	0.62 e	0.90 e	69	Nil	NR	4
Cabletron Systems	CS	81	FB	811	23	3.00 e	3.60 e	23	Nil	B	4
Compaq Computer	CPQ	48	DC	10,866	16	3.90 e	4.50 e	11	Nil	B	4
Conner Peripherals	CNR	21	DC	2,365	10	1.00 e	1.30 e	16	Nil	NR	4
Cray Research	CYR	25	DC	922	10	-1.56 e	1.50 e	16	Nil	B-	3
Data General	DGN	14	SP	1,159	11	-1.23 p	0.60 e	23	Nil	C	4
Dell Computer Corp	DELL	35	JA	3,475	29	2.90 e	3.35 e	10	Nil	B	4
Diebold, Inc	DBD	55	DC	760	14	2.40 e	2.75 e	20	1.7	A-	3
Digital Equipment	DEC	64	JE	13,813	10	0.15 w	3.90 e	16	Nil	C	3
EMC Corp	EMC	15	DC	1,377	23	1.40 e	1.70 e	9	Nil	B	4
Exabyte Corp	EXBT	15	DC	382	20	-0.50 e	1.20 e	12	Nil	NR	3
Hewlett-Packard	HWP	84	OC	31,519	15	4.63 p	5.85 e	14	0.9	A	4
Intergraph Corp	INGR	16	DC	1,041	11	-1.05 e	0.75 e	21	Nil	C	3
Intl Bus. Machines	IBM	91	DC	64,052	13	10.90 e	12.65 e	7	1	B-	5
Komag Inc	KMAG	46	DC	392	15	4.00 e	5.00 e	9	Nil	B-	5
Maxtor Corp	MXTR	7	MR	907	8	-1.75 e	-0.11 e	NM	Nil	C	4
Mentor Graphics	MENT	18	DC	348	15	0.85 e	1.05 e	17	Nil	C	4
MicroTouch Systems	MTSI	12	DC	59	25	0.28 e	0.90 e	13	Nil	NR	3
NetFRAME Systems	NETF	5	DC	89	35	-0.55 e	0.35 e	15	Nil	NR	3
Quantum Corp	QNTM	16	MR	3,368	17	1.70 e	3.00 e	5	Nil	B-	4
Seagate Technology	SEG	48	JE	4,540	13	3.52	5.00 e	10	Nil	B	4
Sequent Computer Sys	SQNT	15	DC	451	20	1.15 e	1.45 e	10	Nil	B-	3
Silicon Graphics	SGI	28	JE	2,228	28	1.28	1.80 e	15	Nil	B	4
Storage Technology	STK	24	DC	1,625	NE	1.00 e	2.20 e	11	Nil	C	3
Stratus Computer	SRA	35	DC	577	11	0.55 e	3.10 e	11	Nil	B+	4

Industry / Company	Ticker	12/95 Price	F-Y End	Rev. ($)	5-Yr. EPS Gr.(%)	EPS 1995	EPS 1996	P/E 1996	Yld. (%)	Com. Stk. Rank	STARS 5=Buy 1=Sell
Sun Microsystems	SUNW	46	JE	5,902	17	1.80	2.55 e	18	Nil	B	5
Symbol Technologies	SBL	40	DC	465	21	1.70 e	2.10 e	19	Nil	B	3
Tandem Computers	TDM	11	SP	2,285	13	0.91	1.25 e	9	Nil	B-	4
Unisys Corp	UIS	6	DC	7,400	10	-0.45 e	0.50 e	11	Nil	B-	4
Conglomerates											
Teledyne Inc	TDY	26	DC	2,391	25	2.90 e	2.40 e	11	1.5	NR	3
Tenneco Inc	TEN	50	DC	12,174	10	4.00 e	4.60 e	11	3.6	B-	3
Textron, Inc	TXT	68	DC	9,683	11	5.45 e	6.05 e	11	2.3	A	4
Containers (Metal & Glass)											
Ball Corp	BLL	28	DC	2,595	12	-0.51 e	2.55 e	11	2.1	B+	2
Crown Cork & Seal	CCK	42	DC	4,452	15	0.96 e	2.25 e	19	Nil	B+	3
Owens-Illinois	OI	15	DC	3,567	12	1.28 e	1.40 e	10	Nil	NR	3
Containers (Paper)											
Bemis Co	BMS	26	DC	1,390	12	1.65 e	1.90 e	13	2.4	A	3
Sealright Co	SRCO	11	DC	295	7	0.50 e	0.65 e	17	4.3	B+	2
Stone Container	STO	14	DC	5,749	6	4.50 e	3.00 e	5	4.1	B-	2
Temple-Inland	TIN	44	DC	2,938	11	5.15 e	5.50 e	8	2.7	B+	2
Cosmetics											
Alberto-Culver Cl B	ACV	34	SP	1,358	NE	1.89 o	2.15 e	16	0.9	A	4
Avon Products	AVP	75	DC	4,267	12	4.20 e	4.80 e	16	2.9	B+	5
Carter-Wallace	CAR	11	MR	664	11	0.65 e	1.10 e	10	1.4	B	3
Gillette Co	G	52	DC	6,070	16	1.85 e	2.15 e	24	1.1	A+	4
Intl Flavors/Fragr	IFF	48	DC	1,315	12	2.24 e	2.50 e	19	2.8	A+	4
Tambrands Inc	TMB	48	DC	645	8	2.35 e	2.70 e	18	3.8	B+	3
Distributors (Consumer Products)											
Cardinal Health	CAH	55	JE	7,806	21	2.01	2.50 e	22	0.2	A-	4
Fleming Cos	FLM	21	DC	15,753	7	1.30 e	1.60 e	13	5.8	B+	2
FoxMeyer Health	FOX	27	MR	5,177	NE	1.85 e	2.05 e	13	Nil	B-	3
McKesson Corp	MCK	51	MR	13,189	10	2.95 e	3.29 e	15	1.9	NR	3
Supervalu Inc	SVU	32	FB	16,564	7	2.35 e	2.50 e	13	3.1	A-	2
Sysco Corp	SYY	33	JE	12,118	15	1.38	1.60 e	20	1.6	A+	4
Electric Companies											
Allegheny Power Sys	AYP	29	DC	2,452	5	1.96 e	2.00 e	14	5.8	A-	3
Amer Electric Pwr	AEP	41	DC	5,505	2	2.85 e	2.95 e	14	5.9	B+	3
Baltimore Gas & El	BGE	29	DC	2,783	3	2.05 e	2.16 e	13	5.4	A	4
Boston Edison	BSE	30	DC	1,549	3	2.50 e	2.60 e	11	6.3	B+	3
Carolina Pwr & Lt	CPL	35	DC	2,877	4	2.40 e	2.50 e	14	5.2	A-	3
Centerior Energy	CX	9	DC	2,421	NE	1.54 e	1.05 e	8	9	B-	1
Central & So. West	CSR	28	DC	3,623	2	2.13 e	2.20 e	13	6.1	A-	4
CINergy Corp	CIN	31	DC	2,924	4	2.12 e	2.20 e	14	5.6	B	3
CMS Energy	CMS	30	DC	3,619	6	2.25 e	2.40 e	12	3.2	B	3
Consolidated Edison	ED	32	DC	6,373	1	2.85 e	2.85 e	11	6.4	A	3
Detroit Edison	DTE	35	DC	3,519	1	2.80 e	2.85 e	12	5.9	B+	3
Dominion Resources	D	41	DC	4,491	2	3.00 e	3.10 e	13	6.2	A-	3
DPL Inc	DPL	25	DC	1,188	3	1.60 e	1.70 e	15	5	B+	3
DQE	DQE	31	DC	1,236	4	2.20 e	2.25 e	14	4.1	B+	3
Duke Power	DUK	47	DC	4,489	3	3.10 e	3.15 e	15	4.3	A-	3
Eastern Util Assoc	EUA	24	DC	564	3	1.60 e	2.40 e	10	6.7	B	3
Entergy Corp	ETR	29	DC	5,963	3	2.35 e	2.40 e	12	6.1	B	3
Florida Progress	FPC	35	DC	2,772	3	2.50 e	2.60 e	14	5.7	A-	4
FPL Group	FPL	46	DC	5,423	4	3.15 e	3.30 e	14	3.7	B	3
Genl Public Util	GPU	34	DC	3,650	3	2.80 e	2.90 e	12	5.5	B	3
Houston Indus	HOU	24	DC	4,002	3	1.70 e	1.85 e	13	6.1	B+	3
Illinova Corp	ILN	30	DC	1,590	6	2.30 e	2.50 e	12	3.7	B	3
IPALCO Enterprises	IPL	38	DC	686	3	2.55 e	2.68 e	14	5.6	B+	3

Industry / Company	Ticker	12/95 Price	F-Y End	Rev. ($)	5-Yr. EPS Gr.(%)	EPS 1995	EPS 1996	P/E 1996	Yld. (%)	Com. Stk. Rank	STARS 5=Buy 1=Sell
Kansas City Pwr & Lt	KLT	26	DC	868	3	1.85 e	1.95 e	13	5.9	B+	3
Long Island Light'g	LIL	16	DC	3,067	NE	2.10 e	2.13 e	8	10.8	B	2
Nevada Power	NVP	22	DC	764	2	1.65 e	1.75 e	13	7.1	B+	2
New England El Sys	NES	40	DC	2,243	2	3.10 e	3.20 e	12	5.9	A-	3
New York State E&G	NGE	26	DC	1,899	1	2.45 e	2.50 e	10	5.4	B	3
Niagara Mohawk Pwr	NMK	10	DC	4,152	NE	1.45 e	1.45 e	7	11.7	B	1
NIPSCO Industries	NI	38	DC	1,676	5	2.60 e	2.86 e	13	4.3	B+	3
Northeast Utilities	NU	24	DC	3,643	2	2.20 e	2.30 e	11	7.2	B	3
Northern States Pwr	NSP	49	DC	2,487	3	3.50 e	3.60 e	14	5.4	A-	3
Ohio Edison	OEC	24	DC	2,368	2	2.03 e	2.08 e	11	6.3	B	3
Oklahoma Gas & Elec	OGE	43	DC	1,355	2	3.05 e	3.10 e	14	6.1	A-	3
Pacific Gas & Elec	PCG	28	DC	10,447	NE	2.90 e	3.00 e	9	6.9	B	2
PacifiCorp	PPW	21	DC	3,507	3	1.65 e	1.60 e	13	5.1	B+	3
PECO Energy	PE	30	DC	4,041	3	2.65 e	2.75 e	11	5.7	B	3
Pinnacle West Capital	PNW	29	DC	1,685	4	2.20 e	2.30 e	13	3.4	B	4
Portland Genl Corp	PGN	29	DC	959	3	1.65 e	2.00 e	15	4.1	B	2
Potomac Electric Pwr	POM	26	DC	1,823	1	0.70 e	1.85 e	14	6.3	B+	4
Public Svc Colorado	PSR	35	DC	2,057	2	2.55 e	2.60 e	14	5.7	B+	3
Public Svc Enterpr	PEG	31	DC	5,916	2	2.65 e	2.75 e	11	7	B+	2
Puget Sound P&L	PSD	23	DC	1,194	3	1.85 e	1.95 e	12	7.9	B+	3
San Diego Gas & El	SDO	24	DC	1,982	2	1.90 e	1.95 e	12	6.5	A-	2
SCANA Corp	SCG	29	DC	1,332	3	1.70 e	1.77 e	16	5	A-	3
SCEcorp	SCE	18	DC	8,345	2	1.65 e	1.68 e	10	5.6	B+	2
Southern Co	SO	25	DC	8,297	3	1.67 e	1.75 e	14	4.9	A-	4
Southwestern Pub Sv	SPS	33	AU	834	1	2.80	2.50 e	13	6.7	A-	2
TECO Energy	TE	26	DC	1,351	4	1.60 e	1.65 e	16	4.1	A	3
Texas Utilities	TXU	41	DC	5,664	4	-0.75 e	3.00 e	14	4.8	B+	4
Unicom Corp	UCM	33	DC	6,278	6	3.10 e	3.00 e	11	4.8	B	1
Union Electric	UEP	42	DC	2,056	2	2.91 e	2.95 e	14	5.9	A-	3
Western Resources	WR	33	DC	1,618	2	2.65 e	2.70 e	12	6	A-	3
Wisconsin Energy Corp	WEC	31	DC	1,742	3	2.15 e	2.15 e	14	4.8	A	3

Electrical Equipment

Industry / Company	Ticker	12/95 Price	F-Y End	Rev. ($)	5-Yr. EPS Gr.(%)	EPS 1995	EPS 1996	P/E 1996	Yld. (%)	Com. Stk. Rank	STARS 5=Buy 1=Sell
AMP Inc	AMP	38	DC	4,027	12	2.00 e	2.40 e	16	2.4	A-	3
Arrow Electronics	ARW	43	DC	4,649	16	4.17 e	4.65 e	9	Nil	B-	3
AVX Corp	AVX	27	MR	989	20	1.50 e	1.80 e	15	0.7	NR	4
Cincinnati Microwave	CNMW	5	DC	65	NE	-0.35 e	0.40 e	11	Nil	C	3
Duracell Intl	DUR	52	JE	2,079	16	1.95	2.20 e	24	2	NR	4
Emerson Electric	EMR	82	SP	10,013	10	4.16 y	4.50 e	18	2.3	A+	4
Genl Electric	GE	72	DC	60,108	11	3.90 e	4.30 e	17	2.5	A+	5
Genl Signal	GSX	32	DC	1,528	11	2.18 e	2.70 e	12	2.9	B	5
Grainger (W.W.)	GWW	66	DC	3,023	11	3.65 e	4.15 e	16	1.3	A	4
Honeywell, Inc	HON	49	DC	6,057	11	2.50 e	3.10 e	16	2.1	B	4
LoJack Corp	LOJN	11	FB	42	40	0.35 e	0.55 e	20	Nil	B-	3
Oak Indus	OAK	19	DC	249	17	1.80 e	1.85 e	10	Nil	B-	5
Philips Electronics NV	PHG	36	DC	33,689	12	4.60 e	5.30 e	7	1.9	NR	3
Sensormatic Elect	SRM	17	JE	889	20	1.02	1.35 e	13	1.2	B+	3
Thomas & Betts	TNB	74	DC	1,076	11	4.15 e	4.75 e	16	3	B+	4
Westinghouse Elec	WX	16	DC	8,848	11	0.20 e	0.50 e	33	1.2	B	4

Electronics (Defense)

Industry / Company	Ticker	12/95 Price	F-Y End	Rev. ($)	5-Yr. EPS Gr.(%)	EPS 1995	EPS 1996	P/E 1996	Yld. (%)	Com. Stk. Rank	STARS 5=Buy 1=Sell
Alliant Techsystems	ATK	51	MR	789	6	3.50 e	4.06 e	12	Nil	NR	3
EG&G Inc	EGG	24	DC	1,333	9	1.02 e	1.30 e	19	2.3	A-	4
Harris Corp	HRS	55	JE	3,444	12	3.95	4.35 e	13	2.4	B+	4
Loral Corp	LOR	35	MR	5,484	10	1.95 e	2.12 e	17	0.9	A+	5

Electronics (Instruments)

Industry / Company	Ticker	12/95 Price	F-Y End	Rev. ($)	5-Yr. EPS Gr.(%)	EPS 1995	EPS 1996	P/E 1996	Yld. (%)	Com. Stk. Rank	STARS 5=Buy 1=Sell
AMETEK, Inc	AME	19	DC	808	13	1.30 e	1.55 e	12	1.2	B	4
Perkin-Elmer	PKN	38	JE	1,064	15	1.57	1.95 e	19	1.8	B	4
Tektronix Inc	TEK	49	MY	1,472	13	2.63	3.40 e	14	1.2	B-	4
Thermo Electron	TMO	52	DC	1,585	18	1.65 e	1.95 e	27	Nil	B+	4
Varian Associates	VAR	48	SP	1,576	16	3.96	3.80 e	13	0.5	B+	3

Industry / Company	Ticker	12/95 Price	F-Y End	Rev. ($)	5-Yr. EPS Gr.(%)	EPS 1995	EPS 1996	P/E 1996	Yld. (%)	Com. Stk. Rank	STARS 5=Buy 1=Sell
Electronics (Semiconductors)											
Advanced Micro Dev	AMD	17	DC	2,135	15	2.75 e	2.45 e	7	Nil	B-	3
Altera Corp	ALTR	50	DC	199	24	1.86 e	2.80 e	18	Nil	B-	4
Analog Devices	ADI	35	OC	942	23	1.50 p	2.05 e	17	Nil	B	3
Applied Materials	AMAT	39	OC	3,062	24	2.56 p	3.90 e	10	Nil	B	5
Atmel Corp	ATML	22	DC	375	27	1.12 e	1.55 e	14	Nil	NR	4
Avnet, Inc	AVT	45	JE	4,300	14	3.32	4.25 e	11	1.3	A	4
Chips/Technologies	CHPS	9	JE	105	20	0.50	0.86 e	10	Nil	B-	3
Cirrus Logic	CRUS	20	MR	889	25	1.70 e	2.63 e	8	Nil	B-	3
Cypress Semiconductor	CY	13	DC	406	27	1.15 e	1.52 e	8	Nil	B	3
Cyrix Corp	CYRX	23	DC	246	25	1.60 e	2.45 e	9	Nil	NR	4
Exar Corp	EXAR	15	MR	159	20	1.50 e	1.85 e	8	Nil	B-	4
Helix Technology	HELX	40	DC	87	NE	2.07 e	2.90 e	14	2.5	B+	5
Integrated Circuit Sys	ICST	12	JE	104	15	0.45	1.50 e	8	Nil	B	5
Integrated Device Tech	IDTI	13	MR	422	22	1.68 e	2.08 e	6	Nil	B-	3
Intel Corp	INTC	57	DC	11,521	17	4.18 e	5.10 e	11	0.2	B	5
Linear Technology Corp	LLTC	39	JE	265	28	1.11	1.76 e	22	0.4	B+	4
LSI Logic	LSI	33	DC	902	24	1.84 e	2.60 e	13	Nil	B-	5
Maxim Integrated Prod	MXIM	39	JE	251	32	0.58	1.37 e	28	Nil	B	3
Micron Technology	MU	40	AU	2,953	27	3.95	6.30 e	6	0.5	B	2
Motorola, Inc	MOT	57	DC	22,245	18	3.14 e	3.90 e	15	0.7	A	4
Natl Semiconductor	NSM	22	MY	2,379	13	2.02	2.45 e	9	Nil	B-	4
Photronics, Inc	PLAB	27	OC	125	21	1.66 p	1.75 e	15	Nil	B	4
Sierra Semiconductor	SERA	14	DC	109	23	0.78 e	0.95 e	15	Nil	NR	5
Solectron Corp	SLR	44	AU	2,066	20	1.82	2.30 e	19	Nil	B+	4
Teradyne Inc	TER	25	DC	677	22	1.97 e	2.45 e	10	Nil	B-	3
Texas Instruments	TXN	52	DC	10,315	16	5.67 e	6.70 e	8	1.3	B	3
Ultratech Stepper	UTEK	26	DC	91	30	1.17 e	1.75 e	15	Nil	NR	4
VLSI Technology	VLSI	18	DC	587	19	1.01 e	1.85 e	10	Nil	B-	3
Xilinx Inc	XLNX	31	MR	355	26	1.27 e	1.90 e	16	Nil	B	4
Engineering & Construction											
CBI Indus	CBI	33	DC	1,891	12	1.18 e	1.70 e	19	1.4	B	1
Fluor Corp	FLR	66	OC	9,301	15	2.78 p	3.30 e	20	1	B+	3
Foster Wheeler	FWC	43	DC	2,271	15	1.25 e	2.35 e	18	1.8	A	4
Jacobs Engr Group	JEC	25	SP	1,723	14	1.27	1.45 e	17	Nil	B+	4
Entertainment											
Disney (Walt) Co	DIS	59	SP	12,112	17	2.60	2.60 e	23	0.6	A	5
King World Prod'ns	KWP	39	AU	574	10	3.14	3.45 e	11	Nil	B+	4
Time Warner Inc	TWX	38	DC	7,396	10	-0.55 e	-0.20 e	NM	0.9	B-	3
Viacom Inc Cl B	VIA.B	47	DC	7,363	16	0.60 e	1.20 e	39	Nil	NR	3
Financial (Misc.)											
Alliance Cap Mgmt L.P.	AC	23	DC	601	5	1.90 e	2.15 e	11	7.4	NR	4
AMBAC Inc	ABK	47	DC	202	12	4.50 e	5.00 e	9	1.2	NR	3
Amer Express	AXP	41	DC	14,282	12	3.20 e	3.65 e	11	2.1	B	5
Amer General	AGC	35	DC	4,841	10	3.45 e	3.85 e	9	3.5	B+	4
Block (H & R)	HRB	41	AP	1,360	14	1.01	1.90 e	21	3.1	A	5
Capstead Mortgage	CMO	23	DC	604	NE	1.65 e	2.45 e	9	7.1	NR	3
Countrywide Credit Indus	CCR	22	FB	603	11	1.95 e	2.25 e	10	1.4	B+	2
Eaton Vance	EAVN	28	OC	168	11	3.27 p	3.35 e	8	2.4	A-	4
Federal Home Loan	FRE	84	DC	6,923	15	5.75 e	6.60 e	13	1.4	NR	4
Federal Natl Mtge	FNM	124	DC	18,573	12	8.60 e	9.50 e	13	2.1	A-	4
Franklin Resources	BEN	50	SP	885	14	3.24 p	3.45 e	15	0.8	A	3
Green Tree Finl	GNT	26	DC	497	16	1.80 e	2.10 e	13	0.9	B+	5
SunAmerica Inc	SAI	48	SP	1,064	16	2.84	3.43 e	14	0.8	A-	4
T.Rowe Price Assoc	TROW	49	DC	382	15	2.50 e	2.85 e	17	1.7	A-	2
Transamerica Corp	TA	73	DC	5,355	11	5.70 e	6.25 e	12	2.7	B	3
United Asset Mgmt	UAM	38	DC	492	12	2.15 e	2.45 e	16	3.1	A	5

Industry / Company	Ticker	12/95 Price	F-Y End	Rev. ($)	5-Yr. EPS Gr.(%)	EPS 1995	EPS 1996	P/E 1996	Yld. (%)	Com. Stk. Rank	STARS 5=Buy 1=Sell
Foods											
Archer-Daniels-Midland	ADM	18	JE	12,672	11	1.48	1.45 e	12	1.1	A+	3
Campbell Soup	CPB	60	JL	7,278	11	2.80	3.15 e	19	2.3	B	5
ConAgra Inc	CAG	41	MY	24,109	12	2.06	2.35 e	18	2.3	A+	3
CPC Intl	CPC	69	DC	7,425	11	3.65 e	4.10 e	17	2.2	A+	4
Dean Foods	DF	28	MY	2,630	10	2.01	1.85 e	15	2.6	A	2
Dole Food Co	DOL	35	DC	3,842	14	2.10 e	2.15 e	16	1.1	B	4
Dreyer's Gr Ice Cr	DRYR	33	DC	564	16	0.02 e	1.45 e	23	0.7	B	3
Flowers Indus	FLO	12	JE	1,129	12	0.75	0.80 e	15	4.7	B+	3
Genl Mills	GIS	58	MY	5,027	11	2.33	3.10 e	19	3.2	A	3
Grand Metropolitan ADS	GRM	29	SP	12,232	14	2.00 e	2.10 e	14	3.4	NR	3
Heinz (H.J.)	HNZ	33	AP	8,087	9	1.59	1.80 e	18	3.2	A+	4
Hershey Foods	HSY	65	DC	3,606	10	3.40 e	3.85 e	17	2.2	A	4
Hormel Foods	HRL	25	OC	3,046	9	1.57 p	1.80 e	14	2.4	A+	3
IBP, Inc	IBP	51	DC	12,075	14	5.75 e	6.40 e	8	0.3	NR	4
Interstate Bakeries	IBC	22	MY	1,223	17	1.05	0.85 e	26	2.2	NR	3
Intl Multifoods	IMC	20	FB	2,295	7	1.60 e	1.85 e	11	3.9	B+	4
Kellogg Co	K	77	DC	6,562	11	3.35 e	3.85 e	20	2	A+	3
McCormick & Co	MCCRK	24	NV	1,695	11	1.30 e	1.45 e	17	2.3	A	3
Michael Foods	MIKL	12	DC	506	31	0.90 e	1.00 e	12	1.7	NR	3
Nabisco Holdings A	NA	33	DC	7,025	17	1.25 e	1.55 e	21	1.6	NR	3
Pioneer Hi-Bred Intl	PHB	56	AU	1,532	11	2.16	2.65 e	21	1.4	B+	3
Quaker Oats	OAT	35	JE	6,365	10	6.00 y	0.95 e	36	3.3	A-	1
Ralston-Purina Group	RAL	62	SP	5,622	10	2.76 py	3.45 e	18	1.9	B+	4
Sara Lee Corp	SLE	32	JE	17,719	10	1.62	1.85 e	17	2.3	A	4
Smucker (J.M.) Cl A	SJM.A	22	AP	628	NE	1.25 o	1.20 e	18	2.3	A	3
Tyson Foods Cl A	TYSNA	26	SP	5,511	12	1.51 o	1.65 e	16	0.4	A	3
Unilever ADR	UL	85	DC	46,758	12	5.40 e	5.85 e	14	2.1	NR	3
Unilever N.V.	UN	141	DC	46,576	11	9.30 e	10.20 e	14	2.4	A	3
Univl Foods	UFC	40	SP	793	10	2.54 p	2.40 e	17	2.4	A	4
Wrigley, (Wm) Jr	WWY	53	DC	1,597	12	1.92 e	2.15 e	24	1.2	A+	3
Gold Mining											
Barrick Gold	ABX	26	DC	936	14	0.85 e	1.00 e	26	0.4	A-	3
Battle Mtn Gold	BMG	9	DC	230	5	0.10 e	0.15 e	57	0.5	B-	3
Echo Bay Mines	ECO	10	DC	378	2	-0.30 e	-0.05 e	NM	0.7	B-	3
Hecla Mining	HL	7	DC	129	6	-2.30 e	-0.10 e	NM	Nil	C	3
Homestake Mining	HM	16	DC	705	4	0.25 e	0.40 e	39	1.2	B-	3
Horsham Corp	HSM	13	DC	2,493	16	0.59 e	0.80 e	17	0.5	NR	3
Newmont Mining	NEM	45	DC	597	11	1.35 e	1.25 e	36	1	B	3
Placer Dome Inc	PDG	24	DC	899	14	0.30 e	0.65 e	37	1.2	B-	3
Santa Fe Pacific Gold	GLD	12	DC	376	11	0.35 e	0.45 e	27	0.4	NR	3
Hardware & Tools											
Black & Decker Corp	BDK	35	DC	5,248	14	1.95 e	2.25 e	16	1.1	B	4
Snap-On Inc	SNA	45	DC	1,194	11	2.75 e	3.10 e	15	2.3	B+	3
Stanley Works	SWK	52	DC	2,511	8	2.10 e	3.25 e	16	2.7	B+	3
Health Care (Diversified)											
Abbott Laboratories	ABT	42	DC	9,156	12	2.15 e	2.40 e	17	2	A+	4
Amer Home Products	AHP	97	DC	8,966	9	6.40 e	5.60 e	17	3.1	A+	4
Bristol-Myers Squibb	BMY	86	DC	11,984	8	5.10 e	5.45 e	16	3.4	A+	4
Johnson & Johnson	JNJ	86	DC	15,734	12	3.70 e	4.15 e	21	1.5	A+	5
Mallinckrodt Group	MKG	36	JE	2,212	12	2.32	2.55 e	14	1.7	B	3
Warner-Lambert	WLA	97	DC	6,417	7	5.55 e	5.70 e	17	2.6	A-	4
Health Care (Drugs)											
BioChem Pharma	BCHXF	40	DC	110	86	-0.15 e	0.08 e	502	Nil	NR	4
Biogen Inc	BGEN	62	DC	156	32	0.15 e	1.00 e	62	Nil	B-	4
Centocor Inc	CNTO	31	DC	67	30	-0.90 e	-0.46 e	NM	Nil	C	5
Cephalon Inc	CEPH	41	DC	22	0	-1.40 e	-1.25 e	NM	Nil	NR	3

Industry / Company	Ticker	12/95 Price	F-Y End	Rev. ($)	5-Yr. EPS Gr.(%)	EPS 1995	EPS 1996	P/E 1996	Yld. (%)	Com. Stk. Rank	STARS 5=Buy 1=Sell
Chiron Corp	CHIR	111	DC	454	29	-12.90 e	1.30 e	85	Nil	C	3
Elan Corp ADS	ELN	49	MR	193	28	2.40 e	3.00 e	16	Nil	NR	4
Forest Labs	FRX	45	MR	393	18	2.30 e	2.60 e	17	Nil	B+	3
Genentech Inc	GNE	53	DC	795	20	1.35 e	1.45 e	37	Nil	NR	3
Genzyme Corp-Genl Div	GENZ	62	DC	311	23	1.85 e	2.30 e	27	Nil	C	4
Glaxo Wellcome plc ADR	GLX	28	JE	8,484	6	1.55 e	1.70 e	17	3.5	NR	5
Immunex Corp	IMNX	17	DC	144	30	-0.50 e	-0.35 e	NM	Nil	C	3
IVAX Corp	IVX	29	DC	1,135	20	1.10 e	1.40 e	20	0.2	B-	4
Lilly (Eli)	LLY	56	DC	5,712	10	2.30 e	2.60 e	22	2.4	A	4
Merck & Co	MRK	66	DC	14,970	11	2.70 e	3.10 e	21	2	A+	5
Mylan Labs	MYL	24	MR	396	18	1.10 e	1.25 e	19	0.6	A-	4
Perrigo Co	PRGO	12	JE	717	12	0.58	0.70 e	17	Nil	NR	3
Pfizer, Inc	PFE	63	DC	8,281	14	2.50 e	2.90 e	22	1.6	A-	5
Pharmacia & Upjohn	PNU	39	DC	6,823	13	1.80 e	2.10 e	18	2.7	NR	4
Rhone-Poulenc Rorer	RPR	53	DC	4,175	9	3.25 e	3.45 e	15	2.2	B+	4
Roberts Pharmaceutical	RPCX	18	DC	112	27	0.07 e	0.75 e	24	Nil	B-	3
Schering-Plough	SGP	55	DC	4,657	11	2.80 e	3.15 e	17	2.1	A+	4
SmithKline Beecham ADS	SBE	56	DC	0	12	2.70 e	3.10 e	18	2.4	NR	4
Teva Pharm Indus ADR	TEVIY	46	DC	588	24	1.55 e	1.90 e	24	0.4	NR	4
Health Care (HMOs)											
Coastal Physician Grp	DR	14	DC	749	20	0.10 e	0.80 e	17	Nil	NR	3
Coventry Corp	CVTY	21	DC	747	20	0.70 e	1.10 e	19	Nil	NR	3
FHP Int'l Corp	FHPC	29	JE	3,909	13	0.29	1.20 e	24	Nil	B	3
HealthCare COMPARE	HCCC	44	DC	187	20	1.88 e	2.25 e	19	Nil	B	3
Healthsource Inc	HS	36	DC	584	25	0.82 e	1.07 e	34	Nil	B	3
Humana Inc	HUM	27	DC	3,576	20	1.20 e	1.60 e	17	Nil	B+	4
Oxford Health Plans	OXHP	74	DC	721	28	1.40 e	2.00 e	37	Nil	NR	3
PacifiCare Health Sys B	PHSYB	87	SP	3,731	18	3.62 o	4.25 e	20	Nil	B+	4
U.S. HealthCare	USHC	47	DC	2,975	15	2.40 e	2.85 e	16	2.3	B+	4
United Amer Healthcare	UAH	10	JE	69	NE	1.01	1.20 e	8	Nil	B	4
United Dental Care	UDCI	41	DC	83	NE	0.67 e	1.00 e	41	Nil	NR	2
United Healthcare	UNH	65	DC	3,769	20	2.15 e	3.00 e	22	Nil	B	4
Wellpoint Hlth Networks A	WLP	32	DC	2,792	12	2.25 e	2.40 e	13	Nil	NR	3
Health Care (Misc.)											
Advocat Inc	AVC	11	DC	103	18	0.97 e	1.18 e	9	Nil	NR	4
ALZA Corp	AZA	25	DC	279	13	0.87 e	1.05 e	23	Nil	B	3
Amgen Inc	AMGN	59	DC	1,648	15	1.95 e	2.30 e	26	Nil	B-	5
Beverly Enterprises	BEV	11	DC	2,984	15	0.64 e	0.95 e	11	Nil	B-	3
Caremark International	CK	18	DC	2,426	18	1.05 e	1.40 e	13	0.2	NR	5
Health Care & Retirement	HCR	35	DC	615	19	1.55 e	1.80 e	19	Nil	NR	3
Horizon/CMS Healthcare	HHC	25	MY	1,626	22	0.79 f	0.68 e	37	Nil	B	4
Manor Care	MNR	35	MY	1,322	16	1.51	1.75 e	20	0.2	A-	4
NovaCare	NOV	5	JE	905	10	0.95	0.55 e	9	Nil	B	3
Heavy Duty Trucks & Parts											
Cummins Engine	CUM	37	DC	4,737	6	4.00 e	3.00 e	12	2.7	B-	2
Dana Corp	DCN	29	DC	6,614	11	2.65 e	2.40 e	12	3.1	B	2
Eaton Corp	ETN	54	DC	6,052	11	5.25 e	5.50 e	10	2.9	B+	3
Navistar Intl	NAV	11	OC	6,342	7	1.83 p	1.00 e	11	Nil	B-	2
PACCAR Inc	PCAR	42	DC	4,285	8	6.25 e	4.25 e	10	2.3	B+	2
Wabash National	WNC	22	DC	562	25	1.40 e	1.70 e	13	0.5	NR	3
Homebuilding											
Centex Corp	CTX	35	MR	3,278	10	1.75 e	2.25 e	15	0.5	B+	4
Kaufman & Broad Home	KBH	15	NV	1,336	13	0.65 e	0.90 e	17	2	B+	3
Lennar Corp	LEN	25	NV	818	13	1.95 e	2.15 e	12	0.3	A-	5
Pulte Corp	PHM	34	DC	1,756	11	1.75 e	2.40 e	14	0.7	A-	4
Ryland Group	RYL	14	DC	1,643	12	0.10 e	0.75 e	19	4.2	B+	3
Toll Brothers	TOL	23	OC	646	15	1.47 p	1.65 e	14	Nil	B	4

Industry / Company	Ticker	12/95 Price	F-Y End	Rev. ($)	5-Yr. EPS Gr.(%)	EPS 1995	EPS 1996	P/E 1996	Yld. (%)	Com. Stk. Rank	STARS 5=Buy 1=Sell
U.S. Home	UH	29	DC	995	12	3.07 e	3.25 e	9	Nil	NR	5
Hospital Management											
Columbia/HCA Hlthcare	COL	51	DC	20,095	16	2.37 e	3.35 e	15	0.2	NR	4
Community Psych Ctrs	CMY	12	NV	424	14	-0.11 e	0.80 e	15	Nil	B	4
Foundation Health	FH	43	JE	2,460	17	0.90	3.15 e	14	Nil	NR	5
Health Mgmt Assoc A	HMA	26	SP	531	21	0.88 p	1.10 e	24	Nil	B	4
HEALTHSOUTH Corp	HRC	29	DC	1,127	24	1.07 e	1.30 e	22	Nil	B	4
Integrated Health Svcs	IHS	25	DC	684	21	2.48 e	3.20 e	8	Nil	NR	3
Magellan Health Svcs	MGL	24	SP	1,152	14	-1.54	2.40 e	10	Nil	NR	4
Mariner Health Group	MRNR	17	DC	216	24	0.65 e	1.20 e	14	Nil	NR	5
Mid Atlantic Medical Svcs	MME	24	DC	750	21	1.30 e	1.60 e	15	Nil	NR	4
OrNda Healthcorp	ORN	23	AU	1,843	22	1.53	1.75 e	13	Nil	NR	4
PhyCor Inc	PHYC	51	DC	242	32	0.60 e	0.85 e	59	Nil	NR	4
Physician Corp of Amer	PCAM	17	DC	825	17	0.50 e	0.70 e	24	Nil	NR	3
Quantum Hlth Resources	QHRI	10	DC	275	27	0.16 e	0.55 e	18	Nil	NR	3
Tenet Healthcare	THC	21	MY	3,318	12	1.04 y	1.65 e	13	Nil	NR	3
TheraTx Inc	THTX	12	DC	127	21	0.97 e	1.25 e	10	Nil	NR	4
Value Health Inc	VH	28	DC	976	28	1.75 e	2.20 e	12	Nil	NR	4
Vencor Inc	VC	33	DC	400	23	1.45 e	1.85 e	18	Nil	B	3
Hotel-Motel											
Aztar Corp	AZR	8	DC	541	18	0.20 e	0.60 e	13	Nil	NR	3
Boomtown Inc	BMTN	5	SP	232	NE	-0.31 p	0.70 e	7	Nil	NR	3
Circus Circus Enterp	CIR	28	JA	1,170	14	1.32 e	1.75 e	16	Nil	B+	4
Harrah's Entertainment	HET	24	DC	1,339	21	1.38 e	1.60 e	15	Nil	NR	3
Hilton Hotels	HLT	62	DC	1,506	12	3.20 e	3.70 e	17	1.9	B+	3
Host Marriott	HMT	13	DC	1,501	15	-0.12 e	-0.10 e	NM	Nil	C	4
Intl Game Technology	IGT	11	SP	621	13	0.71 p	0.85 e	13	1.1	B	3
Marriott International	MAR	38	DC	8,415	17	1.85 e	2.10 e	18	0.7	NR	3
Mirage Resorts	MIR	35	DC	1,254	21	1.65 e	1.80 e	19	Nil	B-	3
Prime Hospitality	PDQ	10	DC	134	25	0.50 e	0.70 e	14	Nil	NR	5
Household Furnishings & Appliances											
Armstrong World Indus	ACK	62	DC	2,753	11	4.15 e	5.80 e	11	2.3	B+	4
Ethan Allen Interiors	ETH	20	JE	476	12	1.56 wy	1.65 e	12	Nil	NR	3
Fedders Corp	FJC	6	AU	316	NE	0.72	0.75 e	8	1.3	B-	4
Heilig-Meyers	HMY	18	FB	1,152	17	1.00 e	1.15 e	16	1.5	A+	2
La-Z Boy Chair	LZB	31	AP	850	11	2.01	2.20 e	14	2.4	A-	3
Leggett & Platt	LEG	24	DC	1,858	15	1.60 e	1.80 e	13	1.6	A	4
Maytag Corp	MYG	20	DC	3,373	9	-0.10 e	1.50 e	14	2.7	B-	3
Shaw Indus	SHX	15	DC	2,789	13	0.57 e	0.95 e	16	2	A	4
Whirlpool Corp	WHR	53	DC	8,104	11	3.00 e	4.40 e	12	2.5	B	4
Zenith Electronics	ZE	7	DC	1,469	NE	-1.65 e	0.50 e	14	Nil	C	2
Household Products											
Clorox Co	CLX	72	JE	1,984	11	3.78	4.20 e	17	2.9	A	3
Colgate-Palmolive	CL	70	DC	7,588	12	1.05 e	4.60 e	15	2.6	B+	4
Dial Corp	DL	30	DC	3,547	11	0.08 e	2.00 e	15	2.1	B+	4
Kimberly-Clark	KMB	83	DC	7,364	10	4.10 e	5.00 e	17	2.1	A+	4
Procter & Gamble	PG	83	JE	33,434	12	3.71	4.30 e	19	1.9	A	4
Housewares											
Newell Co	NWL	26	DC	2,075	15	1.45 e	1.65 e	16	1.8	A+	4
Premark Intl	PMI	51	DC	3,451	12	4.05 e	4.40 e	12	2.1	B+	4
Rubbermaid, Inc	RBD	26	DC	2,169	13	0.41 e	1.50 e	17	2.1	A+	3
Insurance Brokers											
Alexander & Alex Sv	AAL	19	DC	1,324	14	1.20 e	1.65 e	12	0.5	B-	3
Marsh & McLennan	MMC	89	DC	3,435	11	5.80 e	6.10 e	15	3.6	A+	4

Industry / Company	Ticker	12/95 Price	F-Y End	Rev. ($)	5-Yr. EPS Gr.(%)	EPS 1995	EPS 1996	P/E 1996	Yld. (%)	Com. Stk. Rank	STARS 5=Buy 1=Sell
Investment Banking/Brokerage											
Oppenheimer Cap L.P.	OCC	28	A P	34	11	2.02	2.44 e	11	7.8	NR	4
Travelers Group	TRV	63	DC	18,465	13	4.50 e	5.00 e	13	1.2	B+	4
Leisure Time											
Bally Entertainment	BLY	14	DC	942	13	0.55 e	0.80 e	18	Nil	C	3
Brunswick Corp	BC	24	DC	2,700	16	1.37 e	1.90 e	13	2	B	3
Carnival Corp A	CCL	24	NV	1,998	16	1.59 op	1.75 e	14	1.4	B+	4
Handleman Co	HDL	6	A P	1,226	7	0.84	0.20 e	29	3.4	B+	1
Harley-Davidson	HDI	29	DC	1,542	16	1.45 e	1.75 e	16	0.6	B+	5
Outboard Marine	OM	20	SP	1,229	16	2.56	2.35 e	9	1.9	B-	2
Life Insurance											
AFLAC Inc	AFL	44	DC	6,111	14	3.50 e	4.00 e	11	1.1	A	4
Conseco Inc	CNC	63	DC	1,862	10	4.90 e	7.00 e	9	0.1	B+	4
Equitable Cos	EQ	24	DC	6,447	17	1.75 e	2.10 e	11	0.8	NR	3
Jefferson-Pilot	J P	47	DC	1,269	10	3.00 e	3.33 e	14	2.7	A	3
Lincoln Natl Corp	LNC	54	DC	6,984	9	2.85 e	4.65 e	12	3.4	B+	3
Provident Companies	PVT	34	DC	2,762	8	2.75 e	3.25 e	10	2.1	B	3
Providian Corp	PVN	41	DC	2,959	10	4.00 e	4.40 e	9	2.4	A-	3
Torchmark Corp	TMK	45	DC	1,923	10	4.00 e	4.50 e	10	2.5	A+	3
UNUM Corp	UNM	55	DC	3,624	12	3.90 e	4.30 e	13	1.9	NR	3
USLIFE Corp	USH	30	DC	1,651	9	2.93 e	3.20 e	9	3.1	B+	3
Machine Tools											
Cincinnati Milacron	CMZ	26	DC	1,197	14	3.25 e	2.15 e	12	1.3	B-	4
Giddings & Lewis	GIDL	17	DC	619	11	1.00 e	1.30 e	13	0.7	NR	3
Machinery (Diversified)											
Briggs & Stratton	B GG	43	J E	1,340	10	3.62	2.85 e	15	2.3	A-	2
BW/IP Inc	BWIP	17	DC	449	11	1.16 e	1.50 e	11	2.6	NR	4
Case Corp	CSE	46	DC	4,405	12	4.00 e	4.40 e	10	0.4	NR	4
Caterpillar Inc	CAT	59	DC	14,328	11	5.40 e	5.90 e	10	2.3	B	3
Cooper Indus	CBE	37	DC	4,588	10	2.45 e	2.70 e	14	3.5	A-	3
Deere & Co	DE	35	OC	10,291	12	2.71 p	3.20 e	11	2.2	B	3
Duriron Co	DURI	23	DC	345	14	1.15 e	1.40 e	17	1.9	B+	3
Harnischfeger Indus	HPH	33	OC	2,214	13	1.32 py	2.65 e	13	1.2	B	4
Ingersoll-Rand	IR	35	DC	4,507	11	2.45 e	2.90 e	12	2.1	B+	3
JLG Indus	JLGI	30	JL	269	10	1.46	2.00 e	15	0.1	B	4
NACCO Indus Inc Cl A	NC	56	DC	1,865	22	6.60 e	7.30 e	8	1.2	B+	4
Pentair, Inc	PNTA	50	DC	1,649	12	2.90 e	3.45 e	14	1.6	A-	4
Stewart & Stevenson	SSSS	25	J A	1,138	13	1.85 e	1.75 e	14	1.2	B	3
Tecumseh Products Cl A	TECUA	52	DC	1,533	11	5.70 e	5.80 e	9	2	B+	3
Timken Co	TKR	38	DC	1,930	12	3.40 e	4.45 e	9	3.1	B	3
Varity Corp	VAT	37	J A	2,268	20	3.30 e	4.00 e	9	Nil	B-	4
Major Regional Banks											
Banc One Corp	ONE	38	DC	7,857	11	3.20 e	3.60 e	10	3.6	A+	3
Bancorp Hawaii	BOH	36	DC	941	7	2.90 e	3.05 e	12	3.1	A	2
Bank of Boston	BKB	46	DC	4,566	9	4.45 e	4.80 e	10	3.2	B-	4
Bank South Corp	BKSO	30	DC	533	11	1.45 e	1.60 e	19	1.8	B-	3
Barnett Banks Inc	BBI	59	DC	3,097	9	5.25 e	5.50 e	11	3.1	A-	3
BayBanks Inc	BBNK	98	DC	865	10	6.85 e	7.30 e	13	2.4	B+	3
Boatmen's Bancshares	BOAT	41	DC	2,107	8	3.35 e	3.70 e	11	3.6	A	3
City National	CYN	14	DC	215	NE	0.97 e	1.05 e	13	2	C	3
Comerica Inc	CMA	40	DC	2,559	9	3.52 e	3.80 e	11	3.5	A-	3
Commerce Bancshares	CBSH	38	DC	621	8	2.86 e	3.10 e	12	1.7	A+	3
CoreStates Financial	CFL	38	DC	2,497	9	3.20 e	4.10 e	9	4.4	B+	3
Crestar Financial	CF	59	DC	1,180	9	5.00 e	5.35 e	11	3	B+	4
Fifth Third Bancorp	FITB	73	DC	1,178	13	4.30 e	4.80 e	15	2.1	A+	4
First Bank System	FBS	50	DC	2,375	10	4.15 e	4.60 e	11	2.9	B-	4

Industry / Company	Ticker	12/95 Price	F-Y End	Rev. ($)	5-Yr. EPS Gr.(%)	EPS 1995	EPS 1996	P/E 1996	Yld. (%)	Com. Stk. Rank	STARS 5=Buy 1=Sell
First Commerce	FCOM	32	DC	475	10	2.73 e	3.35 e	10	4.3	B+	4
First Empire State	FES	218	DC	871	7	17.31 e	19.10 e	11	1.2	A+	4
First Fidelity Bancorp	FFB	75	DC	2,553	8	5.60 e	5.90 e	13	2.6	B	3
First Hawaiian	FHWN	30	DC	562	6	2.48 e	2.65 e	11	3.9	A	3
First Interstate Bancorp	I	137	DC	4,246	13	11.25 e	12.25 e	11	2.3	B	3
First of America Bk	FOA	44	DC	1,791	8	3.80 e	4.20 e	11	3.9	A-	4
First Security	FSCO	39	DC	980	10	2.90 e	3.10 e	12	2.9	A	4
First Tenn Natl	FTEN	61	DC	1,058	9	4.75 e	5.50 e	11	3.5	A-	5
First Union Corp	FTU	56	DC	6,254	9	5.70 e	6.25 e	9	3.7	A	4
First Virginia Banks	FVB	42	DC	588	7	3.35 e	3.60 e	12	3.3	A	3
Fleet Financial Group	FLT	41	DC	4,445	9	4.20 e	4.50 e	9	4.2	B+	3
Hibernia Corp Cl A	HIB	11	DC	496	10	1.03 e	0.85 e	13	2.6	B-	3
Huntington Bancshares	HBAN	24	DC	1,455	8	1.95 e	2.05 e	12	3.3	A-	4
Integra Finl Corp	ITG	63	DC	1,099	8	4.90 e	5.10 e	12	3.1	B+	3
KeyCorp	KEY	36	DC	5,373	9	3.40 e	3.70 e	10	3.9	A+	3
Marshall & Ilsley	MRIS	26	DC	1,179	9	1.94 e	2.10 e	12	2.5	A-	2
MBNA Corp	KRB	37	DC	1,853	21	2.30 e	2.90 e	13	2.2	NR	5
Mellon Bank Corp	MEL	54	DC	3,957	10	4.50 e	5.05 e	11	4	B-	3
Mercantile Bancorp	MTL	46	DC	1,023	9	4.00 e	4.40 e	10	2.8	B+	5
Mercantile Bankshares	MRBK	28	DC	455	8	2.15 e	2.35 e	12	3.3	A	3
Meridian Bancorp	MRDN	47	DC	1,226	9	3.05 e	3.40 e	14	3.1	A-	3
Midlantic Corp	MIDL	66	DC	1,078	8	4.35 e	4.60 e	14	1.9	B-	3
NationsBank Corp	NB	70	DC	13,113	10	7.05 e	7.90 e	9	3.3	A-	4
Natl City Corp	NCC	33	DC	2,905	9	2.93 e	3.20 e	10	3.9	A-	4
Northern Trust	NTRS	56	DC	1,479	10	3.65 e	4.05 e	14	2.2	B+	4
Norwest Corp	NOB	33	DC	6,032	11	2.80 e	3.15 e	10	2.9	A-	4
Old Kent Finl	OKEN	41	DC	875	8	3.25 e	3.70 e	11	3.1	A+	4
PNC Bank Corp	PNC	32	DC	4,684	8	2.40 e	2.75 e	12	4.3	B	3
Regions Financial	RGBK	43	DC	929	11	3.71 e	4.10 e	10	3	A+	4
Republic New York	RNB	62	DC	2,560	8	4.85 e	6.75 e	9	2.3	B+	3
Signet Banking	SBK	24	DC	1,375	9	2.00 e	2.20 e	11	3.3	B	3
Star Banc Corp	STB	60	DC	687	10	4.50 e	5.10 e	12	2.6	A+	4
State Str Boston	STT	45	DC	1,886	12	2.95 e	3.25 e	14	1.6	A+	3
Summit Bancorp'n	SUBN	32	DC	394	NE	2.10 e	2.30 e	14	2.6	A-	3
SunTrust Banks	STI	69	DC	3,252	10	4.95 e	5.35 e	13	2.3	A+	3
Synovus Financial	SNV	29	DC	693	13	1.48 e	1.72 e	17	1.8	A+	4
U.S. Bancorp	USBC	34	DC	1,936	9	2.80 e	3.00 e	11	3.3	A	3
U.S. Trust	USTC	50	DC	457	12	3.20 e	3.60 e	14	Nil	A-	4
UJB Financial	UJB	36	DC	1,062	10	3.00 e	3.30 e	11	3.5	A-	4
Union Bank	UBNK	54	DC	1,246	6	5.30 e	5.70 e	10	2.5	A-	4
Union Planters	UPC	32	DC	758	10	3.02 e	3.30 e	10	3.1	B	4
Wachovia Corp	WB	46	DC	2,750	9	3.55 e	3.80 e	12	3.1	A-	3
Wells Fargo	WFC	216	DC	4,965	10	19.00 e	21.00 e	10	2.1	B+	3
Wilmington Trust Corp	WILM	31	DC	421	10	2.65 e	2.90 e	11	3.8	A+	4
Zions Bancorp	ZION	80	DC	427	9	5.42 e	6.00 e	13	2	B+	3

Manufactured   Housing

Industry / Company	Ticker	12/95 Price	F-Y End	Rev. ($)	5-Yr. EPS Gr.(%)	EPS 1995	EPS 1996	P/E 1996	Yld. (%)	Com. Stk. Rank	STARS 5=Buy 1=Sell
Clayton Homes	CMH	21	JE	758	18	0.92	1.12 e	19	0.3	B+	5
Fleetwood Enterpr	FLE	26	AP	2,856	12	1.82	1.75 e	15	2.3	B+	3
Oakwood Homes	OH	38	SP	821	18	1.97 p	2.40 e	16	0.2	A-	4

Manufacturing   (Diversified)

Industry / Company	Ticker	12/95 Price	F-Y End	Rev. ($)	5-Yr. EPS Gr.(%)	EPS 1995	EPS 1996	P/E 1996	Yld. (%)	Com. Stk. Rank	STARS 5=Buy 1=Sell
AlliedSignal Inc	ALD	48	DC	12,817	12	3.10 e	3.55 e	13	1.6	B+	4
Crane Co	CR	37	DC	1,653	14	2.45 e	2.70 e	14	2	B+	3
Dover Corp	DOV	37	DC	3,085	14	2.45 e	2.65 e	14	1.6	A	3
Illinois Tool Works	ITW	59	DC	3,461	12	3.30 e	3.80 e	16	1.1	A+	3
Johnson Controls	JCI	69	SP	8,330	12	4.53	5.00 e	14	2.3	A-	3
Millipore Corp	MIL	41	DC	497	15	1.85 e	2.20 e	19	0.7	B+	4
Pall Corp	PLL	27	JL	823	15	1.04 y	1.20 e	22	1.5	A	4
Parker-Hannifin	PH	34	JE	3,214	11	2.96	3.30 e	10	2.1	B+	4
TRINOVA Corp	TNV	29	DC	1,795	12	3.20 e	3.40 e	8	2.5	B-	4
Tyco International	TYC	36	JE	4,535	18	1.43 y	2.00 e	18	0.5	B+	4

Industry / Company	Ticker	12/95 Price	F-Y End	Rev. ($)	5-Yr. EPS Gr.(%)	EPS 1995	EPS 1996	P/E 1996	Yld. (%)	Com. Stk. Rank	STARS 5=Buy 1=Sell
Medical Products & Supplies											
Acuson Corp	ACN	12	DC	350	9	0.25 e	0.45 e	28	Nil	B	2
Allergan, Inc	AGN	33	DC	947	12	1.12 e	2.10 e	15	1.4	NR	3
AMSCO Intl	ASZ	15	DC	483	11	1.00 e	1.15 e	13	Nil	NR	3
Bard (C.R.)	BCR	32	DC	1,018	12	1.65 e	2.00 e	16	1.9	A-	3
Bausch & Lomb	BOL	40	DC	1,851	9	2.25 e	2.65 e	15	2.6	A-	3
Baxter International	BAX	42	DC	9,324	9	2.35 e	2.60 e	16	2.6	B+	4
Becton, Dickinson	BDX	75	SP	2,713	11	3.59	4.05 e	19	1.2	A+	4
Biomet, Inc	BMET	18	MY	452	20	0.69	0.85 e	21	Nil	B+	4
Boston Scientific	BSX	49	DC	449	20	0.48 e	1.65 e	30	Nil	NR	5
Cordis Corp	CORD	101	JE	443	18	3.00	3.90 e	26	Nil	B-	3
Hillenbrand Indus	HB	34	NV	1,577	12	1.65 e	1.95 e	17	1.7	A	3
Medtronic, Inc	MDT	56	AP	1,742	19	1.27	1.85 e	30	0.4	A+	5
Nellcor Puritan Bennett	NELL	58	JE	264	17	2.20	2.70 e	21	Nil	B+	4
St. Jude Medical	STJM	43	DC	360	15	1.80 e	2.10 e	20	Nil	B+	4
Stryker Corp	STRY	53	DC	682	18	1.80 e	2.15 e	24	0.1	A-	3
U.S. Surgical	USS	21	DC	919	19	1.05 e	1.20 e	18	0.3	B+	3
Metals (Misc.)											
ASARCO Inc	AR	32	DC	2,032	5	5.60 e	5.00 e	6	2.5	B-	4
Cyprus Amax Minerals	CYM	26	DC	2,788	10	1.30 e	4.45 e	6	3	B-	4
Freep't McMoRan C&G B	FCX	28	DC	1,212	NE	1.05 e	1.50 e	19	3.2	NR	4
Inco Ltd	N	33	DC	2,484	8	2.05 e	3.25 e	10	1.2	B-	3
Phelps Dodge	PD	62	DC	3,289	13	10.30 e	9.75 e	6	2.8	B	4
Miscellaneous											
Corning Inc	GLW	32	DC	4,799	13	-0.29 e	1.60 e	20	2.2	A-	3
Danaher Corp	DHR	32	DC	1,289	16	1.80 e	2.00 e	16	0.2	B	3
Hanson plc ADR	HAN	15	SP	17,660	10	1.50 e	1.50 e	10	6.8	NR	5
Harsco Corp	HSC	58	DC	1,357	12	3.65 e	4.35 e	13	2.6	B+	4
Ionics Inc	ION	44	DC	222	18	1.30 e	1.60 e	27	Nil	B+	4
Kennametal, Inc	KMT	32	JE	984	14	2.58	3.00 e	11	1.8	B+	4
Litton Indus	LIT	45	JL	3,320	8	2.84	3.05 e	15	Nil	B	3
Minnesota Min'g/Mfg	MMM	66	DC	15,079	10	3.40 e	3.90 e	17	2.8	A+	4
PRI Automation	PRIA	35	SP	64	25	1.16 p	1.60 e	22	Nil	NR	3
Money Center Banks											
Bank of New York	BK	49	DC	4,251	9	4.55 e	5.00 e	10	2.9	B	4
BankAmerica Corp	BAC	65	DC	16,531	9	6.30 e	7.10 e	9	2.8	B	5
Bankers Trust NY	BT	67	DC	7,503	8	2.10 e	6.40 e	10	6	B+	2
Chase Manhattan	CMB	60	DC	11,817	8	5.60 e	6.50 e	9	2.9	B	4
Chemical Banking Corp	CHL	59	DC	12,685	8	6.55 e	7.15 e	8	3.4	B-	4
Citicorp	CCI	67	DC	31,650	10	7.10 e	7.90 e	9	1.7	B-	5
Morgan (J.P.)	JPM	80	DC	11,915	9	6.35 e	7.00 e	11	4	B+	4
Multi-Line Insurance											
20th Century Indus	TW	20	DC	1,180	20	0.85 e	1.45 e	14	Nil	C	3
Berkley (W.R.)	BKLY	54	DC	831	12	2.75 e	3.40 e	16	0.8	B+	3
Chubb Corp	CB	97	DC	5,710	11	7.00 e	7.70 e	13	2	A	4
GEICO Corp	GEC	70	DC	2,716	12	3.45 e	3.85 e	18	1.5	A	3
Genl Re Corp	GRN	155	DC	3,837	13	9.25 e	10.45 e	15	1.2	A	5
Hartford Stm Boiler Ins	HSB	50	DC	604	9	3.00 e	3.25 e	15	4.5	B+	3
Loews Corp	LTR	78	DC	13,515	20	6.00 e	7.00 e	11	1.2	A-	3
MBIA Inc	MBI	75	DC	440	12	6.40 e	7.25 e	10	1.8	NR	4
NAC Re Corp	NRC	36	DC	478	13	2.35 e	2.80 e	13	0.5	B+	3
Ohio Casualty	OCAS	39	DC	1,559	10	2.50 e	3.50 e	11	3.9	B+	3
Progressive Corp,Ohio	PGR	49	DC	2,415	13	3.10 e	3.45 e	14	0.4	B+	3
SAFECO Corp	SAFC	35	DC	3,537	10	2.65 e	3.05 e	11	3	A-	3
St. Paul Cos	SPC	56	DC	4,701	9	5.00 e	5.70 e	10	2.8	A-	4
Transatlantic Holdings	TRH	73	DC	1,005	14	5.30 e	6.25 e	12	0.6	B+	5
USF&G Corp	FG	17	DC	3,221	10	1.35 e	1.55 e	11	1.1	B-	3

Industry / Company	Ticker	12/95 Price	F-Y End	Rev. ($)	5-Yr. EPS Gr.(%)	EPS 1995	EPS 1996	P/E 1996	Yld. (%)	Com. Stk. Rank	STARS 5=Buy 1=Sell
Natural Gas											
Atlanta Gas Light	ATG	20	SP	1,063	4	0.50	1.35 e	15	5.3	B+	3
British Gas ADS	BRG	39	DC	15,129	12	3.30 e	3.55 e	11	5.8	NR	1
Brooklyn Union Gas	BU	29	SP	1,216	4	1.90	1.95 e	15	4.8	A-	3
Coastal Corp	CGP	37	DC	10,215	13	2.35 e	2.50 e	15	1	B+	4
Columbia Gas System	CG	44	DC	2,833	7	5.45 e	2.60 e	17	Nil	NR	4
Consolidated Nat Gas	CNG	45	DC	3,036	8	0.20 e	2.40 e	19	4.2	B+	4
El Paso Natural Gas	EPG	29	DC	870	7	2.50 e	2.60 e	11	4.5	NR	3
Enron Corp	ENE	38	DC	8,905	13	2.10 e	2.25 e	17	2.2	B+	3
ENSERCH Corp	ENS	16	DC	1,857	10	0.40 e	0.75 e	22	1.2	B	3
MCN Corp	MCN	23	DC	1,546	8	1.50 e	1.60 e	15	4	NR	4
NICOR Inc	GAS	28	DC	1,609	4	1.90 e	2.05 e	13	4.6	B+	3
NorAm Energy	NAE	9	DC	2,801	10	0.38 e	0.43 e	21	3.1	B	3
Northern Border Ptnrs L.P.	NBP	23	DC	212	4	1.90 e	1.95 e	12	9.4	NR	2
Nova Corp	NVA	8	DC	3,724	12	1.73 ie	1.70 ei	5	Nil	B	3
ONEOK Inc	OKE	23	AU	950	6	1.58	1.65 e	14	5	B	3
Pacific Enterprises	PET	28	DC	2,664	5	2.10 e	2.15 e	13	4.8	B-	3
Panhandle East'n	PEL	28	DC	4,585	8	2.00 e	2.20 e	13	3.2	B	4
Peoples Energy	PGL	32	SP	1,033	3	1.78	2.15 e	15	5.6	B+	3
Questar Corp	STR	34	DC	670	8	2.10 e	2.30 e	15	3.5	A-	3
Seagull Energy	SGO	22	DC	408	16	0.21 e	0.20 e	111	Nil	B-	3
Sonat, Inc	SNT	36	DC	1,774	9	2.62 e	1.70 e	21	3	B	3
TransCanada P.L.	TRP	14	DC	5,204	9	1.75 ei	1.75 ei	8	Nil	B	2
Williams Cos	WMB	44	DC	1,751	12	2.60 e	3.05 e	14	2.4	B+	5
Office Equipment & Supplies											
Alco Standard	ASN	46	SP	9,892	19	1.67	2.25 e	20	1.2	B+	3
Moore Corp Ltd	MCL	19	DC	2,401	17	2.70 e	1.00 e	19	5	B-	2
Pitney Bowes	PBI	47	DC	3,271	10	2.65 e	2.95 e	16	2.5	A+	3
Reynolds & Reynolds A	REY	39	SP	911	17	1.85	2.20 e	18	1.2	B+	5
Wallace Computer Svc	WCS	55	JL	713	13	2.46	3.55 e	15	1.5	A	4
Xerox Corp	XRX	137	DC	17,837	18	8.80 e	10.45 e	13	2.1	B-	4
Oil & Gas Drilling											
Global Marine	GLM	9	DC	359	13	0.30 e	0.55 e	16	Nil	NR	5
Helmerich & Payne	HP	30	SP	326	13	0.40	1.05 e	28	1.6	B	3
Nabors Industries	NBR	11	SP	573	15	0.58 po	0.70 e	16	Nil	B-	5
Noble Drilling Corp	NDCO	9	DC	352	18	-0.02 e	0.25 e	36	Nil	NR	3
Rowan Cos	RDC	10	DC	438	9	-0.23 e	0.20 e	48	Nil	C	5
Oil (Domestic Integrated)											
Amerada Hess	AHC	53	DC	6,602	17	-0.13 e	1.35 e	39	1.1	B-	5
Ashland Inc	ASH	35	SP	11,179	12	0.08	3.15 e	11	3.1	B	4
Atlantic Richfield	ARC	111	DC	15,035	9	8.25 e	8.55 e	13	4.9	B+	4
Kerr-McGee	KMG	64	DC	3,353	14	-0.69 e	3.10 e	20	2.5	B	3
Louisiana Land/Exp	LLX	43	DC	802	27	0.49 e	1.15 e	37	0.5	B-	4
Murphy Oil	MUR	42	DC	1,768	10	1.40 e	2.00 e	21	3.1	B	3
Occidental Petrol'm	OXY	21	DC	9,236	8	1.75 e	1.70 e	13	4.6	B-	2
Pennzoil Co.	PZL	42	DC	2,563	13	-5.84 e	1.15 e	37	2.3	B-	2
Phillips Petroleum	P	34	DC	12,211	14	2.05 e	2.20 e	16	3.5	B	3
Quaker State Corp	KSF	13	DC	755	18	0.45 e	0.80 e	16	3.1	B-	5
Sun Co	SUN	27	DC	7,702	14	2.41 e	2.25 e	12	3.6	NR	3
Tosco Corp	TOS	38	DC	6,366	14	1.95 e	2.95 e	13	1.6	B	3
Ultramar Corp	ULR	26	DC	2,475	11	1.22 e	2.25 e	11	4.2	NR	3
Unocal Corp	UCL	29	DC	7,965	13	1.13 e	1.60 e	18	2.7	B	4
USX-Marathon Grp	MRO	20	DC	12,757	15	1.21 e	1.30 e	15	3.4	NR	4
Oil (Exploration & Production)											
Anadarko Petroleum	APC	54	DC	482	18	0.39 e	1.10 e	49	0.5	B	3
Apache Corp	APA	30	DC	546	13	0.40 e	1.00 e	30	0.9	B-	4
Burlington Resources	BR	39	DC	1,055	13	-2.00 e	0.90 e	44	1.4	NR	3

Industry / Company	Ticker	12/95 Price	F-Y End	Rev. ($)	5-Yr. EPS Gr.(%)	EPS 1995	EPS 1996	P/E 1996	Yld. (%)	Com. Stk. Rank	STARS 5=Buy 1=Sell
Enron Oil & Gas	EOG	24	DC	572	14	0.95 e	1.05 e	23	0.5	NR	3
Mesa Inc	MXP	4	DC	229	8	-1.05 e	-1.10 e	NM	Nil	C	2
Noble Affiliates	NBL	30	DC	358	11	-0.01 e	0.95 e	31	0.5	B	3
Oryx Energy Co	ORX	13	DC	1,072	9	1.51 e	0.70 e	19	Nil	NR	2
Pogo Producing	PPP	28	DC	174	16	0.35 e	0.65 e	43	0.4	B-	2
Santa Fe Energy Res	SFR	10	DC	391	9	0.12 e	0.25 e	39	Nil	NR	3
Sceptre Resources	SRL	6	DC	248	0	0.35 ie	0.55 ei	11	Nil	B-	4
Union Texas Petroleum	UTH	19	DC	748	12	1.15 e	1.25 e	16	1	B	3

Oil (International Integrated)

Industry / Company	Ticker	12/95 Price	F-Y End	Rev. ($)	5-Yr. EPS Gr.(%)	EPS 1995	EPS 1996	P/E 1996	Yld. (%)	Com. Stk. Rank	STARS 5=Buy 1=Sell
Amoco Corp	AN	72	DC	26,048	9	4.30 e	4.65 e	15	3.3	B	3
British Petrol ADS	BP	102	DC	51,618	11	6.00 e	7.40 e	14	2.7	NR	5
Chevron Corp	CHV	52	DC	30,340	10	2.87 e	3.50 e	15	3.8	B	3
Elf Aquitaine ADS	ELF	37	DC	40,952	17	1.80 e	2.35 e	16	2.7	NR	3
ENI S.p.A. ADS	E	34	DC	31,032	NE	3.45 e	4.00 e	9	Nil	NR	4
Exxon Corp	XON	81	DC	99,683	7	5.08 e	5.30 e	15	3.6	B+	4
Imperial Oil Ltd	IMO	36	DC	9,011	20	2.93 ei	3.10 ei	12	Nil	B	4
Mobil Corp	MOB	112	DC	66,757	10	6.50 e	7.40 e	15	3.3	B+	5
Norsk Hydro A.S. ADS	NHY	42	DC	10,412	22	3.58 e	3.90 e	11	1.3	NR	3
Repsol S.A. ADS	REP	33	DC	18,005	14	3.25 e	3.60 e	9	2.8	NR	4
Royal Dutch Petrol	RD	141	DC	0	8	8.81 e	8.80 e	16	3.2	A	4
Shell Transp/Trad ADR	SC	82	DC	38,644	9	4.89 e	5.87 e	14	3.5	A-	4
Texaco Inc	TX	79	DC	32,540	10	4.10 e	4.50 e	17	4	B	4
TOTAL B ADS	TOT	34	DC	25,256	16	1.75 e	2.15 e	16	1.8	NR	4
YPF Soc. Anonima ADS	YPF	22	DC	4,201	14	2.35 e	2.10 e	10	3.6	NR	3

Oil Well Equipment & Services

Industry / Company	Ticker	12/95 Price	F-Y End	Rev. ($)	5-Yr. EPS Gr.(%)	EPS 1995	EPS 1996	P/E 1996	Yld. (%)	Com. Stk. Rank	STARS 5=Buy 1=Sell
Baker Hughes Inc	BHI	24	SP	2,637	16	0.67 y	1.00 e	24	1.8	B	5
Dresser Industries	DI	24	OC	5,629	13	1.17 py	1.35 e	18	2.7	B	4
Halliburton Co	HAL	51	DC	5,741	17	2.00 e	2.50 e	20	1.9	B-	5
Input/Output Inc	IO	58	MY	135	21	1.31	1.65 e	35	Nil	NR	4
McDermott Intl	MDR	22	MR	3,044	12	0.70 e	1.40 e	16	4.5	B-	1
Schlumberger Ltd	SLB	69	DC	6,697	16	2.72 e	3.30 e	21	2.1	B+	4
Smith Intl	SII	24	DC	654	13	1.12 e	1.20 e	20	Nil	B-	3
Tidewater Inc	TDW	32	MR	539	22	1.25 e	1.55 e	20	1.5	B	4
Western Atlas	WAI	51	DC	2,166	15	1.85 e	2.30 e	22	Nil	NR	4

Paper & Forest Products

Industry / Company	Ticker	12/95 Price	F-Y End	Rev. ($)	5-Yr. EPS Gr.(%)	EPS 1995	EPS 1996	P/E 1996	Yld. (%)	Com. Stk. Rank	STARS 5=Buy 1=Sell
Boise Cascade	BCC	35	DC	4,140	7	5.60 e	5.75 e	6	1.7	B-	3
Bowater, Inc	BOW	36	DC	1,359	7	5.77 e	7.25 e	5	1.6	B-	4
Champion Intl	CHA	42	DC	5,318	7	7.80 e	8.25 e	5	0.4	B-	3
Chesapeake Corp	CSK	30	DC	991	20	3.85 e	4.55 e	7	2.7	B-	4
Consolidated Papers	CDP	56	DC	1,028	16	4.90 e	6.00 e	9	2.6	B+	3
Federal Paper Board	FBO	52	DC	1,570	12	5.05 e	5.95 e	9	3	B	3
Georgia-Pacific	GP	69	DC	12,738	9	11.15 e	9.50 e	7	2.9	B-	2
Glatfelter (P. H.)	GLT	17	DC	478	13	1.55 e	1.85 e	9	4	B	4
Intl Paper	IP	38	DC	14,966	23	4.70 e	5.00 e	8	2.6	B+	3
James River Corp	JR	24	DC	5,417	7	0.88 e	2.00 e	12	2.4	B-	3
Jefferson Smurfit	JJSC	10	DC	3,233	15	2.30 e	2.50 e	4	Nil	NR	3
Louisiana Pacific	LPX	24	DC	3,040	10	2.10 e	2.40 e	10	2.3	B+	3
Mead Corp	MEA	52	DC	4,558	9	6.30 e	7.25 e	7	2.1	B-	3
Potlatch Corp	PCH	40	DC	1,471	8	3.85 e	4.50 e	9	4.1	B+	3
Rayonier Inc	RYN	33	DC	1,070	15	4.80 e	4.70 e	7	2.9	NR	3
Sonoco Products	SON	26	DC	2,300	13	1.75 e	1.95 e	13	2.2	A-	3
Union Camp	UCC	48	DC	3,396	10	6.55 e	5.80 e	8	3.7	B	2
Westvaco Corp	W	28	OC	3,272	14	2.80 y	3.50 e	8	3.1	B	4
Weyerhaeuser Co	WY	43	DC	10,398	11	5.00 e	6.00 e	7	3.6	B+	4
Willamette Indus	WMTT	56	DC	3,008	12	9.60 e	10.00 e	6	2.1	B+	3

Personal Loans

Industry / Company	Ticker	12/95 Price	F-Y End	Rev. ($)	5-Yr. EPS Gr.(%)	EPS 1995	EPS 1996	P/E 1996	Yld. (%)	Com. Stk. Rank	STARS 5=Buy 1=Sell
Beneficial Corp	BNL	47	DC	2,137	12	3.75 e	4.90 e	10	4	B+	3

Industry / Company	Ticker	12/95 Price	F-Y End	Rev. ($)	5-Yr. EPS Gr.(%)	EPS 1995	EPS 1996	P/E 1996	Yld. (%)	Com. Stk. Rank	STARS 5=Buy 1=Sell
Household Intl	HI	60	DC	4,603	15	4.15 e	4.90 e	12	2.2	B+	3
Mercury Finance	MFN	13	DC	252	23	0.63 e	0.79 e	17	2.2	A-	4
Student Loan Mktg	SLM	66	DC	2,852	12	4.65 e	5.20 e	13	2.4	A	3
Photography/Imaging											
Eastman Kodak	EK	67	DC	13,557	12	3.85 e	4.20 e	16	2.3	B	4
Polaroid Corp	PRD	47	DC	2,313	11	-2.75 e	2.20 e	22	1.2	B	2
Pollution Control											
Browning-Ferris Indus	BFI	29	SP	5,779	14	1.93	2.20 e	13	2.3	A-	4
Gundle/SLT Environmental	GUN	6	DC	130	NE	-0.25 e	0.30 e	19	Nil	NR	3
Laidlaw Inc Cl B	LDW.B	10	AU	2,517	13	0.48 o	0.60 e	17	Nil	B+	3
Rollins Environ Sv	REN	3	SP	217	11	-0.30	-0.15 e	NM	Nil	C	2
Sanifill Inc	FIL	33	DC	173	21	1.40 e	1.65 e	20	Nil	B	3
Wheelabrator Tech	WTI	17	DC	1,325	12	1.10 e	1.20 e	14	0.6	NR	4
WMX Technologies	WMX	30	DC	10,097	11	1.60 e	2.05 e	15	2	A-	3
Property-Casualty Insurance											
Aetna Life & Casualty	AET	69	DC	17,525	8	2.50 e	7.00 e	10	3.9	B-	3
Allstate Corp	ALL	41	DC	21,464	11	3.50 e	3.75 e	11	1.8	NR	5
Amer Intl Group	AIG	93	DC	22,442	14	5.10 e	5.85 e	16	0.3	A+	5
Aon Corp	AOC	50	DC	4,157	10	3.58 e	3.85 e	13	2.7	A-	3
CIGNA Corp	CI	103	DC	18,392	9	-0.85 e	10.00 e	10	2.9	B+	3
CNA Financial	CNA	114	DC	11,000	13	7.65 e	8.65 e	13	Nil	B-	3
ITT Hartford Group	HIG	48	DC	11,102	NE	4.00 e	4.75 e	10	3.3	NR	4
Kemper Corp	KEM	50	DC	1,602	10	4.00 e	4.50 e	11	1.8	B	3
Publishing											
Amer Greetings Cl A	AGREA	28	FB	1,869	12	1.50 e	2.10 e	13	2.3	A	3
Banta Corp	BNTA	44	DC	811	13	2.60 e	2.90 e	15	1.4	A-	3
Dun & Bradstreet	DNB	65	DC	4,896	8	3.80 e	4.05 e	16	4	A	4
Gartner Group A	GART	48	SP	229	27	0.56 e	0.70 e	68	Nil	NR	2
Gibson Greetings	GIBG	16	DC	549	8	-2.90 e	1.20 e	13	Nil	B	4
Harcourt General	H	42	OC	3,035	13	2.16 p	2.50 e	17	1.6	B+	4
Houghton Mifflin	HTN	43	DC	483	15	-0.50 e	3.15 e	14	2.2	A-	4
Marvel Entertainment Grp	MRV	13	DC	515	22	0.25 e	0.80 e	16	Nil	NR	3
Meredith Corp	MDP	42	JE	885	19	1.44 oy	1.60 e	26	0.9	B	3
Reader's Digest Assn A	RDA	51	JE	3,069	11	2.35 o	2.60 e	20	3.5	A-	3
Reuters Hldgs ADS	RTRSY	55	DC	3,625	16	2.35 e	2.70 e	20	1.5	NR	4
Scholastic Corp	SCHL	78	MY	750	13	2.38 o	2.90 e	27	Nil	NR	4
Western Publishing	WPGI	8	JA	403	NE	-3.30 e	-1.40 e	NM	Nil	C	2
Publishing (Newspapers)											
Belo (A.H.)Cl A	BLC	35	DC	628	14	1.80 e	2.20 e	16	0.9	B+	4
Dow Jones & Co	DJ	40	DC	2,091	13	2.00 e	2.25 e	18	2.3	A	3
Gannett Co	GCI	61	DC	3,825	11	3.40 e	3.50 e	18	2.2	A	3
Hollinger Intl A	HOLI	11	DC	423	17	0.60 e	0.90 e	12	0.9	NR	5
Knight-Ridder Inc	KRI	63	DC	2,649	10	3.00 e	3.50 e	18	2.3	A-	3
McClatchy Newspapers A	MNI	23	DC	471	11	1.20 e	1.35 e	17	1.6	B	3
Media General Cl A	MEG.A	30	DC	626	16	1.85 e	2.20 e	14	1.5	B	3
New York Times Cl A	NYT.A	30	DC	2,358	14	1.40 e	1.60 e	19	1.8	B+	3
News Corp Ltd ADS	NWS	21	JE	8,993	13	1.36 w	1.45 e	15	0.3	NR	4
Times Mirror A	TMC	34	DC	3,357	13	-3.39 e	1.65 e	21	0.7	B-	3
Tribune Co.	TRB	61	DC	2,155	14	3.95 e	4.45 e	14	1.8	B+	4
Washington Post B	WPO	282	DC	1,614	10	17.65 e	18.75 e	15	1.5	B+	4
Railroads											
Burlington Northern Santa Fe	BNI	78	DC	4,995	12	5.65 e	6.50 e	12	1.5	NR	4
Canadian Pacific, Ord	CP	18	DC	7,053	21	1.45 ei	2.05 ei	9	Nil	B-	3
Conrail Inc	CRR	70	DC	3,733	11	5.55 e	5.95 e	12	2.4	B	4
CSX Corp	CSX	46	DC	9,608	12	2.65 e	3.85 e	12	2.2	B+	4

Industry / Company	Ticker	12/95 Price	F-Y End	Rev. ($)	5-Yr. EPS Gr.(%)	EPS 1995	EPS 1996	P/E 1996	Yld. (%)	Com. Stk. Rank	STARS 5=Buy 1=Sell
GATX Corp	GMT	49	DC	1,155	15	4.55 e	5.00 e	10	3.2	A-	4
Illinois Central Corp	IC	38	DC	594	13	2.95 e	3.45 e	11	3	NR	5
Kansas City So. Ind	KSU	46	DC	1,098	16	2.15 e	3.10 e	15	0.6	B	3
Norfolk Southern	NSC	79	DC	4,581	9	5.30 e	5.95 e	13	2.6	A	3
Southern Pacific Rail	RSP	24	DC	3,143	17	0.20 e	1.00 e	24	Nil	NR	3
Union Pacific	UNP	66	DC	7,798	11	3.05 e	4.15 e	16	2.6	A-	3
Restaurants											
Boston Chicken	BOST	32	DC	96	36	0.63 e	0.90 e	36	Nil	NR	3
Brinker Intl	EAT	15	JE	1,042	16	0.98	1.00 e	15	Nil	B+	2
Buffets Inc	BOCB	14	DC	410	16	0.82 e	0.95 e	14	Nil	B+	4
Consolidated Products	COPI	15	SP	187	22	0.86	0.91 e	16	Nil	NR	4
Cracker Brl Old Ctry	CBRL	17	JL	783	19	1.09	1.20 e	14	0.1	A	3
DAKA Intl	DKAI	28	JE	321	NE	2.03	2.10 e	13	Nil	B-	4
Intl Dairy Queen A	INDQA	23	NV	341	10	1.40 e	1.55 e	15	Nil	B+	4
Luby's Cafeterias	LUB	22	AU	419	9	1.55	1.65 e	13	3.2	A	3
McDonald's Corp	MCD	45	DC	8,321	14	1.95 e	2.20 e	21	0.5	A+	3
Morrison Restaurants	RI	14	MY	1,035	16	1.73	1.05 e	13	2.6	A	3
Outback Steakhouse	OSSI	36	DC	452	29	1.17 e	1.55 e	23	Nil	NR	3
Ryan's Family Stk Hse	RYAN	7	DC	448	13	0.61 e	0.70 e	10	Nil	B+	4
Sbarro Inc	SBA	22	DC	296	12	1.05 e	1.80 e	12	3.5	B+	3
Shoney's Inc	SHN	10	OC	1,166	11	0.66 e	0.90 e	11	Nil	B	2
Sizzler International	SZ	4	AP	462	NE	0.24	0.19 e	22	Nil	NR	2
Wendy's Intl	WEN	21	DC	1,398	18	1.12 e	1.30 e	16	1.1	B+	4
Retail (Department Stores)											
Dillard Dept Str A	DDS	29	JA	5,546	12	2.30 e	2.65 e	11	0.4	A+	3
Federated Dept Stores	FD	27	JA	8,316	14	0.75 e	2.10 e	13	Nil	NR	3
Kohl's Corp	KSS	53	JA	1,554	20	1.95 e	2.65 e	20	Nil	NR	3
May Dept Stores	MA	42	JA	12,223	11	3.20 e	3.50 e	12	2.7	A+	3
Mercantile Stores	MST	46	JA	2,820	8	2.90 e	3.40 e	14	2.2	B+	3
Neiman-Marcus Group	NMG	24	JL	1,888	19	0.70	1.13 e	21	Nil	NR	3
Nordstrom, Inc	NOBE	41	JA	3,894	13	2.30 e	2.70 e	15	1.2	A+	3
Penney (J.C.)	JCP	48	JA	20,380	9	3.95 e	4.45 e	11	4	A-	3
Retail (Drug Stores)											
Eckerd Corp	ECK	45	JA	4,549	12	2.85 e	3.25 e	14	Nil	NR	4
Genovese Drug Str A	GDX.A	11	JA	570	10	0.95 e	0.90 e	13	2.1	A	3
Longs Drug Stores	LDG	48	JA	2,558	6	2.52 e	2.70 e	18	2.3	A-	3
Revco D.S.	RXR	28	MY	4,432	20	0.95 y	1.15 e	25	Nil	NR	3
Rite Aid	RAD	34	FB	4,534	11	1.95 e	2.00 e	17	1.9	A-	4
Walgreen Co	WAG	30	AU	10,395	13	1.30	1.47 e	20	1.4	A+	3
Retail (Food Chains)											
Albertson's, Inc	ABS	33	JA	11,895	13	1.85 e	2.05 e	16	1.5	A+	3
Amer Stores	ASC	27	JA	18,355	9	2.15 e	2.35 e	11	2	A	3
Giant Food Cl A	GFS.A	32	FB	3,696	10	1.70 e	1.85 e	17	2.3	A-	3
Great Atl & Pac Tea	GAP	23	FB	10,332	11	1.05 e	1.15 e	20	0.8	B-	2
Kroger Co	KR	37	DC	22,959	13	2.70 e	3.15 e	12	Nil	B	5
Safeway Inc	SWY	52	DC	15,627	17	2.60 e	3.00 e	17	Nil	NR	4
Stop & Shop Cos	SHP	23	JA	3,789	13	1.55 e	1.90 e	12	Nil	NR	3
Whole Foods Market	WFMI	14	SP	496	20	0.58 p	0.80 e	17	Nil	NR	3
Winn-Dixie Stores	WIN	37	JE	11,788	11	1.55	1.75 e	21	2.4	A+	3
Retail (General Merchandise)											
Caldor Corp	CLD	3	JA	2,749	14	-2.50 e	0.50 e	7	Nil	D	3
Dayton Hudson	DH	75	JA	21,311	11	4.95 e	6.20 e	12	2.3	A	3
Dollar General	DG	21	JA	1,449	21	1.28 e	1.60 e	13	0.9	A	4
Family Dollar Stores	FDO	14	AU	1,547	14	1.03	1.10 e	12	2.9	A-	2
K mart	KM	7	JA	34,313	13	0.05 e	0.70 e	10	Nil	B+	2
MacFrugals Bargains	MFI	14	JA	682	11	1.55 e	1.75 e	8	Nil	B	4

Industry / Company	Ticker	12/95 Price	F-Y End	Rev. ($)	5-Yr. EPS Gr.(%)	EPS 1995	EPS 1996	P/E 1996	Yld. (%)	Com. Stk. Rank	STARS 5=Buy 1=Sell
Sears,Roebuck	S	39	DC	54,559	12	2.50 e	3.00 e	13	2.3	B-	4
Wal-Mart Stores	WMT	22	JA	82,494	15	1.30 e	1.50 e	15	0.8	A+	3
Retail (Specialty)											
AutoZone Inc	AZO	29	AU	1,808	24	0.93	1.15 e	25	Nil	B+	4
Barnes & Noble	BKS	29	JA	1,623	30	1.15 e	1.50 e	19	Nil	NR	3
Bed Bath & Beyond	BBBY	39	FB	440	24	1.10 e	1.40 e	28	Nil	NR	4
Best Buy Co	BBY	16	FB	5,080	19	1.30 e	1.50 e	11	Nil	B	3
Circuit City Stores	CC	28	FB	5,583	17	1.95 e	2.30 e	12	0.4	A	3
Dart Group Cl A	DARTA	94	JA	967	NE	1.50 e	2.50 e	37	0.1	B-	4
Hi-Lo Automotive	HLO	5	DC	235	11	0.40 e	0.50 e	10	Nil	NR	2
Home Depot	HD	48	JA	12,477	26	1.50 e	1.90 e	25	0.4	A	3
Home Shopping Network	HSN	9	DC	1,127	0	-0.30 e	0.25 e	36	Nil	B-	3
Intelligent Electronics	INEL	6	JA	3,208	15	-0.42 e	0.73 e	8	6.6	NR	2
Jostens Inc	JOS	24	JE	665	12	1.12 y	1.45 e	17	3.6	B+	3
Lands' End	LE	14	JA	992	12	0.85 e	1.05 e	13	Nil	B+	2
Lowe's Cos	LOW	34	JA	6,111	22	1.45 e	1.70 e	20	0.5	A-	3
Melville Corp	MES	31	DC	11,286	8	-5.60 e	2.51 e	12	4.9	A-	3
OfficeMax Inc	OMX	22	JA	1,841	30	1.50 e	0.90 e	25	Nil	NR	5
Pep Boys-Man,Mo,Ja	PBY	26	JA	1,407	19	1.40 e	1.70 e	15	0.7	A+	3
Price/Costco Inc	PCCW	15	AU	18,247	12	0.68	1.25 e	12	Nil	NR	3
Sports Authority	TSA	20	JA	839	25	1.07 e	1.35 e	15	Nil	NR	4
Tandy Corp	TAN	42	DC	4,944	13	3.55 e	4.30 e	10	1.9	B	3
Toys R Us	TOY	22	JA	8,746	13	1.75 e	2.05 e	11	Nil	B+	3
Tractor Supply	TSCO	20	DC	330	20	1.35 e	1.70 e	12	Nil	NR	4
Waban Inc	WBN	19	JA	3,650	13	2.20 e	2.50 e	7	Nil	NR	4
Woolworth Corp	Z	13	JA	8,293	8	0.40 e	1.10 e	12	Nil	B-	3
Retail (Specialty-Apparel)											
AnnTaylor Stores	ANN	10	JA	659	18	0.05 e	0.75 e	14	Nil	NR	2
Charming Shoppes	CHRS	3	JA	1,273	9	-0.50 e	0.10 e	29	Nil	B+	2
Designs Inc	DESI	7	JA	266	13	0.80 e	0.95 e	7	Nil	NR	3
Gap Inc	GPS	42	JA	3,723	14	2.30 e	2.75 e	15	1.1	A	4
Intimate Brands A	IBI	15	JA	2,108	23	0.88 e	1.10 e	14	3.2	NR	4
Limited Inc	LTD	17	JA	7,321	14	1.05 e	1.20 e	14	2.3	A+	4
Talbots Inc	TLB	29	JA	880	17	1.80 e	2.10 e	14	0.9	NR	3
TJX Companies	TJX	19	JA	3,843	8	0.95 e	1.10 e	17	1.4	B	3
Savings & Loans											
Ahmanson (H F) & Co	AHM	27	DC	3,381	15	3.50 e	2.30 e	12	3.3	B	3
Calif Federal Bank A	CAL	16	DC	1,109	9	1.30 e	1.50 e	11	Nil	C	3
Charter One Finl	COFI	31	DC	424	11	3.15 e	3.30 e	9	2.6	NR	3
Coast Svgs Finl	CSA	35	DC	538	6	1.70 e	2.15 e	16	Nil	B-	3
Dime Bancorp	DME	12	DC	1,216	11	0.80 e	1.25 e	9	Nil	NR	3
Glendale Federal Bank	GLN	18	JE	1,221	8	1.28 w	0.30 e	59	Nil	NR	4
Golden West Finl	GDW	55	DC	1,914	10	3.95 e	4.75 e	12	0.6	B+	5
Great Westn Finl	GWF	25	DC	2,998	11	1.55 e	2.40 e	11	3.6	B-	3
Greenpoint Finl	GNPT	27	DC	491	13	2.55 e	3.10 e	9	2.9	NR	4
Roosevelt Finl	RFED	19	DC	522	11	1.60 e	2.05 e	9	2.8	NR	5
Standard Fedl Bancorp'n	SFB	39	DC	830	11	3.70 e	4.00 e	10	1.8	NR	3
Washington Federal	WFSL	26	SP	353	10	1.97	2.30 e	11	3.7	A	3
Washington Mutual	WAMU	29	DC	1,316	13	2.60 e	2.90 e	10	2.7	B	4
Shoes											
Brown Group	BG	14	JA	1,462	4	0.55 e	1.45 e	10	7	B-	3
L.A. Gear, Inc	LA	2	NV	416	NE	-1.15 e	-0.25 e	NM	Nil	C	1
NIKE, Inc Cl B	NKE	70	MY	4,761	14	2.72 o	3.65 e	19	0.8	A	4
Reebok Intl	RBK	28	DC	3,280	11	2.70 e	3.12 e	9	1	B+	4
Stride Rite	SRR	7	NV	524	14	0.21 e	0.60 e	12	2.7	A-	2
Wolverine World Wide	WWW	32	DC	378	20	1.40 e	1.65 e	19	0.4	B	4

Industry / Company	Ticker	12/95 Price	F-Y End	Rev. ($)	5-Yr. EPS Gr.(%)	EPS 1995	EPS 1996	P/E 1996	Yld. (%)	Com. Stk. Rank	STARS 5=Buy 1=Sell
Specialized Services											
Cintas Corp	CTAS	45	MY	615	18	1.34	1.60 e	28	0.4	A+	3
Ecolab Inc	ECL	30	DC	1,208	13	1.50 e	1.70 e	18	1.8	B	4
Flightsafety Intl	FSI	50	DC	301	13	2.70 e	3.10 e	16	1.1	A	3
Interpublic Grp Cos	IPG	43	DC	1,984	13	2.20 e	2.60 e	17	1.4	A+	4
Kelly Services A	KELYA	28	DC	2,363	14	1.81 e	2.05 e	14	2.8	A	4
Manpower Inc	MAN	28	DC	4,296	18	1.70 e	2.05 e	14	0.4	NR	4
Natl Service Indus	NSI	32	AU	1,971	10	1.93	2.10 e	15	3.5	A	3
Ogden Corp	OG	21	DC	2,110	1	1.50 e	1.55 e	14	5.8	B+	3
Olsten Corp	OLS	40	DC	2,260	17	2.07 e	2.45 e	16	0.8	B+	5
Rollins Inc	ROL	22	DC	605	1	1.36 e	1.50 e	15	2.5	A-	3
Safety-Kleen	SK	16	DC	791	1	0.85 e	0.95 e	16	2.3	B+	3
Service Corp Intl	SRV	44	DC	1,117	16	1.70 e	2.05 e	21	1	A-	3
ServiceMaster L.P.	SVM	30	DC	2,985	13	2.20 e	2.50 e	12	3.1	A+	3
Specialty Printing											
Deluxe Corp	DLX	29	DC	1,748	7	1.10 e	1.30 e	22	5.1	A	2
Donnelley(RR)& Sons	DNY	39	DC	4,889	12	2.00 e	2.35 e	17	1.8	A-	4
Harland (John H.)	JH	21	DC	521	9	1.60 e	1.80 e	12	4.8	A	3
Steel											
Allegheny Ludlum	ALS	19	DC	1,077	14	1.65 e	1.80 e	10	2.8	NR	3
Armco Inc	AS	6	DC	1,438	5	0.15 e	0.60 e	10	Nil	C	4
Bethlehem Steel	BS	14	DC	4,819	7	1.30 e	2.20 e	6	Nil	C	4
Birmingham Steel	BIR	15	JE	886	16	1.74	1.25 e	12	2.6	B	4
Chaparral Steel Co	CSM	17	MY	532	5	0.67	1.20 e	14	1.1	NR	4
Inland Steel Indus	IAD	25	DC	4,497	8	2.65 e	2.90 e	9	0.7	C	4
J & L Specialty Steel	JL	19	DC	712	13	2.15 e	2.15 e	9	1.9	NR	4
LTV Corp	LTV	14	DC	4,529	1	1.75 e	1.95 e	7	Nil	NR	4
Natl Steel B	NS	13	DC	2,700	NE	2.03 e	2.40 e	5	Nil	NR	4
Nucor Corp	NUE	57	DC	2,976	19	3.05 e	3.50 e	16	0.4	A	4
Quanex Corp	NX	19	OC	891	23	2.20 yp	2.25 e	9	3	B	3
Rouge Steel A	ROU	24	DC	1,236	5	4.40 e	2.25 e	11	0.5	NR	5
Texas Indus	TXI	53	MY	831	39	3.88	6.10 e	9	0.7	B	4
USX-U.S. Steel Group	X	31	DC	6,066	12	3.70 e	5.70 e	5	3.2	NR	4
Worthington Indus	WTHG	21	MY	1,484	15	1.29	1.15 e	18	2.1	A-	4
Telecommunications (Long Distance)											
AT&T Corp	T	65	DC	75,094	1	2.71 e	3.88 e	17	2	A-	3
Comsat Corp	CQ	19	DC	827	7	1.65 e	1.75 e	11	4.1	B	3
MCI Communications	MCIC	26	DC	13,338	12	0.80 e	1.73 e	15	0.1	B	5
MIDCOM Communications	MCCI	18	DC	155	NE	-0.37 e	0.30 e	61	Nil	NR	4
Sprint Corp	FON	40	DC	12,662	1	2.75 e	2.84 e	14	2.5	B	3
WorldCom Inc	WCOM	35	DC	2,221	19	1.38 e	1.75 e	20	Nil	B	4
Telephone											
ALLTEL Corp	AT	30	DC	2,962	11	1.85 e	1.95 e	15	3.5	A	4
Ameritech Corp	AIT	59	DC	12,570	7	3.75 e	3.65 e	16	3.6	A-	4
BCE Inc	BCE	35	DC	21,670	3	2.15 ei	2.45 ei	14	Nil	B+	2
Bell Atlantic Corp	BEL	67	DC	13,791	7	4.22 e	4.10 e	16	4.1	A-	5
BellSouth Corp	BLS	44	DC	16,845	7	2.23 e	2.45 e	18	3.3	B+	4
Century Tel Enterp	CTL	32	DC	540	12	1.96 e	2.18 e	15	1	A	4
Cincinnati Bell	CSN	35	DC	1,228	16	0.40 e	1.90 e	18	2.3	B+	3
Frontier Corp	FRO	30	DC	985	13	0.95 e	1.73 e	17	2.8	B+	3
GTE Corp	GTE	44	DC	19,944	8	2.60 e	2.78 e	16	4.2	B+	3
MFS Communications	MFST	53	DC	287	NE	-4.25 e	-4.35 e	NM	Nil	NR	4
NYNEX Corp	NYN	54	DC	13,307	6	2.80 e	3.42 e	16	4.3	B+	3
Pacific Telesis Group	PAC	34	DC	9,235	3	2.45 e	2.50 e	13	6.5	B+	2
SBC Communications	SBC	57	DC	11,619	9	3.10 e	3.40 e	17	2.8	A	5
Southern New Eng Telecom	SNG	40	DC	1,717	6	2.60 e	2.92 e	14	4.4	A-	3
Telecom Corp New Zealand	ADSNZT	69	MR	1,860	14	4.00 e	4.50 e	15	5	NR	4

Industry / Company	Ticker	12/95 Price	F-Y End	Rev. ($)	5-Yr. EPS Gr.(%)	EPS 1995	EPS 1996	P/E 1996	Yld. (%)	Com. Stk. Rank	STARS 5=Buy 1=Sell
Telefonica de Espana ADS	TEF	42	DC	11,986	12	3.25 e	3.82 e	11	2.8	NR	3
Telefonos de Mexico L ADS	TMX	32	DC	5,843	11	3.15 e	3.95 e	8	2.7	NR	4
Telephone & Data Sys	TDS	40	DC	731	31	1.83 e	1.55 e	25	0.9	B+	3
U S West Communic Grp	USW	36	DC	10,953	5	2.35 e	2.45 e	15	6	B+	3
Textiles											
Burlington Industries	BUR	13	SP	2,209	8	1.05 p	1.30 e	10	Nil	NR	3
De Rigo ADS	DER	23	DC	131	23	1.00 e	1.40 e	16	Nil	NR	4
Fieldcrest Cannon	FLD	17	DC	1,064	9	-0.65 e	2.30 e	7	Nil	B	3
Fruit of The Loom A	FTL	24	DC	2,298	12	-2.00 e	1.75 e	14	Nil	NR	3
Gucci Group N.V.	GUC	39	JA	264	20	1.20 e	1.70 e	23	Nil	NR	3
Guilford Mills	GFD	20	SP	783	10	2.41 p	2.65 e	8	2.9	B+	4
Hancock Fabrics	HKF	9	JA	367	12	0.45 e	0.60 e	15	3.5	NR	4
Hartmarx Corp	HMX	4	NV	718	9	0.07 e	0.20 e	22	Nil	B-	4
Kellwood Co	KWD	20	AP	1,365	15	0.53	2.00 e	10	2.9	B	4
Liz Claiborne	LIZ	28	DC	2,163	10	1.55 e	1.75 e	16	1.6	A-	4
Oshkosh B'Gosh Cl A	GOSHA	18	DC	363	13	0.85 e	0.95 e	18	1.6	B	3
Oxford Indus	OXM	17	MY	657	8	1.22	1.10 e	15	4.7	B+	3
Phillips-Van Heusen	PVH	10	JA	1,255	10	0.04 e	1.00 e	10	1.5	A	3
Quiksilver, Inc	QUIK	34	OC	173	30	1.45 p	1.85 e	18	Nil	B	4
Russell Corp	RML	28	DC	1,098	12	1.40 e	1.85 e	15	1.7	A-	3
Springs Industries A	SMI	41	DC	2,069	10	3.75 e	4.10 e	10	3.1	B+	3
Triarc Cos Cl A	TRY	11	DC	1,063	35	0.50 e	0.30 e	37	Nil	C	2
V.F. Corp	VFC	53	DC	4,972	11	2.40 e	4.60 e	11	2.7	A-	3
Tobacco											
Amer Brands	AMB	45	DC	13,147	8	2.80 e	3.15 e	14	4.4	A	5
Philip Morris Cos	MO	90	DC	65,125	14	6.50 e	7.60 e	12	4.4	A+	5
RJR Nabisco Holdings(New)	RN	31	DC	15,366	15	2.25 e	2.55 e	12	4.8	NR	3
Univl Corp	UVV	24	JE	3,281	13	0.73	1.60 e	15	4.1	B	3
UST Inc	UST	33	DC	1,223	14	2.15 e	2.45 e	14	4.4	A+	3
Toys											
Acclaim Entertainment	AKLM	12	AU	567	22	0.86	0.55 e	22	Nil	NR	3
Hasbro Inc	HAS	31	DC	2,670	13	1.80 e	2.55 e	12	1	B+	4
Mattel, Inc	MAT	31	DC	3,205	15	1.60 e	1.90 e	16	0.7	B	4
Tyco Toys	TTI	5	DC	753	11	-0.51 e	0.10 e	45	Nil	C	4
Transportation (Misc.)											
Air Express Intl	AEIC	23	DC	997	14	1.50 e	1.75 e	13	0.8	B+	3
Airborne Freight	ABF	27	DC	1,971	11	1.00 e	1.80 e	15	1.1	B	3
Federal Express	FDX	74	MY	9,392	14	5.27	5.70 e	13	Nil	B-	4
Pittston Services Group	PZS	31	DC	1,872	4	2.25 e	2.60 e	12	0.6	B	4
Ryder System	R	25	DC	4,686	11	1.80 e	2.35 e	11	2.4	B	3
Truckers											
Consolidated Freightways	CNF	27	DC	4,680	10	1.70 e	2.20 e	12	1.5	B-	3
Hunt(JB)Transport	JBHT	17	DC	1,208	12	0.25 e	0.85 e	20	1.1	B+	2
Roadway Services	CBB	49	DC	4,572	11	0.93 e	2.80 e	17	2.8	B+	2
Yellow Corp	YELL	12	DC	2,867	9	-0.40 e	0.75 e	17	Nil	B-	2

5

The Outlook for
the Economy
and the Market

Shareholders entered 1996 happy but suspicious. No one foresaw the spectacular performance in 1995, but never before has it pushed forward with such persistence. Is disillusionment ahead, or are so-called structural changes, such as corporate efficiency, labor insecurity, consumer price sensitivity, fiscal responsibility, and investor buy-and-hold discipline, really creating a new era for stocks?

The answer is somewhere in between. For U.S. companies, while new technology and improving productivity remain priorities, finding excess costs is becoming more difficult and attention is shifting back to the top line -- revenues. Employees are still anxious, but some signs of wage progress are appearing.

We do not expect the delicate balance between corporate staff reductions and consumer buying power to be upset in the near future, and we are still looking for relatively slow GDP growth along with basically flat inflation and interest rates. But the risk in this forecast is underestimating the vigor of the economy.

In 1995, the economy weathered the slowdown induced by the Fed's high interest rates in 1994. By the summer of 1995, housing was rebounding, consumer spending was seeing some growth, and exports were outpacing even optimistic forecasts. The economy started 1996 with very low inflation, low unemployment, and enough momentum to keep on advancing for a quarter or two.

The Secret to Further Gains

The secret to further gains for both stocks and bonds is interest rates. If the Fed lowers interest rates again, as we expect, 1996 will see continued improvements in the economic picture and in the markets. If the Fed proves reluctant to ease or is overly fearful of imagined inflation demons, both stocks and the economy could be in for some rough sledding.

As we head into 1996, we have a 2% economy, consisting of 2% inflation and 2% or so of growth. While the Fed may be pleased with 2% inflation, the rest of us are anything but satisfied with 2% growth. The near-term answer to getting out of the rut is to lower interest rates. Without lower interest rates, we see the economy gradually deteriorating, setting the stage for a downturn late in 1996 or early in 1997. Unemployment will creep up, consumer spending growth will slowly dissipate, and almost any unexpected setback could tip things over the edge.

Yet lower interest rates won't prevent a recession forever, but it should keep the current expansion going through 1996. With somewhat lower interest rates, a rise in unemployment will be stemmed, corporate layoffs will be less severe and consumer confidence should remain strong.

Continued Demand for Stocks

Demand for stocks has been stimulated by growing 401(k), IRA, and Keogh contributions, and there is little question that small investors lately have tended to buy on dips, rather than sell into them, as was generally the case in the past. With each uptick in the market, aging baby boomers have become more convinced they have made the right decision in stashing money away into stocks and stock mutual funds for their retirement. Also, longtime investors, who already saw large paper profits mushroom in 1995, will still be reluctant to liquidate holdings as even a reduced capital gains tax would take a huge chunk out of portfolios.

Nevertheless, too much is being made of the changing nature and objectives of today's investors. Indeed, not long ago the concern was that so many novice shareowners posed a threat of panic selling on any pronounced pullback.

As a result of the tenacity of the market advance in recent years, the resolve of investors has not really been tested. The largest setback for the S&P 500 during 1995 was only 2.4%, the smallest for any year since the end of World War II. The biggest drop anytime in the past five years was 9% in 1994, and the average of the largest pullbacks in each of these years was 6% -- considerably less than the 13% average in the last half-century. Indeed, this stock market advance has gone on five years without a correction of 10% or more, which is unprecedented. Of the past 50 years, 25 suffered setbacks of more than 10% and 15 of them saw 15%-plus drops.

Upward momentum has been maintained partly because of an extraordinarily favorable news background: a smooth economic soft landing, promises of cuts in the deficit and in the capital gains tax, low inflation, declining interest rates, and surprisingly good corporate profits.

Upon entering 1996, however, stock valuations are already high. We would not want to see the P/E ratio of the S&P 500 get much above the current level of 17.5 (based on trailing 12-month earnings). On the same basis, P/Es at the peaks of the nine preceding postwar bull markets have ranged from under 10 in 1981 to more than 22 in 1987, but have been clustered in the 17-19 area.

For stocks to rise without P/E expansion would require, of course, improvement in profits. Our analysts are looking for an 18% gain in 1996 earnings on the S&P 500, while on a top-down, or macroeconomic basis, we are estimating only a 5% rise. Our analysts were pretty much on target in 1995, but the macro estimate may be closer to the mark this year, assuming the current sharply reduced payout ratio (dividends relative to earnings) of only 38% is at least partly a sign that corporations are concerned about profit prospects. Historically, when the payout ratio falls to a cyclical low, which it did in 1995, earnings in the following years are flat or down.

Also suffering from the reduced payout ratio but still a clear-cut indication of generous valuations, the dividend yield on the S&P 500 is at 2.25% -- down from prior record lows around 2.63% at market tops in August 1987 and January 1973.

Presidents and the Market

The fourth years of presidential terms have usually been good for stocks, though third years, such as 1995, have been the best by far. Since 1928, the fourth year of a president's term has seen the stock market advance 7.6% on average, versus a 12.4% average gain during the president's third year in office. And years ending in "6" have been good for the market, but not as good as years ending in "5." Going back to the mid-1930s, gains in the stock market during years ending in "6" have produced gains of about 7% on average, versus an average rise of nearly 29% for the market during those years ending in "5."

But what about those years that end in "6" <u>and</u> occur during the president's fourth year in office? The results will astound you. The four election years of 1916, 1936, 1956, and 1976 each posted positive results for stocks with an average advance of 13.7% for the S&P 500 index. In addition, each of these years was then followed by a sell-off in stocks that averaged 22.4%. Therefore, should history repeat itself and stocks rise in 1996, look out for 1997!

The Market Outlook for 1996

We do not see any major problems near term, either from a fundamental standpoint or on the technical front. Greed or fear will gain the upper hand at some point, but for now, the bull market remains intact.

That's not to say, however, that we expect big gains in 1996, particularly since the market may have to work its way back from a correction during the year. Out forecast is that the S&P 500 will end the year at 645, about 5% above its year-end 1995 close. In addition, we expect two cuts from the Fed during the first half of 1996, taking Fed funds to 4.75% or 5% at mid-year. This will trim the yield on three-month bills under 5% and push the long bond a touch below the 5.75% low set in 1993. But the bond party will be over with the coming of summer.

The S&P Economic Outlook
(Seasonally Adjusted Annual Rates)

	1994 (%)	1995e (%)	1996e (%)
Gross Domestic Product			
Annual rate of increase	6.2	5.0	4.8
Annual rate of increase - real GDP	4.1	3.3	2.7
Annual rate of increase - GDP deflator	2.1	1.7	2.0
Components of Real GDP			
Personal Consumption Expenditures	3.5	3.0	3.4
Durable goods	8.6	5.9	5.8
Nondurable goods	2.9	2.2	2.7
Services	2.5	2.6	3.0
Nonresidential Fixed Investment	13.7	14.5	6.3
Producers' Durable Equipment	17.6	16.0	6.0
Residential Fixed Investment	8.3	(1.7)	3.3
Net change in business inventories	40.7	36.5	17.3
Gov't Purchase of Goods & Services	(0.8)	0.1	(0.4)
Federal	(5.3)	(3.5)	(5.3)
State & Local	2.1	2.1	2.3
Exports	9.0	10.6	9.0
Imports	13.4	11.1	8.5
Income & Profits			
Personal Income	6.1	6.1	4.9
Disposable personal income	5.8	5.8	5.4
Savings rate	4.1	4.4	4.2
Corporate profits before taxes	13.4	9.1	0.9
Corporate profits after taxes	11.3	9.7	1.5
Earnings per share (S&P 500 on trailing 4Q)	39.8	19.1	4.8
Prices & Interest Rates (Averge for period)			
Consumer Price Index	2.6	2.9	2.9
Treasury bills	4.2	5.5	4.6
10 year notes	7.1	6.6	5.7
30 year bonds	7.4	6.9	6.0
New issue rate - corporate bonds	8.0	7.6	6.7
Other Key Indicators			
Industrial Production Index	5.3	3.4	2.9
Capacity utilization rate	83.4	83.4	83.0
Housing starts	11.5	(6.5)	0.8
Auto sales	5.9	(3.3)	2.5
Unemployment rate	6.1	5.6	5.5
U.S. dollar (Quarterly % chg. at quarterly rates)	(1.5)	(5.9)	0.3

6

Sector Investing Through Mutual Funds

It frequently has been said that mutual funds maintain marital harmony, because it is easier to replace an underperforming mutual fund manager than it is to replace an underperforming spouse. So if you prefer mutual funds to individual stocks, but would like to practice sector investing, don't despair. There are plenty of sector funds available.

Sector funds are mutual funds that emphasize the purchase of stocks in a specific industry or overall sector. There are more than 100 such funds. When investors attempt to find these funds, however, they typically must start with the fund family and then see if that family offers a sector fund. In an attempt to reverse this process, and keep within the framework of this book, many of these funds have been assigned to one or more of the corresponding sectors/industries in the S&P 500.

In situations where the fund invests in all industries of a particular sector, that sector-specific fund has been assigned to one or more of the corresponding S&P 500 sectors and is shown in bold type face. If a fund invests in only one or a select few industries within a sector, but not the entire sector, this industry-specific fund is grouped with its corresponding industries. No fund has been assigned to both individual industries and an overall sector. Funds are either industry-specific or sector-specific.

Along with the name of the fund and the corresponding sectors or industries, you will find the one-year and five-year total returns (share price appreciation plus dividends reinvested).

Please be aware that this list is by no means all-inclusive. In addition, these industry and sector funds are not likely to invest in only those companies found in the S&P 500. Shares of other domestic and international industry-related (as well as non-industry-related) companies may be bought and sold by the sector fund manager. Be sure to order the fund's prospectus and read it carefully. This will tell you about the full range of companies that the fund may own, as well as the fund's performance, expenses, minimum investment levels, limits to the number of switches per year, and other important information.

Sector Funds Listing

S&P Sector S&P Industry	Distributor	Fund Name	Total Returns (%) 1995	5-Yr.
Basic Materials	Benham Group	Natural Resources	14.4	NA
	Colonial Funds	Natural Resources A	13.1	NA
	Dean Witter	Natural Resources	23.4	10.3
	Eaton Vance - Marathon	Golden Natural Resources	21.8	10.7
	Fidelity Distributors	Select Industrial Materials	15.4	18.3
	G.T. Global	Natural Resources A	7.1	NA
	John Hancock	Global Resources	1.4	6.9
	Merrill Lynch Funds	Natural Resources A	10.0	5.7
	Prudential Mutual Funds	Global Natural Resources A	26.5	10.9
	Putnam Mutual Funds	Natural Resources A	24.7	9.5
	State Street Research	Global Resources A	22.6	6.3
	T. Rowe Price	New Era	20.8	11.4
Aluminum	...	...	...	...
Chemicals	Fidelity Distributors	Select Chemical	21.4	18.9
Chemicals (Diversified)	Fidelity Distributors	Select Chemical	21.4	18.9
Chemicals (Specialty)	Fidelity Distributors	Select Chemical	21.4	18.9
Containers (Metal & Glass)	...	...	...	...
Containers (Paper)	Fidelity Distributors	Select Paper & Forest Products	22.0	20.0
Gold Mining	Benham Group	Gold Equities Index	9.3	6.0
	Blanchard Group of Funds	Precious Metals	4.4	7.2
	Bull & Bear	Gold Investors	−5.4	4.6
	Dean Witter	Precious Metals	5.0	4.5
	Fidelity Distributors	Select American Gold	11.2	8.8
	Fidelity Distributors	Select Precious Metals	−3.3	9.9
	Franklin Distributors	Gold	−1.3	6.6
	Gabelli Funds	Gold	3.1	NA
	IDS Financial Services	Precious Metals	25.2	12.5
	Invesco Funds Group	Strategic Portfolio - Gold	12.7	3.6
	John Hancock	Gold & Government B	2.8	3.1
	Keystone Distributors	Precious Metals Holdings	−1.4	10.0
	Lexington Funds	Goldfund	−1.9	4.9
	Lexington Funds	Strategic Investments	−14.7	2.3
	Lexington Funds	Strategic Silver	−5.9	−3.7
	MFS Funds	Gold & Natural Resources B	−6.0	2.3
	Monitrend	Gold	−5.8	−17.9
	Oppenheimer Fund Mgmt.	Gold & Special Minerals	−1.5	6.2
	PIMCO Advisors	Precious Metals A	−3.5	NA
	Pioneer Funds	Gold Shares	2.5	6.1
	Rydex Funds	Precious Metals	11.5	NA
	Scudder Investor Services	Gold	13.2	7.2
	Smith Barney Shearson	Precious Metals & Minerals A	−10.6	4.2
	SoGen Funds	Gold	1.3	NA
	United Funds	Gold & Government	9.8	7.1
	United Services Advisors	Gold Shares	−26.8	−7.9
	United Services Advisors	World Gold	15.9	11.0
	USAA Investment Trust	Gold	4.0	5.6
	Van Eck Securities	Gold/Resources	4.3	7.5
	Van Eck Securities	International Investors Gold	−8.9	6.9
	Vanguard Group	Spec. Port.-Gold & Prec. Metals	−4.5	8.0
Metals (Miscellaneous)	...	...	...	...
Paper & Forest Products	Fidelity Distributors	Select Paper & Forest Products	22.0	20.0
Steel	...	...	...	...

Sector Funds Listing

S&P Sector S&P Industry	Distributor	Fund Name	Total Returns (%) 1995	5-Yr.
Capital Goods	**Fidelity Distributors**	**Select Industrial Equipment**	**27.9**	**21.8**
Aerospace/Defense	Fidelity Distributors	Select Defense & Aerospace	47.4	19.6
Electrical Equipment	Fidelity Distributors	Select Electronics	69.4	35.2
Engineering & Construction	Fidelity Distributors	Select Construction & Housing	28.8	19.4
Heavy Duty Trucks & Parts	Fidelity Distributors	Select Automotive	13.4	21.1
Machine Tools	...	...	...	...
Machinery (Diversified)	...	...	...	...
Manufacturing (Diversified)	Fidelity Distributors	Select Industrial Materials	15.4	18.3
Pollution Control	Fidelity Distributors	Select Environmental Services	26.1	3.8
	Invesco Funds Group	Strategic Port.-Environmental	41.1	NA
Consumer Cyclical	**Fidelity Distributors**	**Select Consumer Products**	**28.3**	**17.4**
Auto Parts	Fidelity Distributors	Select Automotive	13.4	21.1
Automobiles	Fidelity Distributors	Select Automotive	13.4	21.1
Broadcast Media	Fidelity Distributors	Select Leisure	27.0	20.6
	Fidelity Distributors	Select Multimedia	33.7	26.3
	Invesco Funds Group	Strategic Portfolio - Leisure	15.8	23.0
Building Materials	Fidelity Distributors	Select Construction & Housing	28.8	19.4
Entertainment	Fidelity Distributors	Select Leisure	27.0	20.6
	Fidelity Distributors	Select Multimedia	33.7	26.3
	Invesco Funds Group	Strategic Portfolio - Leisure	15.8	23.0
Hardware & Tools	Fidelity Distributors	Select Construction & Housing	28.8	19.4
Homebuilding	Fidelity Distributors	Select Construction & Housing	28.8	19.4
Hotel-Motel	Fidelity Distributors	Select Leisure	27.0	20.6
	Invesco Funds Group	Strategic Portfolio - Leisure	15.8	23.0
Household Furn. & Appl.	Fidelity Distributors	Select Construction & Housing	28.8	19.4
Leisure Time	Fidelity Distributors	Select Leisure	27.0	20.6
	Invesco Funds Group	Strategic Portfolio - Leisure	15.8	23.0
Manufactured Housing	Fidelity Distributors	Select Construction & Housing	28.8	19.4
Publishing	Fidelity Distributors	Select Leisure	27.0	20.6
	Fidelity Distributors	Select Multimedia	33.7	26.3
	Invesco Funds Group	Strategic Portfolio - Leisure	15.8	23.0
Publishing (Newspapers)	Fidelity Distributors	Select Leisure	27.0	20.6
	Fidelity Distributors	Select Multimedia	33.7	26.3
	Invesco Funds Group	Strategic Portfolio - Leisure	15.8	23.0
Restaurants	Fidelity Distributors	Select Food & Agriculture	36.6	17.5
	Fidelity Distributors	Select Leisure	27.0	20.6
	Invesco Funds Group	Strategic Portfolio - Leisure	15.8	23.0
Retail (Department Stores)	Fidelity Distributors	Select Retailing	12.0	19.8
Retail (General Merchandise)	Fidelity Distributors	Select Retailing	12.0	19.8
Retail (Specialty)	Fidelity Distributors	Select Retailing	12.0	19.8
Retail (Specialty-Apparel)	Fidelity Distributors	Select Retailing	12.0	19.8
Shoes	...	...	...	...
Textiles	...	...	...	...
Toys	Fidelity Distributors	Select Leisure	27.0	20.6
	Invesco Funds Group	Strategic Portfolio - Leisure	15.8	23.0
Consumer Staples	**Fidelity Distributors**	**Select Consumer Products**	**28.3**	**17.4**
Beverages (Alcoholic)	Fidelity Distributors	Select Food & Agriculture	36.6	17.5
Beverages (Soft Drinks)	Fidelity Distributors	Select Food & Agriculture	36.6	17.5

Sector Funds Listing

| S&P Sector | | | Total Returns (%) | |
S&P Industry	Distributor	Fund Name	1995	5-Yr.
Cosmetics	...	...	...	...
Distributors (Cons.Prods.)	Fidelity Distributors	Select Food & Agriculture	36.6	17.5
Foods	Fidelity Distributors	Select Food & Agriculture	36.6	17.5
Health Care (Diversified)	Capstone Group	Medical Research	61.2	22.6
	Dean Witter	Health Sciences Trust	62.3	NA
	Fidelity Distributors	Select Health Care	45.9	22.4
	G.T. Global	Health Care A	37.0	14.0
	Invesco Funds Group	Strategic Port.-Health Sciences	58.9	19.4
	Merrill Lynch Funds	Health Care A	49.9	NA
	Putnam Mutual Funds	Health Sciences Trust A	47.0	17.6
	Vanguard Group	Spec. Portfolio - Health Care	45.2	20.7
Health Care (Drugs)	Capstone Group	Medical Research	61.2	22.6
	Dean Witter	Health Sciences Trust	62.3	NA
	Fidelity Distributors	Select Health Care	45.9	22.4
	G.T. Global	Health Care A	37.0	14.0
	Invesco Funds Group	Strategic Port.-Health Sciences	58.9	19.4
	Merrill Lynch Funds	Health Care A	49.9	NA
	Putnam Mutual Funds	Health Sciences Trust A	47.0	17.6
	Vanguard Group	Spec. Portfolio - Health Care	45.2	20.7
Health Care (Miscellaneous)	Capstone Group	Medical Research	61.2	22.6
	Dean Witter	Health Sciences Trust	62.3	NA
	Fidelity Distributors	Select Biotechnology	49.1	17.0
	Fidelity Distributors	Select Health Care	45.9	22.4
	Fidelity Distributors	Select Medical Delivery	32.2	20.9
	G.T. Global	Health Care A	37.0	14.0
	Invesco Funds Group	Strategic Port.-Health Sciences	58.9	19.4
	Merrill Lynch Funds	Health Care A	49.9	NA
	Putnam Mutual Funds	Health Sciences Trust A	47.0	17.6
	Vanguard Group	Spec. Portfolio - Health Care	45.2	20.7
Hospital Management	Capstone Group	Medical Research	61.2	22.6
	Dean Witter	Health Sciences Trust	62.3	NA
	Fidelity Distributors	Select Health Care	45.9	22.4
	Fidelity Distributors	Select Medical Delivery	32.2	20.9
	G.T. Global	Health Care A	37.0	14.0
	Invesco Funds Group	Strategic Port.-Health Sciences	58.9	19.4
	Merrill Lynch Funds	Health Care A	49.9	NA
	Putnam Mutual Funds	Health Sciences Trust A	47.0	17.6
	Vanguard Group	Spec. Portfolio - Health Care	45.2	20.7
Household Products	Fidelity Distributors	Select Construction & Housing	28.8	19.4
Housewares	Fidelity Distributors	Select Construction & Housing	28.8	19.4
Medical Products & Supplies	Capstone Group	Medical Research	61.2	22.6
	Dean Witter	Health Sciences Trust	62.3	NA
	Fidelity Distributors	Select Health Care	45.9	22.4
	G.T. Global	Health Care A	37.0	14.0
	Invesco Funds Group	Strategic Port.-Health Sciences	58.9	19.4
	Merrill Lynch Funds	Health Care A	49.9	NA
	Putnam Mutual Funds	Health Sciences Trust A	47.0	17.6
	Vanguard Group	Spec. Portfolio - Health Care	45.2	20.7
Retail (Drug Stores)	Fidelity Distributors	Select Retailing	12.0	19.8
Retail (Food Chains)	Fidelity Distributors	Select Retailing	12.0	19.8
Tobacco .	Fidelity Distributors	Select Food & Agriculture	36.6	17.5

Sector Funds Listing

S&P Sector			Total Returns (%)	
S&P Industry	**Distributor**	**Fund Name**	**1995**	**5-Yr.**
Energy	**Benham Group**	**Natural Resources**	14.4	NA
	Colonial Funds	**Natural Resources A**	13.1	NA
	Dean Witter	**Natural Resources**	23.4	10.3
	Eaton Vance - Marathon	**Golden Natural Resources**	21.8	10.7
	Fidelity Distributors	**Select Energy**	21.4	7.2
	G.T. Global	**Natural Resources A**	7.1	NA
	Invesco Funds Group	**Strategic Portfolio - Energy**	19.8	1.7
	John Hancock	**Global Resources**	1.4	6.9
	Merrill Lynch Funds	**Natural Resources A**	10.0	5.7
	Prudential Mutual Funds	**Global Natural Resources A**	26.5	10.9
	Putnam Mutual Funds	**Natural Resources A**	24.7	9.5
	State Street Research	**Global Resources A**	22.6	6.3
	T. Rowe Price	**New Era**	20.8	11.4
	United Services Advisors	**Global Resources**	9.0	3.6
	Vanguard Group	**Spec. Portfolio - Energy**	25.3	10.7
Oil & Gas Drilling	Fidelity Distributors	Select Energy Service	40.9	6.3
	Fidelity Distributors	Select Natural Gas	30.4	NA
Oil (Domestic Integrated)	...	...	...	...
Oil (Exploration & Prod'n)	Fidelity Distributors	Select Energy Service	40.9	6.3
Oil (International Integrated)	...	...	...	...
Oil Well Equip. & Services	Fidelity Distributors	Select Energy Service	40.9	6.3
Financials	**Century Shares Trust**	**Century Shares**	35.2	16.7
	Fidelity Distributors	**Select Financial Services**	47.4	31.0
	G.T. Global	**Financial Services A**	19.1	NA
	Invesco Funds Group	**Strategic Portfolio - Financial**	39.8	28.0
	PaineWebber	**Regional Financial A**	47.7	30.0
Insurance Brokers	Fidelity Distributors	Select Insurance	34.8	19.5
Investment Bank/Brokerage	Fidelity Distributors	Select Broker & Invest. Mgmt.	23.6	23.9
Life Insurance	Fidelity Distributors	Select Insurance	34.8	19.5
Major Regional Banks	Fidelity Distributors	Select Home Finance	53.5	39.1
	Fidelity Distributors	Select Regional Banks	46.8	32.1
	John Hancock	Regional Bank B	47.6	33.8
	PaineWebber	Regional Financial A	47.7	30.0
Money Center Banks	Fidelity Distributors	Select Home Finance	53.5	39.1
	Fidelity Distributors	Select Regional Banks	46.8	32.1
	John Hancock	Regional Bank B	47.6	33.8
	PaineWebber	Regional Financial A	47.7	30.0
Multi-Line Insurance	Fidelity Distributors	Select Insurance	34.8	19.5
Personal Loans	Fidelity Distributors	Select Home Finance	53.5	39.1
Property-Casualty Insurance	Fidelity Distributors	Select Insurance	34.8	19.5
Savings & Loans	Fidelity Distributors	Select Home Finance	53.5	39.1
	PaineWebber	Regional Financial A	47.7	30.0
Services				
Specialized Services	...	...	...	...
Specialty Printing	...	...	...	...

Sector Funds Listing

S&P Sector S&P Industry	Distributor	Fund Name	Total Returns (%) 1995	5-Yr.
Technology	**Alliance Capital**	**Technology A**	45.8	32.3
	Fidelity Distributors	**Select Technology**	43.7	28.8
	First American	**Technology C**	41.0	NA
	Franklin Distributors	**DynaTech**	26.1	15.0
	Invesco Funds Group	**Strategic Portfolio - Tech.**	45.8	30.0
	John Hancock	**Global Technology**	46.5	24.5
	Kemper Financial Services	**Technology A**	42.8	20.4
	Merrill Lynch Funds	**Technology A**	5.9	NA
	Seligman Financial Svcs	**Communications & Info. A**	43.4	37.0
	Seligman Financial Svcs	**Global Technology A**	45.1	NA
	T. Rowe Price	**Science & Technology**	55.5	33.6
	United Funds	**Science & Technology**	55.6	23.1
Communication Equip. Mfrs.	Fidelity Distributors	Select Developing Communications	17.4	27.5
	G.T. Global	Telecommunications A	8.6	NA
	Montgomery Securities	Global Communications	16.9	NA
Computer Software & Svcs.	Fidelity Distributors	Select Software & Services	46.1	30.9
Computer Systems	Fidelity Distributors	Select Computers	51.7	30.3
Electronics (Defense)	Fidelity Distributors	Select Defense & Aerospace	47.4	19.6
Electronics (Instrumentation)	Fidelity Distributors	Select Electronics	69.4	35.2
Electronics (Semiconductors)	Fidelity Distributors	Select Electronics	69.4	35.2
Office Equipment & Supplies	Fidelity Distributors	Select Computers	51.7	30.3
Photography/Imaging	Fidelity Distributors	Select Leisure	27.0	20.6
Telecom. (Long Dist.)	Fidelity Distributors	Select Telecommunications	29.7	21.5
	G.T. Global	Telecommunications A	8.6	NA
	Montgomery Securities	Global Communications	16.9	NA
	Smith Barney Shearson	Telephone Growth A	8.5	14.8
	Smith Barney Shearson	Telephone Income A	42.8	13.2
Transportation	**Fidelity Distributors**	**Select Transportation**	15.2	24.2
Airlines	Fidelity Distributors	Select Air Transportation	59.5	19.0
Railroads	...	...	...	...
Transportation (Miscellaneous)		...	...	......
Truckers	...	...	...	...
Utilities	**AAL Mutual**	**Utilities**	29.2	NA
	AIM Funds	**Global Utilities A**	27.7	11.1
	America's Utility Fund	**Utilities**	32.3	NA
	Benham Group	**Utilities Income**	35.6	NA
	Cappiello-Rushmore	**Utility Income**	29.8	NA
	Colonial Funds	**Global Utilities A**	18.0	NA
	Colonial Funds	**Utilities A**	34.8	15.0
	Dean Witter	**Utilities**	28.4	11.0
	Dean Witter	**Global Utilities**	14.3	NA
	Eaton Vance - Marathon	**Total Return Trust**	26.2	NA
	Eaton Vance - Traditional	**Total Return Trust**	27.4	10.1
	Evergreen Funds	**Utility A**	30.8	NA
	Federated Securities	**Utility**	25.5	12.8
	Federated Securities	**World Utility**	23.4	NA
	Fidelity Distributors	**Select Utilities**	34.4	13.4

Sector Funds Listing

S&P Sector			Total Returns (%)	
S&P Industry	Distributor	Fund Name	1995	5-Yr.
	Fidelity Distributors	Utilities Income	30.6	14.0
	Flagship Group	Utility A	26.8	NA
	Franklin Distributors	Utilities	30.7	11.8
	Galaxy Funds	Utility Index	37.1	NA
	IDS Financial Services	Utilities Income	23.4	13.0
	Invesco Funds Group	Strategic Portfolio - Utilities	25.3	14.1
	John Hancock	Utilities	22.3	NA
	Lindner Funds	Utility	23.9	NA
	Merrill Lynch Funds	Global Utility A	23.7	11.6
	MFS Funds	Utilities A	32.5	NA
	Midwest	Utility	26.5	12.1
	PaineWebber	Utility Income A	28.3	NA
	Princor Funds	Utilities A	33.9	NA
	Prudential Mutual Funds	Global Utility A	23.4	13.3
	Prudential Mutual Funds	Utility A	25.7	12.2
	Putnam Mutual Funds	Utilities Growth & Income A	31.1	11.3
	Smith Barney Shearson	Utility B	30.8	11.3
	Strong Funds	American Utilities	37.0	NA
	Vanguard Group	Spec. Portfolio - Utilities Inc.	34.0	NA
Electric Companies	Dreyfus Service Corp.	Edison Electric Index	29.6	NA
Natural Gas	Fidelity Distributors	Select Natural Gas	30.4	NA
	Rushmore	American Gas Index	30.5	9.6
Telephone	Fidelity Distributors	Select Telecommunications	29.7	21.5
	G.T. Global	Telecommunications A	8.6	NA
	Montgomery Securities	Global Communications	16.9	NA
	Smith Barney Shearson	Telephone Growth A	8.5	14.8
	Smith Barney Shearson	Telephone Income A	42.8	13.2
Other	MFS Financial Services	Managed Sectors A	33.1	NA
	Dean Witter Distributors	American Value	42.2	20.6

Total Returns Courtesy of Lipper Analytical Services

Appendix A

The S&P 500 Composite Index

S&P 500 Composite Index

Sectors, Industries, and Companies and Their Percentage of the Overall Index as of 12/29/95

Sector/Industry Ticker/Company	% of 500
Basic Materials	*6.06*
Aluminum	**0.44**
AL Alcan Aluminium Ltd	0.15
AA Aluminum Co. of America	0.20
RLM Reynolds Metals.	0.09
Chemicals	**2.28**
APD Air Products & Chemicals	0.13
DOW Dow Chemical	0.40
DD Du Pont (E.I.)	0.85
EMN Eastman Chemical	0.11
GR Goodrich (B.F.)	0.04
HPC Hercules, Inc.	0.14
MTC Monsanto Company	0.31
PX Praxair, Inc	0.10
ROH Rohm & Haas	0.09
UK Union Carbide	0.11
Chemicals (Diversified)	**0.38**
AVY Avery Dennison Corp	0.06
EC Engelhard Corp	0.07
FMC FMC Corp	0.05
PPG PPG Industries	0.20
Chemicals (Specialty)	**0.44**
GRA Grace (W.R.) & Co.	0.13
GLK Great Lakes Chemical	0.10
MII Morton International	0.12
NLC Nalco Chemical	0.04
SIAL Sigma-Aldrich	0.05
Containers (Metal & Glass)	**0.10**
BLL Ball Corp	0.02
CCK Crown Cork & Seal	0.08
Containers (Paper)	**0.11**
BMS Bemis Company	0.03
STO Stone Container	0.03
TIN Temple-Inland	0.05
Gold Mining	**0.53**
ABX Barrick Gold Corp	0.20
ECO Echo Bay Mines Ltd	0.03
HM Homestake Mining	0.05
NEM Newmont Mining	0.09
PDG Placer Dome Inc.	0.13
GLD Santa Fe Pacific Gold Corp	0.03

Sector/Industry Ticker/Company	% of 500
Metals (Miscellaneous)	**0.39**
AR ASARCO Inc	0.04
CYM Cyprus Amax Minerals Co.	0.05
FCX Freeport-McMoran C&G	0.12
N Inco, Ltd.	0.09
PD Phelps Dodge	0.09
Paper & Forest Products	**1.11**
BCC Boise Cascade.	0.04
CHA Champion International	0.09
FBO Federal Paper Board	0.05
GP Georgia-Pacific	0.14
IP International Paper	0.21
JR James River	0.04
LPX Louisiana Pacific	0.06
MEA Mead Corp	0.06
PCH Potlatch Corp	0.03
UCC Union Camp	0.07
W Westvaco Corp	0.06
WY Weyerhaeuser Corp	0.19
WMTT Willamette Industries	0.07
Steel	**0.28**
AS Armco Inc	0.01
BS Bethlehem Steel	0.03
IAD Inland Steel Ind. Inc	0.03
NUE Nucor Corp	0.11
X USX-U.S. Steel Group	0.06
WTHG Worthington Ind	0.04
Capital Goods	*8.42*
Aerospace/Defense	**2.06**
BA Boeing Company	0.59
GD General Dynamics	0.08
LK Lockheed Martin Corp	0.34
MD McDonnell Douglas	0.22
NOC Northrop Grumman Corp	0.08
RTN Raytheon Co	0.25
ROK Rockwell International	0.25
UTX United Technologies	0.25
Electrical Equipment	**3.67**
AMP AMP Inc.	0.18
EMR Emerson Electric	0.40
GE General Electric	2.62
GSX General Signal	0.04
GWW Grainger (W.W.) Inc	0.07
HON Honeywell	0.13
RYC Raychem Corp	0.05

Sector/Industry Ticker/Company	% of 500
TNB Thomas & Betts	0.04
WX Westinghouse Electric	0.14
Engineering & Construction	**0.16**
FLR Fluor Corp	0.12
FWC Foster Wheeler	0.04
Heavy Duty Trucks & Parts	**0.30**
CUM Cummins Engine Co., Inc	0.03
DCN Dana Corp	0.06
ETN Eaton Corp	0.09
IIN ITT Industries	0.06
NAV Navistar International Corp	0.02
PCAR PACCAR Inc	0.04
Machine Tools	**0.03**
CMZ Cincinnati Milacron	0.02
GIDL Giddings & Lewis	0.01
Machinery (Diversified)	**0.76**
BGG Briggs & Stratton	0.03
CAT Caterpillar Inc	0.25
CBE Cooper Industries	0.09
DE Deere & Co	0.20
HPH Harnischfeger Indus	0.04
IR Ingersoll-Rand	0.08
NC NACCO Ind. Cl. A	0.01
TKR Timken Co	0.03
VAT Varity Corp	0.03
Manufacturing (Diversified)	**0.92**
ALD AlliedSignal	0.29
CR Crane Company	0.02
DOV Dover Corp	0.09
ITW Illinois Tool Works	0.15
JCI Johnson Controls	0.06
MIL Millipore Corp	0.04
PLL Pall Corp	0.07
PH Parker-Hannifin	0.06
TNV Trinova Corp	0.02
TYC Tyco International	0.12
Pollution Control	**0.52**
BFI Browning-Ferris Ind.	0.14
LDW.B Laidlaw Inc	0.07
WMX WMX Technologies Inc	0.31
Consumer Cyclical	***12.03***
Auto Parts	**0.35**
CTB Cooper Tire & Rubber	0.04
ECH Echlin Inc	0.05
GPC Genuine Parts	0.11

Sector/Industry Ticker/Company	% of 500
GT Goodyear Tire & Rubber	0.15
Automobiles	**2.00**
C Chrysler Corp.	0.46
F Ford Motor	0.68
GM General Motors	0.86
Broadcast Media	**0.99**
CCB Capital Cities/ABC	0.41
CMCSK Comcast Class A Special.	0.10
TCOMA Tele-Communications.	0.28
UMG US West Media Group	0.20
Building Materials	**0.24**
MAS Masco Corp	0.11
OCF Owens-Corning Fiberglas	0.05
SHW Sherwin-Williams	0.08
Entertainment	**1.39**
KWP King World Productions	0.03
TWX Time Warner Inc	0.32
VIA.B Viacom Inc	0.37
DIS Walt Disney Co	0.67
Hardware & Tools	**0.16**
BDK Black & Decker Corp	0.07
SNA Snap-On Inc	0.04
SWK Stanley Works	0.05
Homebuilding	**0.05**
CTX Centex Corp	0.02
KBH Kaufman & Broad Home Corp	0.01
PHM Pulte Corp	0.02
Hotel-Motel	**0.36**
HET Harrah's Entertainment	0.06
HLT Hilton Hotels	0.06
ITT ITT Corp	0.13
MAR Marriott Int'l	0.11
Household Furnishings & Appliances	**0.18**
ACK Armstrong World	0.05
MYG Maytag Corp	0.05
WHR Whirlpool Corp	0.08
Leisure Time	**0.08**
BLY Bally Entertainment Corp	0.01
BC Brunswick Corp	0.05
HDL Handleman Co	0.01
OM Outboard Marine	0.01
Manufactured Housing	**0.03**
FLE Fleetwood Enterprises.	0.03

Sector/Industry Ticker/Company		% of 500
Publishing		**0.36**
DNB	Dun & Bradstreet	0.24
MHP	McGraw-Hill	0.09
MDP	Meredith Corp	0.03
Publishing (Newspapers)		**0.57**
DJ	Dow Jones & Co	0.09
GCI	Gannett Co	0.19
KRI	Knight-Ridder Inc	0.07
NYT.A	New York Times Cl. A	0.06
TMC	Times Mirror	0.08
TRB	Tribune Co	0.08
Restaurants		**0.80**
DRI	Darden Restaurants	0.04
LUB	Luby's Cafeterias	0.01
MCD	McDonald's Corp	0.68
RYAN	Ryan's Family Steak Hse	0.01
SHN	Shoney's Inc	0.01
WEN	Wendy's International	0.05
Retail (Department Stores)		**0.77**
DDS	Dillard Department Stores	0.07
FD	Federated Dept. Stores	0.12
MA	May Dept. Stores	0.23
MST	Mercantile Stores	0.05
NOBE	Nordstrom	0.07
JCP	Penney (J.C.)	0.23
Retail (General Merchandise)		**1.64**
DH	Dayton Hudson	0.12
KM	K mart	0.07
S	Sears, Roebuck & Co	0.33
WMT	Wal-Mart Stores	1.12
Retail (Specialty)		**1.07**
CC	Circuit City Stores	0.06
HD	Home Depot	0.50
LOW	Lowe's Cos	0.12
MES	Melville Corp	0.07
PBY	Pep Boys	0.03
PCCW	Price/Costco Inc	0.06
TAN	Tandy Corp	0.06
TOY	Toys R Us	0.13
Z	Woolworth Corp	0.04
Retail (Specialty-Apparel)		**0.30**
CHRS	Charming Shoppes	0.01
GPS	Gap (The)	0.13
LTD	Limited, The	0.13
TJX	TJX Companies Inc	0.03

Sector/Industry Ticker/Company		% of 500
Shoes		**0.28**
BG	Brown Group	0.01
NKE	NIKE Inc	0.21
RBK	Reebok International	0.05
SRR	Stride Rite	0.01
Textiles		**0.20**
FTL	Froot of the Loom	0.04
LIZ	Liz Claiborne, Inc	0.04
RML	Russell Corp	0.02
SMI	Springs Industries Inc	0.02
VFC	V.F. Corp	0.08
Toys		**0.21**
HAS	Hasbro Inc	0.06
MAT	Mattel, Inc.	0.15
Consumer Staples		***23.52***
Beverages (Alcoholic)		**0.73**
BUD	Anheuser-Busch	0.37
BF.B	Brown-Forman Corp	0.05
ACCOB	Coors (Adolph)	0.03
VO	Seagram Co. Ltd	0.28
Beverages (Soft Drinks)		**2.99**
KO	Coca Cola Co	2.03
PEP	PepsiCo Inc.	0.96
Cosmetics		**0.75**
ACV	Alberto-Culver	0.02
AVP	Avon Products	0.11
G	Gillette Co	0.50
IFF	International Flav/Frag	0.12
Distributors (Consumer Products)		**0.19**
FLM	Fleming Cos. Inc	0.02
SVU	Supervalu Inc	0.05
SYY	Sysco Corp	0.12
Foods		**3.11**
ADM	Archer-Daniels-Midland	0.21
CPC	CPC International.	0.21
CPB	Campbell Soup.	0.33
CAG	ConAgra Inc.	0.21
GIS	General Mills.	0.20
HNZ	Heinz (H.J.)	0.27
HSY	Hershey Foods.	0.11
K	Kellogg Co	0.37
OAT	Quaker Oats.	0.10
RAL	Ralston-Ralston Purina Gp.	0.14
SLE	Sara Lee Corp.	0.34
UN	Unilever N.V.	0.49

Sector/Industry Ticker/Company	% of 500
WWY Wrigley (Wm) Jr.	0.13
Health Care (Diversified)	**3.93**
ABT Abbott Labs	0.72
AGN Allergan, Inc	0.05
AHP American Home Products	0.66
BMY Bristol-Myers Squibb	0.94
JNJ Johnson & Johnson	1.21
MKG Mallinckrodt Group Inc	0.06
WLA Warner-Lambert	0.29
Health Care (Drugs)	**4.18**
LLY Lilly (Eli) & Co	0.68
MRK Merck & Co	1.76
PFE Pfizer, Inc	0.87
PNU Pharmacia & Upjohn, Inc	0.43
SGP Schering-Plough	0.44
Health Care (HMOs)	**0.50**
HUM Humana Inc	0.10
USHC U.S. Healthcare Inc	0.15
UNH United Healthcare Corp	0.25
Health Care (Miscellaneous)	**0.46**
AZA ALZA Corp. Cl. A	0.04
AMGN Amgen	0.34
BEV Beverly Enterprises	0.03
MNR Manor Care	0.05
Hospital Management	**0.59**
COL Columbia/HCA Healthcare Corp	0.49
CMY Community Psych Centers	0.01
THC Tenet Healthcare Corp	0.09
Household Products	**2.05**
CLX Clorox Co	0.08
CL Colgate-Palmolive	0.22
KMB Kimberly-Clark	0.50
PG Procter & Gamble	1.25
Housewares	**0.24**
NWL Newell Co	0.08
PMI Premark International	0.07
RBD Rubbermaid Inc	0.09
Medical Products & Supplies	**1.04**
BCR Bard (C.R.) Inc.	0.04
BOL Bausch & Lomb.	0.05
BAX Baxter International Inc	0.25
BDX Becton, Dickinson.	0.11
BMET Biomet, Inc.	0.04
BSX Boston Scientific	0.17
MDT Medtronic Inc.	0.28

Sector/Industry Ticker/Company	% of 500
STJM St. Jude Medical	0.07
USS U.S. Surgical.	0.03
Retail (Drug Stores)	**0.24**
LDG Longs Drug Stores	0.02
RAD Rite Aid	0.06
WAG Walgreen Co	0.16
Retail (Food Chains)	**0.55**
ABS Albertson's	0.18
ASC American Stores	0.09
GFS.A Giant Food Cl. A	0.04
GAP Great A & P	0.02
KR Kroger Co	0.10
WIN Winn-Dixie	0.12
Tobacco	**1.97**
AMB American Brands Inc	0.18
MO Philip Morris	1.65
UST UST Inc	0.14
Energy	*9.06*
Oil & Gas Drilling	**0.03**
HP Helmerich & Payne	0.01
RDC Rowan Cos	0.02
Oil (Exploration & Production)	**0.16**
BR Burlington Resources	0.11
ORX Oryx Energy Co	0.03
SFR Santa Fe Energy Resources	0.02
Oil (Domestic Integrated)	**1.36**
AHC Amerada Hess	0.11
ASH Ashland Oil	0.05
ARC Atlantic Richfield	0.39
KMG Kerr-McGee	0.07
LLX Louisiana Land & Exploration	0.03
OXY Occidental Petroleum	0.15
PZL Pennzoil Co	0.04
P Phillips Petroleum	0.19
SUN Sun Co., Inc	0.05
MRO USX-Marathon Group	0.12
UCL Unocal Corp	0.16
Oil (International Integrated)	**6.76**
AN Amoco	0.78
CHV Chevron Corp	0.75
XON Exxon Corp	2.17
MOB Mobil Corp	0.96
RD Royal Dutch Petroleum	1.65
TX Texaco Inc	0.45

Sector/Industry Ticker/Company	% of 500	Sector/Industry Ticker/Company	% of 500
Oil Well Equipment & Services	**0.75**	**Money Center Banks**	**2.42**
BHI Baker Hughes	0.08	BAC BankAmerica Corp	0.52
DI Dresser Industries	0.10	BT Bankers Trust N.Y.	0.11
HAL Halliburton Co	0.13	CMB Chase Manhattan	0.24
MDR McDermott International	0.03	CHL Chemical Banking Corp	0.32
SLB Schlumberger Ltd	0.35	CCI Citicorp	0.62
WAI Western Atlas	0.06	FNB First Chicago NBD Corp	0.28
		JPM Morgan (J.P.) & Co	0.33
Financials	*13.13*	**Multi-Line Insurance**	**1.42**
Insurance Brokers	**0.16**	AET Aetna Life & Casualty	0.17
AAL Alexander & Alexander	0.02	AIG American Int'l. Group	0.96
MMC Marsh & McLennan	0.14	CI CIGNA Corp	0.17
		HIG ITT Hartford Group, Inc	0.12
Investment Banking/Brokerage	**1.02**	**Personal Loans**	**0.18**
DWD Dean Witter, Discover & Co	0.17	BNL Beneficial Corp	0.05
MER Merrill Lynch	0.20	HI Household International	0.13
MS Morgan Stanley	0.14		
SB Salomon Inc	0.08	**Property-Casualty Insurance**	**1.30**
TRV Travelers Inc	0.43	ALL Allstate Corp	0.40
		CB Chubb Corp	0.18
Life Insurance	**0.46**	GRN General Re Corp.	0.28
JP Jefferson-Pilot	0.07	LTR Loews Corp	0.20
LNC Lincoln National	0.12	SAFC SAFECO Corp.	0.09
PVN Providian Corp	0.08	SPC St. Paul Cos	0.10
TMK Torchmark Corp	0.07	FG USF&G Corp	0.05
UNM UNUM Corp	0.09		
USH USLIFE Corp	0.03	**Savings & Loans**	**0.21**
		AHM Ahmanson (H.F.) & Co	0.07
Major Regional Banks	**4.07**	GDW Golden West Financial	0.07
ONE Banc One Corp	0.32	GWF Great Western Financial	0.07
BKB Bank of Boston	0.11		
BK Bank of New York	0.21	**Financial (Miscellaneous)**	**1.89**
BBI Barnett Banks Inc	0.12	AXP American Express	0.44
BOAT Boatmen's Bancshares	0.12	AGC American General	0.16
CMA Comerica Inc	0.10	FRE Federal Home Loan Mtg	0.32
CFL CoreStates Financial	0.12	FNM Federal Natl. Mtge	0.74
FBS First Bank System	0.14	KRB MBNA Corp	0.12
FFB First Fidelity Bancorp	0.12	TA Transamerica Corp	0.11
I First Interstate Bancorp	0.23		
FTU First Union Corp	0.21		
FLT Fleet Financial Group	0.22	*Services*	*0.73*
KEY KeyCorp	0.19	**Specialized Services**	**0.53**
MEL Mellon Bank Corp	0.17	HRB Block H&R	0.09
NCC National City Corp	0.11	CU CUC International	0.13
NB NationsBank	0.41	ECL Ecolab Inc	0.04
NOB Norwest Corp	0.25	IPG Interpublic Group	0.07
PNC PNC Bank Corp	0.16	NSI National Service Ind	0.03
RNB Republic New York	0.08	OG Ogden Corp	0.03
STI SunTrust Banks	0.17	SK Safety-Kleen	0.03
USBC U.S. Bancorp	0.11	SRV Service Corp. International	0.11
WB Wachovia Corp	0.17		
WFC Wells Fargo & Co	0.23		

Sector/Industry Ticker/Company	% of 500
Specialty Printing	**0.20**
DLX Deluxe Corp	0.05
DNY Donnelley (R.R.) & Sons	0.13
JH Harland (J.H.)	0.02
Technology	*13.61*
Communication Equipment Mfrs.	**1.03**
ANDW Andrew Corp	0.03
CS Cabletron Systems	0.13
CSCO cisco Systems	0.44
DIGI DSC Communications	0.09
NT Northern Telecom	0.24
SFA Scientific-Atlanta	0.03
TLAB Tellabs, Inc	0.07
Computer Software & Services	**2.71**
ACAD Autodesk, Inc	0.04
AUD Automatic Data Processing Inc	0.23
CEN Ceridian Corp	0.06
CA Computer Associates Intl	0.30
CSC Computer Sciences Corp	0.09
FDC First Data	0.32
MSFT Microsoft Corp	1.12
NOVL Novell Inc	0.12
ORCL Oracle Systems	0.40
SMED Shared Medical Systems	0.03
Computer Systems	**3.04**
AMH Amdahl Corp	0.02
AAPL Apple Computer	0.09
CPQ COMPAQ Computer	0.28
CYR Cray Research	0.01
DGN Data General	0.01
DEC Digital Equipment	0.21
HWP Hewlett-Packard	0.92
INGR Intergraph Corp	0.02
IBM International Bus. Machines	1.14
SGI Silicon Graphics	0.10
SUNW Sun Microsystems	0.19
TDM Tandem Computers Inc	0.03
UIS Unisys Corp	0.02
Electronics (Defense)	**0.16**
EGG E G & G Inc	0.03
LOR Loral Corp	0.13
Electronics (Instrumentation)	**0.07**
PKN Perkin-Elmer	0.03
TEK Tektronix Inc.	0.04

Sector/Industry Ticker/Company	% of 500
Electronics (Semiconductors)	**2.48**
AMD Advanced Micro Devices	0.04
AMAT Applied Materials	0.15
INTC Intel Corp	1.02
LSI LSI Logic	0.09
MU Micron Technology	0.18
MOT Motorola Inc	0.73
NSM National Semiconductor	0.06
TXN Texas Instruments	0.21
Office Equipment & Supplies	**0.63**
ASN Alco Standard	0.11
MCL Moore Corp. Ltd	0.04
PBI Pitney-Bowes	0.16
XRX Xerox Corp	0.32
Photography/Imaging	**0.55**
EK Eastman Kodak	0.50
PRD Polaroid Corp	0.05
Telecommunications (Long Distance)	**2.94**
T AT&T Corp	2.25
MCIC MCI Communications	0.39
FON Sprint Corp	0.30
Transportation	*1.64*
Airlines	**0.30**
AMR AMR Corp	0.12
DAL Delta Air Lines	0.08
LUV Southwest Airlines	0.08
U USAir Group	0.02
Railroads	**1.09**
BNI Burlington Northern Santa Fe	0.24
CSX CSX Corp	0.21
CRR Conrail Inc	0.12
NSC Norfolk Southern Corp	0.22
UNP Union Pacific	0.30
Truckers	**0.09**
CNF Consolidated Freightways	0.03
CBB Roadway Services	0.04
YELL Yellow Corp	0.02
Transportation (Miscellaneous)	**0.16**
FDX Federal Express	0.09
PZS Pittston Services Group	0.03
R Ryder System	0.04

Sector/Industry Ticker/Company		% of 500
Utilities		*9.90*
Electric Companies		**3.74**
AEP	American Electric Power	0.16
BGE	Baltimore Gas & Electric	0.09
CIN	CINergy Corp	0.10
CPL	Carolina Power & Light	0.12
CSR	Central & South West	0.12
ED	Consolidated Edison	0.16
DTE	DTE Holdings	0.11
D	Dominion Resources	0.16
DUK	Duke Power	0.21
ETR	Entergy Corp	0.15
FPL	FPL Group	0.19
GPU	General Public Utilities	0.09
HOU	Houston Industries	0.14
NMK	Niagara Mohawk Power	0.03
NSP	Northern States Power	0.07
OEC	Ohio Edison	0.08
PE	PECO Energy Co	0.15
PPL	PP&L Resources	0.09
PPW	PacifiCorp	0.13
PCG	Pacific Gas & Electric	0.26
PEG	Public Serv. Enterprise Inc	0.16
SCE	SCEcorp	0.17
SO	Southern Co	0.36
TXU	Texas Utilities	0.20
UCM	Unicom Corp	0.15
UEP	Union Electric Co	0.09
Natural Gas		**0.87**
CGP	Coastal Corp	0.09
CG	Columbia Gas System	0.05
CNG	Consolidated Natural Gas	0.09
EFU	Eastern Enterprises	0.02
ENE	Enron Corp	0.21
ENS	ENSERCH Corp	0.02
GAS	NICOR Inc	0.03
NAE	NorAm Energy Corp	0.02
OKE	ONEOK Inc	0.01
PET	Pacific Enterprises	0.05
PEL	Panhandle Eastern	0.09
PGL	Peoples Energy	0.02
SNT	Sonat Inc	0.07
WMB	Williams Cos	0.10

Sector/Industry Ticker/Company		% of 500
Telephone		**5.29**
AT	ALLTEL Corp	0.12
AIT	Ameritech	0.71
BEL	Bell Atlantic	0.64
BLS	BellSouth	0.94
GTE	GTE Corp	0.93
NYN	Nynex	0.50
PAC	Pacific Telesis	0.32
SBC	SBC Communications Inc	0.76
USW	US West Communications Grp	0.37
Other		*1.92*
Conglomerates		**0.35**
TDY	Teledyne Inc	0.04
TGT	Tenneco Inc	0.19
TXT	Textron Inc	0.12
Miscellaneous		**1.57**
ATI	AirTouch Communications	0.30
AGREA	American Greetings Cl A	0.04
GLW	Corning Inc	0.16
DL	Dial Corp	0.06
H	Harcourt General Inc	0.07
HRS	Harris Corp	0.05
JOS	Jostens Inc	0.02
MMM	Minn. Mining & Mfg	0.61
PHYB	Pioneer Hi-Bred International	0.10
TRW	TRW Inc	0.11
WH	Whitman Corp	0.05

Appendix B

Market and Industry Returns by Phase of the Economic Cycle

Market and Industry Returns by Phase of the Economic Cycle

| | Market/Industry Performances (% Change) in the past nine economic: | | | | | |
| | Expansions | | | Contractions | | |
	# of Cycles	Early	Middle	Late	# of Cycles	Early	Late
Basic Materials							
Aluminum	9	28%	23%	8%	9	-13%	5%
Chemicals	9	24	15	3	9	-11	7
Chemicals (Diversified)	2	34	32	18	3	-14	14
Chemicals (Specialty)	0	—	—	—	1	-19	22
Containers (Metal & Glass)	9	22	17	8	9	-8	7
Containers (Paper)	9	29	20	12	9	-13	12
Gold Mining	9	2	16	14	9	7	11
Metals (Miscellaneous)	9	19	11	17	9	-9	7
Paper & Forest Products	9	36	10	9	9	-12	10
Steel	9	26	1	5	9	-11	2
Capital Goods							
Aerospace/Defense	9	33	19	7	9	-9	9
Electrical Equipment	9	24	24	15	9	-15	10
Engineering & Construction	0	—	—	—	1	-29	40
Heavy Duty Trucks & Parts	9	35	11	2	9	-21	2
Machine Tools	9	22	13	11	9	-18	8
Machinery (Diversified)	9	22	14	11	9	-14	6
Manufacturing (Diversified)	0	—	—	—	1	-24	26
Pollution Control	4	48	52	23	5	-27	18
Consumer Cyclical							
Auto Parts	4	30	18	2	4	-23	8
Automobiles	9	38	9	2	9	-15	4
Broadcast Media	8	66	29	13	9	-12	9
Building Materials	9	20	9	11	9	-16	13
Entertainment	9	18	25	15	9	-8	15
Hardware & Tools	2	21	9	12	2	-24	20
Homebuilding	4	25	-1	23	5	-36	30
Hotel-Motel	4	43	23	10	5	-35	15
Household Furn. & Appl.	9	33	8	8	9	-16	11
Leisure Time	4	74	5	6	5	-24	16
Manufactured Housing	4	30	1	-4	5	-26	46
Publishing	9	22	25	6	9	-14	15
Publishing (Newspapers)	4	50	21	8	4	-17	13
Restaurants	4	54	28	22	5	-19	13
Retail (Department Stores)	9	27	4	22	9	-10	14
Retail (General Merchandise)	4	24	6	17	4	-17	19
Retail (Specialty)	1	118	7	120	1	-30	32
Retail (Specialty-Apparel)	0	—	—	—	1	-37	73

Market and Industry Returns by Phase of the Economic Cycle (Continued)

	Market/Industry Performances (% Change) in the past nine economic:					
	Expansions			Contractions		
	# of Cycles	Early	Middle	Late	# of Cycles	Early	Late
Shoes	9	19%	8%	26%	9	-14%	18%
Textiles	9	29	12	7	9	-15	12
Toys	4	44	-15	24	5	-24	15
Consumer Staples						
Beverages (Alcoholic)	9	7	21	17	9	-5	6
Beverages (Soft Drinks)	9	13	23	20	9	-7	13
Cosmetics	6	16	32	22	7	-13	13
Distributors (Cons. Prods.)	1	37	5	94	1	-9	10
Foods	9	21	9	12	9	-4	13
Health Care (Diversified)	0	—	—	—	1	-1	19
Health Care (Drugs)	9	20	22	15	9	-3	8
Health Care (HMOs)	0	—	—	—	0	—	—
Health Care (Miscellaneous)	0	—	—	—	1	13	48
Hospital Management	2	29	-13	71	3	-8	30
Household Products	9	18	14	13	9	0	12
Housewares	0	—	—	—	1	-22	31
Medical Products & Supplies	4	9	26	11	5	-11	12
Retail (Drug Stores)	4	47	24	14	4	-23	25
Retail (Food Chains)	9	13	0	23	9	-6	18
Tobacco	9	10	12	23	9	0	16
Energy						
Oil & Gas Drilling	4	27	2	40	5	-14	4
Oil (Domestic Integrated)	9	25	13	15	9	-9	9
Oil (Exploration & Production)	0	—	—	—	1	0	-15
Oil (International Integrated)	9	27	17	8	9	-8	9
Oil Well Equip. & Services	9	22	26	35	9	-12	6
Financials						
Insurance Brokers	0	—	—	—	1	-15	20
Investment Bank/Brokerage	0	—	—	—	0	—	—
Life Insurance	9	42	2	13	9	-13	19
Major Regional Banks	9	13	5	8	9	-14	13
Money Center Banks	9	11	5	10	9	-11	10
Multi-Line Insurance	4	34	5	22	5	-17	10
Personal Loans	9	23	3	9	9	-15	22
Property-Casualty Insurance	9	28	2	14	9	-11	15
Savings & Loans	5	24	-2	44	6	-21	35
Financial (Miscellaneous)	0	—	—	—	1	-32	38

Market and Industry Returns by Phase of the Economic Cycle (Continued)

| | Market/Industry Performances (% Change) in the past nine economic: | | | | | | |
| | Expansions | | | Contractions | | | |
	# of Cycles	Early	Middle	Late	# of Cycles	Early	Late
Services							
Specialized Services	1	62%	66%	5%	1	-23%	26%
Specialty Printing	0	—	—	—	0	—	—
Technology							
Communication Equip. Mfrs.	2	37	-8	44	3	-14	10
Computer Software & Svcs.	2	59	33	21	3	-26	29
Computer Systems	9	27	19	16	9	-8	14
Electronics (Defense)	0	—	—	—	1	-12	32
Electronics (Instrumentation)	4	27	25	21	4	-15	17
Electronics (Semiconductors)	4	33	17	30	4	-21	13
Office Equipment & Supplies	1	26	31	10	1	-31	44
Photography/Imaging	0	—	—	—	0	—	—
Telecommunications (LD)	0	—	—	—	1	-25	-1
Transportation							
Airlines	9	44	18	-6	9	-16	7
Railroads	9	32	6	6	9	-12	5
Truckers	6	46	23	13	7	-18	16
Transportation (Misc.)	0	—	—	—	1	-29	21
Utilities							
Electric Companies	9	12	3	-1	9	-5	10
Natural Gas	9	19	12	11	9	-5	5
Telephone	0	—	—	—	1	-6	3
Other							
Conglomerates	4	46	7	-16	5	-25	9
Miscellaneous	0	—	—	—	1	-14	17
S&P 500 Composite	*9*	*22*	*12*	*9*	*9*	*-10*	*8*